Praise for *Reading Romantic Poetry*

"These engagements with the nature of poetry are no mystical celebration of a mysterious power – on the contrary: by focusing on specific attempts Professor Stafford underlines the demystifying facet of these poems which lay bare their own artifice to their readers."

CercleS Bulletin

"An excellent, well-written resource for those interested in Romantic poetry ... Stafford brings a new sensibility and fresh eye to the subject ... Highly recommended."

CHOICE

"This is an extremely accomplished, elegant and wide-ranging account of Romantic poetry. The readings of poems are astute and helpful, and the author writes with the tact and good sense of a first-rate appreciative critic, able to bring out the larger implications of details. Foregrounds blend effortlessly with backgrounds; texts and contexts coexist harmoniously and stimulatingly. Fiona Stafford has produced a splendid volume which anyone teaching Romantic poetry would want to read and want their students to read."

Michael O'Neill, Durham University

"A wonderful introduction to the subject by one of Britain's foremost readers and critics of Romantic poetry. Stafford is infinitely sensitive to the poems themselves, but also shows the importance of historical contexts. An excellent study."

Jon Mee, University of Warwick

"A pleasure to read – this is an engaging, sensitive and wide-ranging study. There is real relish here for poetry – a delight in its forms and voices, sounds and rhythms. A wonderful guide to Romantic poetry, offering a rich appreciation of its historical engagements, pleasures and possibilities."

Mina Gorji, University of Cambridge

"A brilliantly informative guide that pinpoints the essential qualities of Romantic verse. With its emphasis on the pleasures of poetry, the artistic inventiveness and intellectual ambition of Romantic writers, and the challenging cultural conditions in which they worked, this is the perfect introduction to Romantic poetry, unmatched in its breadth of reference and critical sensitivity."

David Duff, University of Aberdeen

Reading Poetry

The books in this series include close readings of well known and less familiar poems, many of which can be found in the Blackwell Annotated Anthologies. Each volume provides students and interested faculty with the opportunity to discover and explore the poetry of a given period, through the eyes of an expert scholar in the field.

The series is motivated by an increasing reluctance to study poetry amongst undergraduate students, born out of feelings of alienation from the genre, and even intimidation. By enlisting the pedagogical expertise of the most esteemed critics in the field, the volumes in the *Reading Poetry* series aim to make poetry accessible to a diversity of readers.

Published:

Reading Sixteenth-Century Poetry	Patrick Cheney, Penn State University
Reading Paradise Lost	David Hopkins, University of Bristol
Reading Eighteenth-Century Poetry	Patricia Meyer Spacks, University of Virginia
Reading Romantic Poetry	Fiona Stafford, Oxford University
Reading Victorian Poetry	Richard Cronin, Glasgow University
Reading Modernist Poetry	Michael Whitworth, Oxford University
Reading Postwar British and Irish Poetry	Michael Thurston, Smith College and Nigel Alderman, Mount Holyoke College

Forthcoming:

Reading Shakespeare's Poetry	Dympna Callaghan, Syracuse University
Reading Seventeenth-Century Poetry	Michael Schoenfeldt, University of Michigan

Reading Romantic Poetry

Fiona Stafford

WILEY Blackwell

This paperback edition first published 2014
© 2014 Fiona Stafford

Edition history: John Wiley & Sons, Ltd (hardback, 2012)

Registered Office
John Wiley & Sons, Ltd, The Atrium, Southern Gate, Chichester, West Sussex, PO19 8SQ, UK

Editorial Offices
350 Main Street, Malden, MA 02148-5020, USA
9600 Garsington Road, Oxford, OX4 2DQ, UK
The Atrium, Southern Gate, Chichester, West Sussex, PO19 8SQ, UK

For details of our global editorial offices, for customer services, and for information about how to apply for permission to reuse the copyright material in this book please see our website at www.wiley.com/wiley-blackwell.

The right of Fiona Stafford to be identified as the author of this work has been asserted in accordance with the UK Copyright, Designs and Patents Act 1988.

All rights reserved. No part of this publication may be reproduced, stored in a retrieval system, or transmitted, in any form or by any means, electronic, mechanical, photocopying, recording or otherwise, except as permitted by the UK Copyright, Designs and Patents Act 1988, without the prior permission of the publisher.

Wiley also publishes its books in a variety of electronic formats. Some content that appears in print may not be available in electronic books.

Designations used by companies to distinguish their products are often claimed as trademarks. All brand names and product names used in this book are trade names, service marks, trademarks or registered trademarks of their respective owners. The publisher is not associated with any product or vendor mentioned in this book.

Limit of Liability/Disclaimer of Warranty: While the publisher and author have used their best efforts in preparing this book, they make no representations or warranties with respect to the accuracy or completeness of the contents of this book and specifically disclaim any implied warranties of merchantability or fitness for a particular purpose. It is sold on the understanding that the publisher is not engaged in rendering professional services and neither the publisher nor the author shall be liable for damages arising herefrom. If professional advice or other expert assistance is required, the services of a competent professional should be sought.

Library of Congress Cataloging-in-Publication Data
Stafford, Fiona J.
  Reading Romantic poetry / Fiona Stafford.
     p. cm.
  Includes bibliographical references and index.
  ISBN 978-1-4051-9155-5 (cloth) – ISBN 978-1-118-77300-0 (pbk.)
1. English poetry–19th century–History and criticism. 2. Romanticism–Great Britain.
I. Title.
  PR590.S734 2012
  821'.709145–dc23
                                                              2011042864

A catalogue record for this book is available from the British Library.

Cover image: William Mulready, The Sonnet, 1839. Photo © V&A Images / Alamy.
Cover design by Design Deluxe

Set in 10/13pt Galliard by SPi Publisher Services, Pondicherry, India

Contents

	Preface	vii
1	The Pleasures of Poetry	1
2	Solitude and Sociability	34
3	Common Concerns and Cultural Connections	65
4	Traditions and Transformations: Poets as Readers	95
5	Reading or Listening? Romantic Voices	132
6	Sweet Sounds	162
7	Poems on Pages	193
	References	227
	Index	230

Preface

'Reading Romantic Poetry' may conjure up images of young lovers delighting each other with tender verses or perhaps consoling themselves with songs in the absence of their soul-mates. This book is not, however, a guide to poems that might be suitable for Valentine's Day or for reciting at weddings, even though many of the works that feature are concerned with love in its most varied aspects. What it offers is an introduction to Romantic poetry in the sense used by those interested in literature – in other words, the poetry written during what has come to be known as the 'Romantic period', from around 1785 to 1830. It aims to encourage new readers to respond directly to the verse and to open up fresh approaches to those already familiar with Romantic literature.

At every turn, the reader of Romantic poetry is confronted with urgent questions about the human condition and the surrounding world. All the big questions that perennially confront philosophers, theologians and political theorists are to be found in this period and so reading the poetry encourages renewed engagement with the dilemmas of those who faced them so courageously during a time of revolutionary upheaval and prolonged warfare. Times when great public events are taking place are often times when personal questions seem most pressing; the Romantic period is no exception. Urgent debates over the nature and purpose of art or the state of the nation are to be found amidst personal effusions over falling in love, coming home, becoming a parent or experiencing fears of failure, ageing, loss or exile. Any anthology of Romantic verse offers apparently contradictory opinions on just about every aspect of human experience. Rather than retreat in confusion, or select only a handful of poems in order to establish some straightforward idea of 'Romantic poetry', however, it is much more rewarding to read widely among the different poets of the period and begin to share some of their profound, if often complicated expressions and explorations of poetry, personal experience and the wider world. The chapters below make reference to a range of varied works in the hope of opening different avenues into the rich and remarkable field of Romantic poetry.

The volume of fine poetry written in the closing years of the eighteenth century and the opening decades of the nineteenth means that a book of this kind cannot hope to do justice to 'Romantic Poetry'. There will inevitably be readers who find a personal favorite has been omitted, or insufficient attention devoted to its intricate form, subtle language, or powerful sentiments. Rather than offer exhaustive readings of a few key poems, this book explores different aspects of reading in order to suggest the variety of ways in which any poem from the period might be read and enjoyed. This means that a greater number of poems can be introduced and that those of the better-known poets – William Cowper, Robert Burns, William Blake, William Wordsworth, Samuel Taylor Coleridge, Lord Byron, Percy Bysshe Shelley and John Keats – can be read alongside those by poets who received less attention for much of the twentieth century – Hannah More, Charlotte Smith, Anna Barbauld, Ann Yearsley, John Clare, Felicia Hemans. Since all were part of the same remarkable period of British history, their works are not only worth reading in themselves, but also for their mutual illumination. Collectively, they combine to allow modern readers a much richer and more varied sense of 'Romantic Poetry'.

Since this is an introduction to the poetry of the later eighteenth and early nineteenth centuries – the years represented in Michael O'Neill and Charles Mahoney (eds.) *Romantic Poetry: An Annotated Anthology* and Duncan Wu (ed.) *Romanticism* – the passages quoted have largely been taken from these two widely available anthologies, primarily from the former. Where the poems under discussion are not included in these anthologies, the editions quoted are clearly listed under 'Works Cited' at the end of the book. In the case of Wordsworth, for example, quotations from the poems and prose are largely from the two anthologies, but any not selected by Wu or O'Neill and Mahoney are taken from *William Wordsworth*, ed. Stephen Gill (Oxford: Oxford University Press, 2010). For Shelley, any texts that do not appear in the anthologies are from Timothy Webb's edition of the Poems and Prose, while for Keats, John Barnard's edition has been used. Throughout, ease of consultation has been a guiding principle and so while the critical discussion is informed by the scholarly editions and studies listed in the 'Further Reading sections', most of the quotations are from the more accessible editions easily available to students and general readers.

There is a vast body of critical work to match the richness of the primary material, so anyone intrigued by the discussions below will be able to consider the poems in greater depth through following up related criticism. Since the purpose of the book is to encourage direct responses to the poems themselves, suggestions for additional criticism are gathered into the short bibliographical sections that follow each chapter, along with and acknowledgement of any critical interpretation especially influential on the discussion.

1
The Pleasures of Poetry

It is difficult to get very far, when pursuing Romantic poetry, without coming across references to pleasure – whether it is William Wordsworth explaining to readers of *Lyrical Ballads* that the purpose of poetry is 'to produce excitement in coexistence with an overbalance of pleasure' (Wu, 503), or John Keats describing the activity of writing to his friend, Charles Dilke:

> Talking of Pleasure, this moment I was writing with one hand, and with the other holding to my Mouth a Nectarine – good god how fine – It went down soft pulpy, slushy, oozy – all its delicious embonpoint melted down my throat like a large beatified Strawberry.
> (Keats, *Letters*, II, 179)

In early nineteenth-century Britain, it seems, the very thought of poetry was able to stimulate the most enjoyable ideas. For Samuel Taylor Coleridge, the test of a good poem was the pleasure it generated for readers. When he looked back on his school-days, trying to account for his longstanding love of literature, Coleridge recognized that 'not the poem which we have *read*, but that to which we *return*, with the greatest pleasure, possesses the genuine power, and claims the name of *essential poetry*' (*Biographia Literaria*, I, 23).

Poetry, for its great begetters in the late eighteenth and early nineteenth centuries, was firmly associated with pleasure, from the conception of a new poem to the continuing attraction of the old. And what's more, it was a pleasure to be shared and multiplied, experienced and revisited – something

Reading Romantic Poetry, First Edition. Fiona Stafford.
© 2014 Fiona Stafford. Published 2014 by John Wiley & Sons, Ltd.

intensified, not wearied, by familiarity. For readers encountering Romantic poetry for the first time, therefore, the prospect is enticing, while those returning for the umpteenth do so with the assurance of deep delights in store. This book attempts to introduce new readers to the pleasures of Romantic poetry, but it also hopes to encourage those who already know the poems to return to them with renewed enthusiasm.

The emphasis on poetic enjoyment is evident in many works of the Romantic period, from Samuel Rogers's popular poem of 1792, *The Pleasures of Memory*, to Thomas Campbell's *The Pleasures of Hope*, published in 1809. Though little read today, the very titles of these poems reflect Romantic tastes and attitudes, and in particular, the readiness with which contemporary eyes turned fondly towards the past or gazed ahead into a brighter future. The impulse might be personal or political, and often, during this tumultuous period of history, private concerns had public dimensions – and vice versa, as we shall see. The vividness with which memories, moments and expectations were caught and conveyed in literature means that readers two centuries later can still enter the period, responding to enduring human situations and ethical concerns as well as to issues relating to the specific events in the decades immediately preceding and succeeding 1800.

Romantic poems often acknowledged the complementary satisfactions of the anticipated and the remembered, looking forward to moments of consummate pleasure, or back on experiences of life-changing significance. Keats recreated the intensity of anticipation in 'The Eve of St Agnes', as he presented both Madeline, the isolated young woman, praying for 'visions of delight' as she retires for the night, and 'burning Porphyro', the young man who hides in her bedroom, growing 'faint' with excitement as he watches her undress (47, 159, 224; O'Neill and Mahoney, 423–36). Keats was equally adept at conjuring up a sense of loss in the aftermath of powerful experience, as the pale knight in 'La Belle Dame Sans Merci' demonstrates, through his simple, but haunting words, 'And I awoke and found me here / On the cold hill's side' (43–4; O'Neill and Mahoney, 439). His ode, 'To Autumn', however, insistently directs attention towards the joys of the present, with its warnings against wistful longing for 'the songs of Spring', and wilfully restrained reference to 'full-grown lambs' and 'gathering swallows' (23, 30, 33; O'Neill and Mahoney, 457–8).

In 'Lines written a Few Miles above Tintern Abbey', Wordsworth was able to pay tribute to the competing attractions of past, present and future experience all at once, by pouring out the powerful feelings prompted by returning to a favorite place. The passage of time is obvious from the opening lines 'Five years have passed; five summers, with the length / Of five long winters!' (1–2; O'Neill and Mahoney, 105), but at the same time, the delight of immediate physical experience is also there: 'again I hear / These waters, rolling from their mountain-springs / With a sweet inland murmur' (2–4). Throughout the poem, the double perspectives of present and past play together, until the final section when the speaker's companion is welcomed into the poem, along with hopes for even greater happiness in the future. If the opening line leads readers to expect wistful recollections, 'Tintern Abbey' in fact draws on the evidence of enriching memories to magnify the enjoyment of new experience:

> While here I stand, not only with the sense of
> Present pleasure, but with pleasing thoughts
> That in this moment there is life and food
> For future years.
> (63–6; O'Neill and Mahoney, 107)

Present pleasure was not dependent on the eyes and ears alone, but deepened by memories of earlier, intense experience and amplified by the expectation of recalling this moment in years to come. For Wordsworth, as he gazed on the landscape with grateful recognition, immediate pleasure seemed capable of infinite expansion, even of transfiguration into religious joy.

'Lines written a few miles above Tintern Abbey' was a poem of self-conscious revisiting, but many poems of the period conveyed a similar sense of the long-term value of particularly memorable experiences. The very existence of the poem demonstrated that a fleeting pleasure could be caught and recreated for the benefit of the poet or a future readership. In his passionate essay on the nature and purpose of his chosen art, *A Defence of Poetry*, Percy Bysshe Shelley described poetry as 'the record of the best and happiest moments of the best and happiest minds' (Wu, 1196). When seen out of context, such a definition might provoke charges of self-aggrandisement, but it is an illuminating statement for anyone attempting to understand the experience and motivation of Romantic poets. For Shelley, as for many of his contemporaries, the impulse to create was 'always arising unforeseen and departing unbidden' and so the task of finding forms for such transient moments was fraught with a sense of impending vacancy (Wu, 1196). Not only was composition urgent, but the ensuing poem was somehow inherently elegiac – a mere trace of the original imaginative experience.

Shelley's own poetry often conveyed the compulsion to capture heightened experience, whether in short lyrics such as 'Rarely, rarely comest thou, Spirit of Delight', or in more descriptive verse that seemed hurrying to record his powerful responses to the natural world. Shelley's passionate delight in the physical landscape of Italy, with its dazzling sunlight and strong colors, so different from his native England, is brilliantly caught in 'Julian and Maddalo', a poem written in Venice in 1818, when he was visiting Lord Byron:

> This ride was my delight. – I love all waste
> And solitary places; where we taste
> The pleasure of believing what we see
> Is boundless, as we wish our souls to be:
> And such was this wide ocean, and this shore
> More barren than its billows; - and yet more
> Than all, with a remembered friend I love
> To ride as then I rode; – for the winds drove
> The living spray along the sunny air
> Into our faces; the blue heavens were bare,
> Stripped to their depths by the awakening North;
> And from the waves, sound like delight broke forth
> Harmonizing with solitude, and sent
> Into our hearts aërial merriment.
> (14–27; Shelley, *Poems and Prose*, 89)

The sheer physical enjoyment of the ride, the warmth, the spray and the sounding waves are perfectly captured in couplets, whose regular beat matches the horses' hooves, with metrical variations to suggest the surges of speed along the beach. Such verse seems to carry readers out of their inevitably sedentary situation, transporting them to other places and others' pleasures. 'Julian and Maddalo' invites us to ride along the Adriatic shoreline with Shelley, stripped momentarily of normal concerns and abandoning thought to the bracing pleasures of the wind and sky. The ride is over soon enough, and the verse slows accordingly to match the return 'Homeward, which always makes the spirit tame', but still the intense experience is there on the page, in words that have lasted longer than the traces left by the horse's hooves on the Italian sand.

The capacity of the human spirit to expand in response to natural beauty and powerful sensory experience ('what we see / Is boundless, as we wish our souls to be') is a recurrent theme in Shelley's work – and Romantic poetry more widely. What now seems commonplace was an idea new to the late eighteenth century – that getting out and about in beautiful scenery was good for physical, mental and moral health. Suddenly people were setting off on tours seeking not just historic sites, great houses, art galleries or classical remains, but also breathtaking views of waterfalls and wooded valleys, lofty hills and rocky shores. Nor were soul-expanding sights confined to what had come to be known in the period as 'sublime landscapes' – vast mountains, stormy seas, cliffs and crags. Wordsworth recorded the leap in his heart caused by something as simple as a rainbow, which affected him as strongly in adulthood as it had when he was a boy:

> My Heart Leaps up when I behold
>   A rainbow in the sky
> So was it when my life began
> So is it now I am a man
> So be it when I shall grow old
>   Or let me die!
>   ('The Rainbow', 1–6, Wu, 528)

The survival of instinctive, childhood impulses into maturity affirmed Wordsworth's sense of himself and many of his poems seemed to give thanks for the world and his place within it. They not only recorded special moments of personal meaning, which made internal pledges of continuity, but also offered the possibility of connection to his readers, who might be similarly uplifted by the verse.

Delight in the immediate world is a key-note of Romantic poetry. Travelling often prompted composition, as poets sought words to convey remarkable landscapes, buildings and people to British audiences: *Childe Harold's Pilgrimage*, for example, appealed strongly to people for whom the Continent had long been cut off by years of war. Byron's own trip to Portugal and Spain and then onwards to Albania and Turkey furnished him with a wealth of material for the first two Cantos of *Childe Harold* published in 1812, which he followed up in 1816 and 1818, with reflections drawn from his travels in Switzerland and Italy. Fascination with exotic places fanned the fashion for Orientalism, which is as evident in Coleridge's 'Kubla Khan', Southey's *Thalaba*, Byron's *Eastern Tales*, or Moore's *Lalla Rookh*, as it is in the flamboyant Royal Pavilion at Brighton, commissioned by the Prince Regent. Places remote from Britain offered both imaginative freedom and a relatively safe space in which domestic matters could be addressed under the guise of fantasy. At the same time, texts set in distant lands often reflected serious philosophical, sociological and cultural interests, inherited from the comparative approaches of the Enlightenment. The early nineteenth-century boom in travel literature, botany and international history meant that poets had rich resources for their narratives, which they often handled with considerable care.

Much Romantic literature, however, dealt with more familiar subject matter. John Clare, born and brought up in a Northamptonshire village, found endless variety in the surrounding fields and hedgerows and so his poems recorded the birds, animals and plants he had known all his life. Robert Burns published his first book of poetry when struggling to make a living as a farmer in Ayrshire, a situation reflected in poems that featured his friends, dogs, sheep, and local community. Mary Robinson, on the other hand, whose colorful existence as an actress and companion of men in high places meant a life spent largely in cities was equally inspired by the 'busy sounds / Of summer morning in the sultry smoke / Of noisy London' ('A London Summer Morning', 1–3; Wu, 249). It didn't seem to matter where poets lived or at what level of society, as long as they shared the urge to record their best moments and possessed sufficient skill to do so convincingly. One of the best-selling poems of the age was Robert Bloomfield's *The Farmer's Boy*, an unassuming account of work as a farm labourer, which rapidly ran to six editions, selling some 27,000 copies within two years of its publication in 1800 (St Clair, 582).

Despite the contemporary vogue for sensational Gothic fiction, poetry did not seem to need much in the way of extraordinary stimulation to please an audience, as William Cowper demonstrated in *The Task*, with its domestic descriptions of everything from weather-vanes to window-boxes. In its wonderful account of the pleasures of sitting alone at twilight, watching the fireplace, Cowper introduced one of the major literary topics of the Romantic age:

> Me oft has fancy ludicrous and wild
> Soothed with a waking dream of houses, tow'rs,
> Trees, churches, and strange visages expressed
> In the red cinders, while with poring eye
> I gazed, myself creating what I saw.
> (*The Task*, IV, 286–290; Wu, 20)

The plain language was well suited to the homely scene and, though simple enough to speak to anyone, demonstrated just how rich an imaginative life was open to those who allowed their minds to wander freely. In his gently self-teasing recollection, Cowper was introducing a concern which would exercise all the major poets of the period, by revealing that he was 'creating' what he saw in the cinders, rather than merely reflecting a fixed external object. As M.H. Abrams argued in a wide-ranging analysis that dominated many critical readings during the second half of the twentieth century, the Romantic mind was more like a lamp than a mirror, shedding its own light on the outside world, rather than being merely reflective. In the Romantic period, the most everyday experience could therefore prove to be the stuff of art: Anna Barbauld was even able to transform the 'dreaded Washing-Day' into poetry ('Washing Day', 8; Barbauld, *Poems*, 133).

There was a strong tendency nevertheless to emphasise the benefits of natural surroundings, especially for growing minds and bodies. Barbauld's sense of the world being big with creative possibility, for example, is abundantly evident in a poem urging an unborn child towards birth:

> Haste, little captive, burst thy prison doors!
> Launch on the living world and spring to light!
> Nature for thee displays her various stores,
> Opens her thousand inlets of delight.
> ('To a little invisible Being who is expected
> soon to become visible', 29–32;
> Barbauld, *Poems*, 131–2)

Confident that the natural world was overflowing with delight, Barbauld imagined countless blessings in store for the new baby. Her poem did not probe neonatal psychology as fully as Wordsworth would in *The Prelude*, where the infant mind is considered at length as 'creator and receiver both, / Working but in alliance with the works / Which it beholds' (II, 273–5, *William Wordsworth*, 325). Her poem nevertheless reveals a willingness that began to emerge in the later eighteenth century to seek positive natural influences for children's rapidly developing minds.

Coleridge similarly looked forward to seeing his baby son grow up in a beautiful rural environment, writing in 'Frost at Midnight':

> *thou*, my babe! shalt wander like a breeze
> By lakes and sandy shores, beneath the crags
> Of ancient mountain and beneath the clouds
> (54–56; O'Neill and Mahoney, 223)

In such surroundings, a child must surely thrive spiritually and physically; and Coleridge, conscious that his own youth had been blighted by years at a London boarding school, felt confident in predicting that for his son, 'all seasons' would 'be sweet' (65).

Though familiar enough to modern readers, the tendency to see children as innocent beings, full of creative potential, is another defining characteristic of Romantic poetry, reflecting the influence of eighteenth-century educational theory. The Genevan philosopher, Jean-Jacques Rousseau, had emphasized the benefits of a natural upbringing in his well-known work, *Émile, ou l'Education*, 1762, which built on British empirical theories about the effects of sensory experience and habits of association on intellectual development. Coleridge himself was so impressed with the ideas of the Yorkshire psychologist, David Hartley, that he named his son – the baby in 'Frost at Midnight' – after him. The poem addresses little Hartley Coleridge, while also paying tribute to David Hartley's theory that healthy minds developed from positive associations established in early life, which led eventually to strong faith in God. The 'secret ministry of frost', though sometimes read in more sinister terms, can helpfully be understood as a quiet, but active, natural force, through which the 'Great Universal Teacher' touches those open to his all-embracing love.

Coleridge's eager anticipation of future blessings for his baby, however, is based in reflection on his own, less happy education, 'in the great city, pent 'mid cloisters dim' (52). A boyhood deprived of physical beauty and freedom seemed to have produced to an adult with a mind, restless and self-punishing, as portrayed in the opening depiction of the sleepless speaker, and confirmed abundantly in Coleridge's notebooks and letters. Where Cowper had extolled the pleasures of gazing alone into the fireplace, Coleridge virtually rewrote the lines from *The Task* in 'Frost at Midnight' to show a much less contented response to dying embers:

> The thin blue flame
> Lies on my low-burnt fire, and quivers not;
> Only that film, which fluttered on the grate,
> Still flutters there, the sole unquiet thing.
> Methinks, its motion in this hush of nature
> Gives it dim sympathies with me who live,
> Making it a companionable form,
> Whose puny flaps and freaks the idling Spirit
> By its own moods interprets, every where
> Echo or mirror seeking of itself,
> And makes a toy of Thought.
>
> (13–23)

Coleridge was just as adept as Cowper at finding subjects for poetry in everyday domestic experience, but instead of peaceful, creative, day-dreaming, 'Frost at Midnight' shows a sleepless, isolated spirit, interpreting the film on the grate as an image of himself, 'the sole, unquiet thing'. Despite the apparent emptiness of the late night scene, however, Coleridge still manages a vivid imaginative ascent by pursuing the associated memory of watching the fireplace at school, and using his own troubled experience as the pathway to somewhere far better for his child. The poem is as transformative as the frost on the 'eave-drops', because it reveals just how much is going on in the quiet confines of home. Whatever the speaker's fears over the consequences of negative childhood experience, the poem was in itself a testament to Coleridge's powerful imagination and remarkable ability to recreate some of his inner life for readers.

Coleridge's interest in the relationship between childhood and adult well-being was intensified by becoming a father in 1796, but it also deepened through his conversations with Wordsworth during the same period. His new friend and writing companion had enjoyed just the kind of ideal, unrestricted, rural childhood that Coleridge imagined for his son, as acknowledged in Wordsworth's remarkable autobiographical poem, *The Prelude*. Here, Wordsworth showed that though his faith in the long-term benefits of the natural world, gratefully acknowledged in 'Tintern Abbey', had been sorely tested in the difficult years following the Revolution in France, it had eventually been proved beyond doubt. Wordsworth's long poem recalls the hopeful mood of the early Revolution, when the extreme social injustices of French society were swept away and a new age of liberty, equality and fraternity seemed to be dawning. The ensuing bloodshed, power-struggle and war, however, rapidly destroyed the hopes of the young British idealist, whose personal turmoil was intensified by a passionate relationship and subsequently, an enforced separation from Annette Vallon, the young French woman whom he left behind in France with their baby. Wordsworth, forced to return to England, suffered political disillusionment and private disintegration. When he turned, a few years later, to ponder over his psychological recovery, he began to identify moments from his earliest years, which had somehow provided lifelines in the chaos of his adult experiences. 'There are in our existence spots of time', he wrote in *The Prelude*, through whose lasting impact on the memory,

> our minds
> Are nourished and invisibly repaired;
> A virtue by which pleasure is enhanced,
> That penetrates, enables us to mount
> When high, more high, and lifts us up when fallen.
> (XI, 258, 264–268; *William Wordsworth*, 491)

Such moments, crucial to healthy imaginative development, were 'most conspicuous' in early childhood memories (XI, 277).

The Prelude not only analyzes the growth of the mind, but also recreates many of Wordsworth's own memories in passages of breath-taking descriptive verse, effectively proving its own point. The vivid accounts of wandering among the fells, skating with friends, playing cards or rowing out onto a star-lit lake are told with such energy that readers cannot doubt the poet's assessment,

> happy time
> It was, indeed, for all of us; to me
> It was a time of rapture
> (I, 456–8;
> *William Wordsworth*, 313)

For Wordsworth, as for many of his contemporaries, there was no sharp distinction between the physical and the psychological. Mental experience was largely dependent on physical experience – on the sensory data that poured into the receptive mind from birth. To talk of poetry as a kind of pleasure, then, meant something physical and emotional as well as intellectual, and it is helpful for a modern readership to remember the fullness of experience embodied in the word. The poet who could write of minds being 'nourished' and 'repaired' was not imagining an abstract, spiritual entity, but an essential part of the whole human being. Wordsworth's language may be more restrained than Keats's 'soft, pulpy, slushy, oozy' celebration of literary pleasure, but his understanding of poetry was just as firmly rooted in the senses.

If the idea of 'rapture' in *The Prelude* was largely associated with childhood, however, many other poems of the period celebrated the ecstacies that might occur a little later on. The visionary pursuit of the Poet-protagonist in Shelley's 'Alastor', for example, reaches an explicitly erotic climax when the 'veiled maid' of his dream eventually reveals

> her outspread arms, now bare,
> Her dark locks floating in the breath of night,
> Her beamy bending eyes, her parted lips
> Outstretched, and pale, and quivering eagerly.
> (177–80; O'Neill and
> Mahoney, 325)

In 'The Eve of St Agnes', Keats explored raptures both imaginary and real, as Madeline not only dreams of her lover and but also wakes to find

Porphyro, 'Ethereal, flush'd, and like a throbbing star' and more than ready to melt 'into her dream' (318–20; O'Neill and Mahoney, 434–5).

Often the creative and the sexual impulses were closely allied, as Robert Burns admitted when he described the motivation behind his first composition – a love song inspired by Nelly, the girl he had worked beside in the harvest field. In his 'Epistle to Davie', the '*Pleasures of the Heart*' are far more important than thoughts of wealth or worldly power, and Burns pays tribute to the inspiration of his 'darling Jean!' (*Poems and Songs*, I, 68). It was perhaps not the thought of an individual woman so much as sexual experience that proved so stimulating to Burns's creative spirit, however, as one of other poems in the same volume celebrated a rapturous evening with Annie, 'I kiss'd her owre and owre again, / Amang the rigs o' barley' (*Poems and Songs*, I, 14). Burns continued to express the pleasures of the heart in poems that often combined love and laughter, satire and sentiment. If many of his songs, such as the famous 'Red, Red Rose', delighted those nurturing tender feelings in the drawing room, others entertained people in Clubs and taverns with more explicit suggestions about what might please a lady.

Burns's variety as a love poet was matched only by Byron, who was just as ready to see both the funny and intensely serious sides of youthful passion – at least by the time he wrote *Don Juan*. In the opening Canto, young Juan may be presented as a comical figure as he wanders 'by the glassy brooks / Thinking unutterable things', but the narrator's later comment on the unsurpassed sweetness of 'first and passionate love' still carries emotional conviction (I, 713–4, 1010; Wu, 958, 990). This is a poem that can switch from farce to tragedy in a matter of stanzas, its digressive, conversational narration flexible enough to capture the full range of human experience. Juan's first love for Donna Julia is passionate enough, albeit treated very differently from the idyllic episode with Haidée in Canto II. Since the physical nature of the relationship is emphasised so frankly, it seems entirely fitting that its demise should also be brought about by the uncontrollable body:

> 'And oh! if e'er I should forget, I swear –
>   But that's impossible, and cannot be –
> Sooner shall this blue ocean melt to air,
>   Sooner shall earth resolve itself to sea,
> Than I resign thine image, oh! my fair!
>   Or think of any thing excepting thee;
> A mind diseased no remedy can physic –'
> (Here the ship gave a lurch, and he grew seasick.)

> 'Sooner shall heaven kiss earth' – (Here he fell sicker)
>   'Oh Julia, what is every other woe? –
> (For God's sake let me have a glass of liquor,
>   Pedro, Battista, help me down below!)
> Julia, my love! – you rascal, Pedro, quicker –
>   Oh Julia! – this cursed vessel pitches so –
> Beloved Julia, hear me still beseeching!'
>   (Here he grew inarticulate with reaching.)
>   (II, 145–60; Wu, 992)

Byron was only too aware of how rapidly the pleasures of the flesh could turn to pain, but it was ironies such as this that drove his own fecund imagination. As Juan succumbs to the pains of his first voyage, his creator revels in the cleverness of his poem, its brilliant dramatic comedy and escalating rhymes combining to prompt laughter rather than tears, when love disappears overboard.

Painful Pleasures

Byron knew that pleasurable poetry was not dependent on cheerful subjects and his work, like that of many other fine poets in the Romantic period, also dealt with memories of loss, sadness, despair or disappointment. Indeed, 'the joy of grief' became a critical touchstone in the later eighteenth-century, following the extraordinary, international success of James Macpherson's ancient, isolated, and deeply despondent bard, Ossian. According to some Enlightenment thinkers, including David Hume, sad recollections were generally more pleasurable than happy ones, because of the mind's natural tendency to compare the past with the present. While a bad memory might prompt gratitude for current well-being, thoughts of happier times now gone were likely to produce more melancholy reflections. To gaze back obsessively on 'the times of old', was to emphasise the uncongenial nature of the present, or to deny any hope for a better future. The enormous international popularity of Ossian, however, suggests that many late eighteenth-century readers were deriving deep pleasure from the poems of an old man, left with nothing but memories of a better world now gone. Ossianic gloom appealed partly because it was seen to affect those overflowing with sensibility – the widely admired capacity for fine feeling. Readers moved to tears by an affecting lament were readers possessed of a soul. With the mid-eighteenth-century cult of feeling, poems that dwelled on graveyards, darkness and ruin became very popular, and so the pleasures of memory seemed closely allied to the pleasures of melancholy.

During the Romantic period, however, many of the prevailing cultural trends were questioned, complicated or even rejected, and although the taste for ruins and melancholy was by no means forgotten, the forms it assumed were rather different. Ruined castles and abbeys, no longer necessarily sites for meditations on the transience of human life or vanished societies, were now seized as settings for exciting Gothic narratives, with room for supernatural elements difficult to accommodate in more realistic, modern situations. Poems such as Coleridge's 'Christabel', Scott's *The Lay of the Last Minstrel* or Keats's 'The Eve of St Agnes' all included medieval architecture to create an otherworldly atmosphere, in which anything seemed possible. Darkness and gloom often seemed the most congenial conditions for imaginative freedom, so even a tale filled with terrors offered pleasurable reading, if well told.

From a radical perspective, too, the ruins of monumental buildings might be a cause for celebration as much as sorrow. The great castle of the Bastille in Paris roused passionate feelings across the Channel, long before the start of the French Revolution. In the fifth book of *The Task*, published in 1785, for example, Cowper included an impassioned apostrophe:

> Ye horrid tow'rs, th'abode of broken hearts,
> Ye dungeons and ye cages of despair,
> That monarchs have supplied from age to age
> With music such as suits their sov'reign ears,
> The sighs and groans of miserable men!
> There's not an English heart that would not leap
> To hear that ye were fall'n at last
> 							(*Task*, V, 384–90)

Though Cowper's prediction turned out to be more sweeping than actual events warranted, it is indicative of a growing desire to banish the practices of unenlightened ages and with them the symbols of inhumanity.

If aspects of the past seemed less than admirable, symbols of their distance from the present had strong appeal. In his best known meditation on ruin, Shelley offered contrasting perspectives on the eighteenth-century fascination with ruin and despair. For in the sonnet, 'Ozymandias', the defiant words of an ancient Egyptian king, 'Look on my works, ye mighty, and despair!', are shown to have taken on a new, ironic resonance over centuries of gradual erosion in the desert (11; Wu, 1080). If the words commissioned for the pedestal of the great statue were once meant to subdue any rival contenders for power, their survival next to its broken remains, 'vast and trunkless legs' (2) and a 'shattered visage' (4), half buried in sand, prompts reflections rather different from those expected by Ozymandias.

Shelley's sonnet, with its image of the 'colossal wreck' (13), may encourage melancholy thoughts on the brevity of human life and the inevitable decay of all things, but it also points readers towards an alternative view. The detail of the sculptor's clear understanding of his master, still evident in what is left of the statue – the 'frown / And wrinkled lip, and sneer of cold command' (4–5) – shows that even during the king's life, there were those less delighted than he was by his power. The choice of 'mock' for the sculptor's activity suggests not only straightforward artistic imitation of the king's expression, but also ideas of ridicule and falseness. For the clear-sighted artist, the command to create a permanent image of unjust power might indeed be a cause for despair. And yet, the sonnet reveals that ancient tyranny has eventually been overthrown merely through the passage of time, an idea close to Shelley's heart as he pondered the possibility of bloodless social reform in the aftermath of the French Revolution and Napoleonic wars. These ideas informed his ambitious poetic drama, *Prometheus Unbound*, which depicted the necessary and inevitable overthrow of tyranny, and was composed among the ruins of the Baths of Caracalla, in Rome. With such a context in mind, the words on the statue of Ozymandias remain unchanged, though their meaning is utterly transformed. For those with radical sympathies, the despair of 'the mighty' might well be the spring of hope.

Both 'Ozymandias' and *Prometheus Unbound* drew inspiration from the magnificent ruins of the ancient world, but the Romantic period also saw more domestic explorations of ruin and consolation. In 'The Ruined Cottage', for example, Wordsworth presented an image of a simple home, now emptied of life and crumbling away beneath the weeds. Change and decay are by no means celebrated in this poem, though its treatment of ruin was every bit as innovative as Shelley's in 'Ozymandias'. 'The Ruined Cottage' offered a very different kind of radicalism, which sought to reveal as great a significance in the ruins of something small as in the fall of mighty castles and dynasties. It remained unpublished for several years after its original composition in the 1790s, but when it did appear in 1814, it formed the opening book of Wordsworth's major poem, *The Excursion*.

Wordsworth's poem relates the tale of the last tenant, a young woman called Margaret, who had struggled to support her two young children after being deserted by their father, but eventually, once both have fallen ill and died, gave up hope and followed them to an early grave. The structure of the poem, which is largely told by the elderly pedlar whom the young speaker meets at the site of the ruin, enables Wordsworth to dramatise the natural response of a sympathetic listener, hearing the story for the first time. However, he was also presenting the very different perspective of the older man, whose memory has been tempered by a sense of deep tranquillity fostered over the many years since Margaret's death. Though the old man recounts the story of her short life with great affection and sympathy, he admonishes his young companion towards the end of the poem, saying, 'My Friend, enough to sorrow have you given, / The purposes of wisdom ask no more' (508–9; O'Neill and Mahoney, 121). This is a very different attitude from that of 'Ozymandias' to the ideas of despair associated with physical ruin, but it is also offering alternative perspectives on death and decay. In 'The Ruined Cottage', 'what we feel of sorrow and despair / From ruin and from change' (520–1) are countered by the view of the elderly pedlar, whose larger perspective acts as a guide to the poem's speaker, and therefore the reader.

The pedlar's wisdom is never explained in 'The Ruined Cottage', but his words are left for readers to contemplate, along with the closing description of the 'calm, oblivious tendencies / Of nature' (504). In the 'Ode: Intimations of Immortality', however, Wordsworth offered a conclusion that helps to illuminate the pedlar's tranquillity,

> We will grieve not, rather find
> Strength in what remains behind
> In the primal sympathy
> Which having been must ever be,
> In the soothing thoughts that spring
> Out of human suffering
> In the faith that looks through death,
> In years that bring the philosophic mind.
> (182–9; O'Neill and
> Mahoney, 168)

The faith that is capable of looking 'through death' tempers grief and seeks comfort both from what remains and what is remembered.

The very need to include the pedlar's restraining voice in 'The Ruined Cottage', however, shows that Wordsworth knew only too well the natural impulse to grieve as well as its tendency towards despair. Indeed, in many poems of the period, including several by Wordsworth, the sense of loss seems almost too powerful for consolation. Still the struggle to find order deepens the emotional charge and the complexity of a poem. Byron, grappling with the lacerating sense of separation from his beloved half-sister, Augusta Leigh, with whom he had had a scandalous affair, still clung to the thought of her unconditional love: 'Though human, thou didst not deceive me, / Though woman, thou didst not forsake' ('Stanzas to Augusta', 25–6; O'Neill and Mahoney, 245). In 'Bright Star', Keats, stricken with memories of nursing his younger brother through his final illness and conscious of the likelihood of meeting a similar fate himself, nevertheless took comfort from human love and imagined living for ever, 'pillow'd upon my fair love's ripening breast' (10; O'Neill and Mahoney, 458). Even when the 'deep distress' caused by the death of Wordsworth's shipwrecked brother, John, found such memorable expression in 'Elegiac Stanzas, suggested by a Picture of Peele Castle in a Storm', Wordsworth, too, still resisted utter despair, though his consolation was of a very different kind: 'Not without hope we suffer and we mourn.' (60; O'Neill and Mahoney, 172).

All too often, however, hope seemed to vanish altogether: neither Cowper's 'The Castaway', surrounded by overwhelming waves, nor the speaker of Charlotte Smith's sonnet, 'Written on the Seashore' offer any suggestion of recovery. Byron's 'Darkness' even went so far as to imagine the fate of the entire human race, should the 'bright sun' be extinguished, the earth turned into a 'lump of death – a chaos of hard clay' (72; Wu, 895). So bleak and absolute was Byron's vision, that no one is left to describe the world's death throes, since the last starving, emaciated human beings are shown dying of horror at each other's 'mutual hideousness' (67). Although Byron's cataclysmic dream exceeded the bounds of human experience, his poem was only an extreme version of the dark moods that seemed to descend on many contemporary writers. In Burns's 'Despondency: An Ode', the view backwards with its 'sick'ning Scenes' was just as dismal as the way ahead, which promised nothing but 'dim declining *Age*' and descent into the '*closing tomb!*' (8, 70, 14; *Poems and Songs*, I, 233–4).

'Despondency', 'Melancholy', and 'Dejection' inspired numerous Romantic lyrics, odes and sonnets, none more searing than Coleridge's desolate articulation:

> A grief without pang, void, dark, and drear,
> A stifled, drowsy, unimpassioned grief,
> Which finds no natural outlet, no relief.
> ('Dejection', 21–3; O'Neill and Mahoney, 236)

The very act of writing the poem, however, did seem to offer some 'outlet', making its own existence, if not an embodiment of pleasure, at least a form of pain relief. According to Shelley's *A Defence of Poetry*, the process of composition is in itself elegiac, as we have seen, because it means that the visionary moment is already fading. When the inspiration for a poem was intense misery, however, its retreat was something to welcome rather than lament.

In Coleridge's poem, the situation is further complicated because the feelings of dejection are inseparable from a sense of waning creative power:

> But now afflictions bow me down to earth:
> Nor care I that they rob me of my mirth;
>   But oh! Each visitation
> Suspends what nature gave me at my birth,
> My shaping spirit of Imagination.
>   (82–6)

The ode, accordingly, goes some way to answering its own self-defeating tendencies by existing on the page. Though written in the present tense, the dramatic shifts within 'Dejection' also convey a sense of movement through time, which combine with the strong rhymes to make readers feel by the end of the poem that the worst is in the past, that some order has been restored.

Even when the poem was less explicitly concerned with artistic failure, however, the creation of memorable lines from the experience of misery still constituted a challenge to despair, not just because it signaled that the dire crisis was over, but because it implied some hope of finding a sympathetic reader. The continuing taste for melancholy, most obvious in the overnight success of Byron's *Childe Harold* in 1812, suggests a readership hungry for expressions of powerful feeling. Whether this can be attributed to the restrictive codes of polite society, provoking reactions among those who felt their lives were regulated by others, or whether it reflects the experience of a society afflicted for so many years by war, economic hardship and anxieties about foreign invasion, is difficult to ascertain. Those who grew up in the 1790s and 1810s, however, were subject to both the personal restrictions imposed by society and the various distresses that major international conflict invariably bring. Jane Austen conveys contemporary experience very effectively in *Persuasion*, a post-Waterloo novel, in which the heroine's freedom is severely circumscribed by her social circle, her wide knowledge of poetry a consequence of years of solitary anxiety following her broken engagement to a naval officer.

The preponderance of Romantic poems apparently written in dark moods certainly indicates a readership sympathetic to emotional expressionism. For those suffering from feelings of depression, some comfort might be drawn from finding their own experiences mirrored so memorably, or some diversion found in poems with more uplifting subjects. Those in better heart were equally ready to share the delights described by an accomplished poet, or to be moved to compassion by heartfelt confessions of misery. Poems that spoke of inner feelings seemed to offer a direct connection to others, enabling readers to find emotional closeness and a better understanding of their own hearts. In an age before film, television or radio, the discovery of private, individual experience beyond that of immediate friends and family could only come through literature, and so the emotion embodied in Romantic poetry was revelatory. Poems offered a means to like-minded strangers who could become virtual friends, linked as they were by shared emotions and experiences.

The clarity with which the best poems articulated states of mind also means that they still speak to readers of today, irrespective of changes in society and life-styles. Burns was especially gifted at conveying what seem utterly convincing expressions of personal sorrow in forms that were essentially for sharing. Songs such as 'Auld Lang Syne' have linked audiences around the world and across centuries, inviting individuals to extend their hands in friendship, as they recall their 'auld acquaintance'. Even songs embodying particular emotional situations, such as 'The Banks and Braes of Bonny Doon', 'A Red, Red Rose' or 'Ae Fond Kiss', were still able to speak to wider audiences because of their forms and language:

> Had we never lov'd sae kindly,
> Had we never lov'd sae blindly!
> Never met – or never parted,
> We had ne'er been broken-hearted!
> ('Ae Fond Kiss', 13–16; Burns,
> *Poems and Songs*, II, 592)

Sentiments such as these were easily understood by listeners everywhere, irrespective of their own accents or situations. Burns drew on the oral traditions of rural Scotland, and what he learned from local song-writing helped him to find ways of making the deeply personal fit for a reading, listening, singing, public. Anyone can recognize the experiences captured in Burns's songs, and so sympathetic readers share and contribute to the collective well of feeling. Paradoxically, poems of loss, regret or severance often turned into poems of companionship, as painful feelings were performed for sympathetic audiences.

Byron, too, had the facility for drawing on his own experience and distilling it into stanzas of lasting beauty. 'So we'll go no more a-roving', for example, appears to have had its origins in the post-Carnival exhaustion Byron felt in Venice in 1817, after a string of parties excessive even by his own standards. As he explained to his friend and fellow poet, Thomas Moore, 'I am on the invalid regimen myself. The Carnival – that is, the latter part of it – and sitting up late o' nights, had knocked me up a little. But it is over, and it is now Lent, with all its Abstinence and Sacred Music' (Wu, 932). Rather than turn his mind to the purifying trials of Lent, however, the lyric Byron included in the letter to Moore was a perfectly crafted expression of what he had been feeling:

> So we'll go no more a-roving
>   So late into the night,
> Though the heart be still as loving,
>   And the moon be still as bright.
>
> For the sword outwears its sheath,
>   And the soul wears out the breast,
> And the heart must pause to breathe,
>   And love itself have rest.
>
> Though the night was made for loving,
>   And the day returns too soon,
> Yet we'll go no more a-roving
>   By the light of the moon.
>   (1–12; Wu, 932)

When read independently of the letter which explains the circumstances giving rise to its creation, however, the poem seems to embrace far more than the waning of erotic energy. It seems rather a wistful expression of involuntary but unavoidable ending, of deep pleasure no longer to be enjoyed, for reasons that cannot be fathomed. The 'we' has an inclusiveness that takes the words beyond the individual moment, beyond the private conversation of friends or lovers, opening the feeling to anyone who cares to listen. But it is the kind of poem that resists analysis, because the language is so simple, the images, so immediately recognizable. It is simply there, speaking its truth to readers of all ages.

What is very noticeable in Byron's lyric, however, as in so many Romantic poems, is the satisfying nature of the rhythm. Though the poem is premised on desire and loss, the strong meter and alternation of longer and shorter lines are so perfectly suited to their meaning that the overall reading experience is very powerful. As Wordsworth pointed out in the Preface to *Lyrical Ballads*, 'words metrically arranged' were inherently pleasing, and crucial to the success of a poem (Wu, 503). He was well aware that certain subjects ran the risk of alienating readers, for any 'images and feelings' that 'might have an undue proportion of pain connected with them', were in danger of taking readers 'beyond the bounds of pleasure' (Wu, 503). This was why meter was so important, because the 'co-presence of something regular', especially of a rhythm familiar to the mind when in a less highly charged emotional state, had 'great efficacy in tempering and restraining the passion by an intertexture of ordinary feeling' (Wu, 503). In other words, the most painful ideas could be handled by an accomplished poet, providing that the meter was carefully chosen to avoid excess.

Though fully alert to the regulating powers of poetic rhythm, Wordsworth also recognized, at the same time, that meter could work very differently, to enhance, rather than subdue feeling. Since readers were conditioned by earlier literary experience, they were likely to respond more powerfully to particular rhythms and therefore to the meaning of the poem: 'in the feeling, whether cheerful or melancholy, which he has been accustomed to connect with that particular movement of meter, there will be found something which will greatly contribute to impart passion to the words' (Wu, 503). Wordsworth understood that different rhythms spoke to different emotional needs and moods, so a rapid meter could add to the urgency of a poem, while a slower pace might deepen its reflections.

Such insights from a practising poet are enormously helpful when trying to understand the powerful effects achieved by apparently simple lyrics. For whether the rhythm of a poem such as 'So we'll go no more a-roving' is understood to be tempering painful feelings, or adding immeasurably to the lyric's emotional depth, may depend largely on the attitude and experience of the individual reader. In either case, however, Wordsworth's belief in the essential pleasure of metrical arrangement is fully borne out. The Preface to *Lyrical Ballads* emphasized the emotional effects of poetry, but the sympathy of readers depended as much on the rightness of the rhythm as on the subject matter: a poem had to be in sympathy with its own sense through form and meter. For even lyrics capable of striking the most painful corresponding chords in a reader's imagination could provide an 'overbalance of pleasure' through the beauty of their own acoustic balance and well-made imagery.

Wordsworth himself was often at his best when treating the most upsetting subjects, bringing his distinctive voice to bear on tales of human suffering. In 'Michael', for example, the dreadful blows sustained by the elderly Grasmere shepherd and his wife are conveyed in metrical language as strong and pared down as the way of life celebrated in the poem:

> The Shepherd ended here; and Luke stoop'd down
> And as his Father had requested, laid
> The first stone of the Sheep-fold; at the sight
> The Old Man's grief broke from him; to his heart
> He press'd his son, he kissed him and wept –
> And to the House together they return'd.
> (428–33; O'Neill and Mahoney, 139)

The regularity of the iambic pentameter is varied by the long vowel sounds, which create spondees to slow the lines appropriately – 'first stone', 'Sheep-fold', 'Old Man's' 'grief broke'. These are not lines that can be hurried through, as the reader is halted by words that match the emotion being conveyed. The most demonstrative line, in terms of emotional expression, 'He press'd his son, he kissed him and wept' (432), is also the only line in this passage where the regular meter breaks down, as if not quite able to carry on to a tenth syllable. Moments such as this certainly threaten to carry readers 'beyond the bounds of pleasure', but the emotion is at once matched and brought under control by the measured pace of Wordsworth's poetry.

Wordsworth regarded poetry as a way of paying 'homage to the native and naked dignity of man' (Preface to *Lyrical Ballads*, Wu, 527) – in other words, to the essential qualities of human nature that could be discerned more easily once the more distracting surfaces of life had been stripped away. The human condition was full of pain and suffering, but it was ultimately part of a 'grand, elementary principle of pleasure' (Wu, 527) and the key to this apparent paradox was sympathy. 'Wherever we sympathise with pain', Wordsworth suggested, 'it will be found that the sympathy is produced and carried on by subtle combinations with pleasure' (Preface to *Lyrical Ballads*, 1802, Gill, 68). The stimulation of compassion, often quickest in response to images of suffering and distress, was itself positive, and so even the saddest stories, if sufficiently well-told in the best language and surest rhythm, gave rise to powerful pleasure. The 'pleasures of memory' then, were not necessarily self-soothing reflections on earlier enjoyments, but might also encompass the most harrowing tales, drawn from the past and yet capable of exciting powerful emotions in readers of a later age.

Public and Private

When the second, enlarged edition of *Lyrical Ballads* was published in 1800, Wordsworth sent a copy to one of the leading politicians of the day, Charles James Fox, because he was so concerned about the plight of people in contemporary Britain and hoped that his poems might provoke 'profitable sympathies in many kind and good hearts' (Wordsworth, *Letters*, I, 313). In order to balance the economic hardships caused by prolonged warfare, high taxation, a repressive social system and widespread movement of people towards expanding towns and the armed forces, Wordsworth was offering an increase in 'profitable sympathies'. As an entry in the national ledger, poems may have looked somewhat out of place, but the tone of Wordsworth's letter, like the Preface which had been added to the new edition of *Lyrical Ballads*, could hardly have been more serious. Poetry, by opening the eyes of readers to the feelings of their fellow men and to their own complicated psychological experience, had its special contribution to make to the well-being of the nation.

For modern readers to make sense of Romantic poetry, it is therefore helpful to understand something of the convictions held by its creators, which are often set out quite clearly in their various prefaces, essays and letters. All the poets whose work is discussed in the chapters that follow were very able men and women, many of whom were driven by a strong sense of commitment to society. That they chose to write poetry was rarely a sign of a leisurely life-style: for many, publishing poems was essential to their livelihood, while for those in more privileged circumstances, writing poetry was often part of a general desire to improve the world in which they lived. Anyone who has been lucky enough to see Shelley's gold teething rattle in an exhibition will be aware that his own background was hardly impoverished, but this does not diminish his tireless efforts to expose the injustices of his age, nor his lifelong commitment to the bloodless revolution that might bring about equal rights for all. William Blake, on the other hand, worked hard to earn a living as an engraver, but his poems were similarly radical, often compelled by what he saw in modern

London, with its 'youthful harlots' and child labourers, crying 'weep weep weep weep' ('London', 14, 'The Chimney Sweeper', 3; O'Neill and Mahoney, 28, 38).

While a humanitarian purpose is obvious in poems written about the Slave Trade or the condition of young chimney sweeps, however, it may be less easily visible to readers of later generations in the more personal poems of the period. And yet, contemporary philosophical ideals about sympathy meant that any poem able to awaken a sympathetic response in readers was also contributing to the wider world. To read or write about 'Dejection' was not necessarily to retreat from society, because 'fellow feeling' was coming to be seen as foundational to morality. To sympathize with another's situation, as the Scottish moral philosopher, Adam Smith, had argued influentially in 1759, in *A Theory of Moral Sentiments*, was the first step towards developing a moral conscience and sense of justice. It was by putting ourselves in the place of others and, conversely, by imagining how are own actions might be perceived by an impartial spectator, that we learned to behave in a morally acceptable way. As Burns put it memorably, in 'To a Louse', 'O wad some Pow'r the giftie gie us / *To see oursels as others see us!*' (43–4; *Poems and Songs*, I, 194). And hence what may now seem to be the rather grand claims made by poets in the period for the moral significance of the imagination.

Shelley, for example, was unequivocal about the ethical dimension of his art, arguing eloquently that:

> The great secret of morals is love, or a going out of our own nature, and an identification of ourselves with the beautiful which exists in thought, action, or person not our own. A man to be greatly good, must imagine intensely and comprehensively; he must put himself in the place of another and of many others; the pains and pleasures of his species must become his own. The great instrument of moral good is the imagination – and poetry administers to the effect by acting upon the cause.
>
> (*A Defence of* Poetry, Wu, 1190)

This line of reasoning, which draws on New Testament and Platonic ideals of love as well as eighteenth-century moral philosophy, makes poetry central to moral action because of its association with the imagination. In Shelley's essay, goodness depends on sympathy and the related ability to identify with the feelings of others. The capacity of poems to make the 'pains and pleasures of his species' part of an individual's felt experience has, accordingly, a profound effect on his own attitudes and behavior – and therefore on the lives of those around.

Shelley followed the philosophical arguments of both David Hume and Adam Smith in regarding feeling as fundamental to human action, developing their insights in relation to poetry. Since imaginative literature had a unique capacity to affect the emotions and extend the range of its readers' understanding beyond their own personal experience, Shelley believed that it had a vital role to play in the progress of society. Unlike systems of moral philosophy, however, Shelley argued that poetry 'awakens and enlarges the mind itself', so that a great poem, such as *Paradise Lost*, worked not through any overt didactic message, but by exciting 'the sympathy of succeeding generations of mankind' (*A Defence of Poetry*, Wu, 1190, 1192). As one of the chief means through which the sympathetic imagination could be developed, poetry was crucial to the nation - not only at the moment of publication, but for centuries to come.

In the Preface to *Lyrical Ballads*, Wordsworth, too, wrote passionately about poetry's capacity to awaken hearts to the feelings of fellow men and women, thereby creating sympathetic connections between contemporary strangers, and across the generations: 'the Poet binds together by passion and knowledge the vast empire of human society, as it is spread over the whole earth, and over all time' (Preface to *Lyrical Ballads*, 1802, Gill, 69). Although the language of 'empire' might sound unappealing to modern ears, Wordsworth was using the term metaphorically to convey an image of universal brotherhood sustained by poetry. Many of his own poems revealed the profound human emotions experienced by the kind of people of whom contemporary poetry-readers might not generally have taken much notice: a homeless woman, an elderly traveller, a shepherd, or the mother of a disabled child. Through being given unexpected insights into their powerful feelings, a reader's capacity for sympathetic understanding might be greatly magnified. This was why the poet could be described as 'the rock of defence of human nature; an upholder and preserver, carrying everywhere with him relationship and love' (Preface to *Lyrical Ballads*, 1802, Gill, 69).

According to Wordsworth, the ideal poet acknowledged the beauty of the universe, a task 'light and easy to him who looks at the world in the spirit of love' (Wu, 527). In fact, as numerous contemporary letters and journals testify, the business of writing poetry was often neither light nor very easy, but Wordsworth was attempting to convey the heady, almost intoxicating, pleasure of discovering and communicating affinities with the rest of the world. The poet, in Wordsworth's exhilarating celebration, was presented 'singing a song in which all human beings join with him' (Preface to *Lyrical Ballads*, 1802, Gill, 68) and so to question his account would seem almost a refusal of friendship. As with Shelley, Wordsworth's is a poet's prose, bent on creating for himself a sympathetic audience of readers.

Not all human beings of the period *were* prepared to join in, however. Byron, for one, did not find Wordsworth's enthusiasm for the inner life of the 'low and rustic' especially appealing, though he did admit to the emotional impulse behind poetry ('it is the lava of the imagination whose eruption prevents an earthquake' (Byron, *Letters and Journals*, III, 179). An origin in the passions did not necessarily mean that the resulting poem worked only on the feelings, however, and for Byron, the pleasure of poetry was as much intellectual and rational. His own impulses were often satirical, driven by a desire to expose cant or puncture his more self-satisfied contemporaries with the corrective force of wit and laughter. In his exuberant modern epic, *Don Juan*, the relationship between the modern poet and society is accordingly presented in very different tones from those adopted by Wordsworth or Shelley:

> He was a man who had seen many changes,
>   And always changed as true as any needle;
> His polar star being one which rather ranges,
>   And not the fix'd – he knew the way to wheedle:
> So vile, he 'scaped the doom which oft avenges;
>   And being fluent (save indeed when fee'd ill),
> He lied with such a fervour of intention –
> There was no doubt he earn'd his laureate pension.
>   (*Don Juan*, III, 633–40)

Although Byron was primarily making fun of the current Poet Laureate, Robert Southey, a frequent target of his satire, the more general point about poets adapting to the times and tastes of those who buy their work provides a less idealized image of 'the poet' than that presented by Wordsworth or Shelley.

Throughout *Don Juan*, Byron reflected on the nature of poetry and its connection to contemporary events, lacing his poem with references to well known figures of his day and giving the protagonist an international field for his adventures. Juan is born in Seville, but is subsequently shipwrecked on a Greek island, sold into slavery in Turkey, engaged in battle at the siege of Ismail, before ending up among the fashionable circles of modern

London. Once his hero is moving in English society, Byron has the perfect opportunity for caustic comment on the contemporary literary scene:

> He saw ten thousand living authors pass,
>   That being about their average numeral;
> Also the eighty 'greatest living poets,'
> As every paltry magazine can show *its*.
>   (XI, 429–32)

The poem then considers Byron's own fall from his pre-eminent position as 'The grand Napoleon of rhyme' (440), before running through the various contenders for the title of 'greatest living poet'.

Despite the sceptical tone of many of his literary references, however, Byron was still placing poetry at the heart of modern society and emphasizing its importance through his uncompromising observations. *Don Juan* might debunk the high-flown language of the Lake poets, Wordsworth, Coleridge and Southey, but Byron was still making ambitious claims of his own for the lasting importance of great literature. His description of the poet in Canto III, for example, builds up to a mini-defence of his own art, which, like that of Wordsworth or Shelley, points to its capacity to connect strangers:

> But words are things, and a small drop of ink,
>   Falling like dew, upon a thought, produces
> That which makes thousands, perhaps millions, think;
>   'Tis strange, the shortest letter which man uses
> Instead of speech, may form a lasting link
>   Of ages;
>   (*Don Juan*, III, 793–8)

Byron's emphasis – underlined by the rhymes – was on poetry's capacity to make people think rather than feel, but he was still making just as large a claim for literature as that made by any of his contemporaries. The apparently whimsical meditation on ink, for example, develops a theme that is introduced at the very opening of the poem – that of the dependence of great men on accomplished writers. As Byron points out, lasting glory is conferred not so much by remarkable actions as by 'the historian's style':

> The present century was growing blind
> To the great Marlborough's skill in giving knocks,
> Until his late Life by Archdeacon Coxe.
>   (*Don Juan*, III, 814–6)

The Duke of Marlborough had been the hero of the early eighteenth century, whose great palace had been built by Queen Anne in honor of his victories over the French at Blenheim, but his memory, somewhat eclipsed by the more recent successes of Nelson and Wellington, had suddenly been revived in the year that *Don Juan* was written, in a new biography by Coxe. This is just the same point as that made in the opening Canto, where Byron lists numerous military leaders from the previous century, once famous enough to give their names to inns and buildings, but now slipping from memory. The speed with which heroes turn into has-beens is rammed home by his jibe at the Prince Regent's preference for the army, which seems to threaten even Nelson with obscurity:

> Nelson was once Britannia's god of war,
>   And still should be so, but the tide is turned;
> There's no more to be said of Trafalgar –
>   'Tis with our hero quietly inurned
> Because the army's grown more popular,
>   At which the naval people are concerned,
> Besides, the prince is all for land-service,
> Forgetting Duncan, Nelson, Howe, and Jervis.
>   (I, 25–32; Wu, 938–9)

The power of princes is equally unpredictable, however, as the next stanza shows by speculating on the 'Brave men' who must have fought in the centuries preceding the Trojan War, before concluding, 'But they shone not on poet's page, / And so have been forgotten' (I, 36–7). *Don Juan* may adopt a largely comic tone, but this does not mean it is less concerned about the role of poetry in society than the eloquent manifestos of other Romantic poets.

The relationship between individual and collective experience was a major preoccupation of the period. The world-inverting events of the later eighteenth century, from the American Declaration of Independence in 1776 to the Battle of Waterloo in 1815 combined to ensure a general awareness of living in unprecedented times. In between came war between Britain and America, the Storming of the Bastille, the execution of the French King and Queen, the outbreak of war with Revolutionary France, the rising of the United Irishmen, Napoleon's rise to power in France and conquest over much of Europe, the Act of Union between Britain and Ireland, the Abolition of the Slave Trade, the assassination of the British Prime Minister, and the Regency crisis, which followed the declaration of

George III's insanity. This was a period in which extraordinary public events were taking place with bewildering rapidity and the state and fate of Europe seemed perpetually in flux.

At such a time, when everyone knew their lives were at the mercy of larger forces, it was often unnecessary to spell out the specific circumstances of a poem, since contemporary readers were likely to be subject to the same prevailing mood. Poems that may seem to utter deeply private emotions were often, therefore, articulating the more widespread feelings that gripped many of their readers. Charles Lamb's refrain, 'All, all are gone, the old familiar faces' (Wu, 739), for example, may be primarily an expression of personal dismay, but it also reflects something of the sense of irreversible change, which spread across late eighteenth-century society, in response to shifting politics and economics, changes in land use, the growth of towns and industry, and the acute distresses associated with the long war. Clare's 'The Flitting', too, though prompted by the specific distresses associated with moving away from his native village in 1832, still articulated feelings of displacement that resonated for many.

At times, the influence of public events on private feelings is very obvious, of course, from Burns's indignation over the new legislation controlling whisky sales in 'The Author's Earnest Cry and Prayer' or Coleridge's 'Fears in Solitude', with its ominous subtitle, 'Written in April 1798. During the Alarms of an Invasion', to Shelley's outraged response to the Peterloo massacre in *The Mask of Anarchy* in 1819. Wordsworth's aim in *The Prelude* was to make sense both of his own life and the extraordinary times in which he lived; in doing so, he was offering himself up for the benefit of others – revealing his personal psychological development and his political commitments. It was not until after his death in 1850, however, that *The Prelude* was finally published, which is indicative of the difficulty faced by many Romantic poets in making their political views public. At many moments between 1790 and 1830, printing direct political opinions risked arrest for sedition or libel and so poets were forced to keep their more overtly critical comments hidden or filtered through less direct modes of expression.

Indeed, in many poems the relevance of the individual experience to wider concerns is left understated, perceptible to modern readers largely through contextual information or subtle associations within the text. The New Historicist criticism of Keats, for example, which began to transform understandings of Romantic poetry in the 1980s, drew attention to the implications of his friendship with the radical publisher and poet,

James Leigh Hunt, and revealed hitherto unnoticed political dimensions in many of the major poems. Leigh Hunt had been imprisoned for publishing literature critical of the Prince Regent and his release two years later inspired one of Keats's early sonnets. Hunt's case nevertheless brought home to writers in the 1810s that open comment on political issues could be very dangerous. More covert ways of expressing political sympathies were needed and Thomas Moore, for example, was able to draw attention to the situation in Ireland through his popular *Irish Melodies*, which were sung in elegant drawing rooms throughout the decade.

Caution over free speech was by no means a new development under the Regency, however. From the mid 1790s, when leading radical intellectuals were put on trial for Treason and the Act of Sedition made it almost impossible to publish anything that might be deemed critical of the wartime Government, poets of the period had to be careful about what they published. Rather than remaining silent, however, they often found less direct ways of making their views known. Blake, for example, expressed his opinions on the international situation, on issues such as the Rights of Women, and on the state of his own nation, but he did so in illuminated books that were not only difficult to interpret, but also very rare, since he published them himself. The thousands who read Thomas Paine's *Rights of Man* were not therefore able to share Blake's indignation over the state of the nation, and it has only been in the twentieth century, with mass publication of his work, that the revolutionary dimensions have been fully recognised.

Narrative poems often provided a means of addressing personal matters too sensitive for public exposure, or political views too dangerous to express directly. In *The Prelude*, for example, Wordsworth inserted the tale of 'Vaudracour and Julia' in place of autobiographical revelations about his own French lover, even though the overt sympathies he was expressing with the early days of the Revolution rendered the poem largely unpublishable at its time of composition, in the year of Trafalgar, 1805. *Tam O'Shanter* has been read by critics such as Robert Crawford as a veiled confession of Burns's extra-marital relationship with Ann Park, but in its sympathetic treatment of popular culture and comic portrayal of Satanic rites, it also possessed a distinctly radical charge when it appeared in 1791. Don Juan's succession of love affairs provided an opportunity for the observation of human relations of every kind, with illuminating comparisons between the arrangements operating in different nations. In his comic-epic, Byron was able to draw on extensive personal experience, celebrating past pleasures or settling old scores, while also using sexual relations to expose different kinds of power and its abuse. Keats, too, included topical references to the power of money over matrimony in his apparently fanciful tale of 'Isabella', while the epic fragment, 'Hyperion' was profoundly concerned with the overthrow of an older order and the uncertain future of those witnessing the arrival of the new.

Despite the difficulties of speaking out during a long period of warfare and political turbulence, poetry also offered a voice to numerous men – and women – who might otherwise have remained in obscurity. Poetry was a way of expressing powerful feelings, as the leading practitioners of the art emphasised in their essays, but it was also a medium which allowed expression to people who were denied a university education, professional career or public office because of their gender, religion or class. This was the period in which Ann Yearsley, who had spent her formative years hard at work milking cows, was eventually able to published accomplished poems about the inequities of the Slave Trade. As with pop stars two centuries later, success of the kind enjoyed by Ann Yearsley often depended on a talent-spotting patron, but opportunities were opening up as never before. Poetry was no longer exclusively the pursuit of those with private incomes or classical educations, and with the expansion of cheaper, provincial publishing, more and more people were able to see their work in print. At the same time, the presentation of collections such as John Clare's as the work of a 'peasant poet' meant that anything in the volume could be read in relation to contemporary society: even though his talent was so individual, he was being labelled according to his class.

The later eighteenth century is often seen as the birth time of democracy and it was certainly the moment when British literature began to open doors to anyone with the ability to write poetry. The importance of poetry to those who were to become the leading Romantic writers is abundantly evident in their own verse, essays and letters, but the extent to which poetry transformed the lives of other people is often less well known. During the years between 1780 and 1825, however, people across England, Scotland, Wales and Ireland were not only reading poetry, but writing, too, and their collective achievement was remarkable. When Byron described poetry as lava, whose 'eruption prevented an earthquake', he may have been thinking of his own inner torment, but his comment also applied to the experience of hundreds of contemporary writers, for whom poetry was an outlet for intense social frustration, for political comment and for personal expression. While this might mean that Romantic poetry is seen as a largely conservative force, diffusing the need for political change by alleviating anger over contemporary injustices, it can also be viewed as its leading proponents hoped it would be, as a vital contribution to the gradual improvement of society. For the great reforms of the nineteenth century, which extended the franchise, improved working conditions and prevented child labor may have had something to do with the gradual awakening of sympathy and renewed understanding of the common experience of all humanity that poets in the Romantic period were so keen to promote. The long-term influence of poetry is impossible to trace with any certainty and lies well beyond the scope of this book, but reading the great Romantic statements on the nature of poetry as well as the richly varied poems of the period inevitably raises such thoughts. What is incontrovertible, as should already be apparent, is that during the Romantic period, poetry represented one of the deepest pleasures of existence. And it was a pleasure that did not depend on wealth or status, but accessible to anyone who could read. Once alert to the many dimensions of Romantic poetry, readers of the twenty-first century, too, are able to participate just as fully in its pleasures.

Further Reading

Useful introductions to Romanticism include:

M.H. Abrams (ed.), *English Romantic Poets*, 2nd edn. (London: Oxford University Press, 1975); Simon Bainbridge, *Romanticism: A Sourcebook* (Basingstoke: Palgrave, 2008); Marilyn Butler, *Romantics, Rebels and Reactionaries* (Oxford: Oxford University Press, 1980); Stuart Curran (ed.) *The Cambridge Companion to Romanticism* (Cambridge: Cambridge University Press, 1993); Aidan Day, *Romanticism* (London: Routledge, 1996); Michael Ferber, *Romanticism: A Very Short Introduction* (Oxford: Oxford University Press, 2010); Michael Ferber (ed.) *A Companion to European Romanticism* (Oxford: Blackwell, 2005); Anne K. Mellor, *Romanticism and Gender* (London: Routledge, 1993); Charles Mahoney (ed.), *A Companion to Romanticism* (Oxford: Wiley-Blackwell, 2011); Michael O'Neill, *Literature of the Romantic Period: A Bibliographical Guide* (Oxford: Oxford University Press, 1998); Murray Pittock (ed.) *The Edinburgh Companion to Scottish Romanticism* (Edinburgh: Edinburgh

University Press, 2010); Nicholas Roe (ed.) *Romanticism: An Oxford Guide* (Oxford: Oxford University Press, 2005); Jane Stabler, *Burke to Byron, Barbauld to Baillie, 1790–1830* (Basingstoke: Palgrave, 2002); Duncan Wu, *Romanticism: A Critical Reader* (Oxford: Wiley-Blackwell, 1995).

For an excellent account of eighteenth-century poetry, including discussion of the 'Romantic mode' of 1700–1730, see David Fairer, *English Poetry of the Eighteenth Century 1700–1789* (Harlow: Pearson, 2003), and for a classic account of the Romantic movement, encompassing the eighteenth-century aesthetics, see M.H. Abrams, *The Mirror and the Lamp* (London: Oxford University Press, 1953).

For an influential account of aesthetic pleasures and pains, see Edmund Burke, *A Philosophical Enquiry into our Ideas of the Origin of Our Ideas of the Sublime and the Beautiful* (1757), ed. Adam Phillips (Oxford: Oxford University Press, 1990). David Hume, *A Treatise of Human Nature* (1739), David Hartley, *Observations on Man* (1749) and John Locke, *An Essay upon Human Understanding* (1690) all provide important philosophical foundations for the physical basis of later eighteenth-century aesthetic thought. For the educational implications of empiricism, see John Locke, *Some Thoughts concerning Education* (1693); Jean Jacques Rousseau, *Émile, ou l'Education* (1762). The educational concerns of Romantic poets have been studied by Alan Richardson in *Literature, Education and Romanticism* (Cambridge: Cambridge University Press, 1994); Nicholas Roe, *John Keats and the Culture of Dissent* (Oxford: Oxford University Press, 1997); Anne Stott, *Hannah More: The First Victorian* (Oxford: Oxford University Press, 2003).

Orientalism has been the subject of numerous studies following Edward Said's seminal, if controversial study, *Orientalism* (1978; Harmondsworth: Penguin, 1985). See especially Nigel Leask, *British Romantic Writers and the East* (Cambridge: Cambridge: Oxford University Press, 1992); *Curiosity and the Aesthetics of Travel Writing 1770–*1840 (Oxford: Oxford University Press, 2002); Michael Franklin (ed.), *Sir William Jones: Selected Poetical and Prose Works* (Cardiff: University of Wales Press, 1995).

For useful introductions to some of the major poems mentioned in this chapter, and their contexts, see Drummond Bone (ed.), *The Cambridge*

Companion to Byron (Cambridge: Cambridge University Press, 2004); Gerard Carruthers (ed.) *The Edinburgh Companion to Robert Burns* (Edinburgh: Edinburgh University Press, 2009); Robert Crawford, *The Bard: Robert Burns A Biography* (London: Jonathan Cape, 2009); Richard Cronin, *Shelley's Poetic Thoughts* (London and Basingstoke: Macmillan,1981); Stephen Gill, *The Prelude* (Cambridge: Cambridge University Press, 1991); (ed.), *The Cambridge Companion to William Wordsworth* (Cambridge: Cambridge University Press, 2003); Jerome McGann, *Fiery Dust: Byron's Poetic Development* (Chicago: University of Chicago Press, 1968); Timothy Morton (ed.) *The Cambridge Companion to Shelley* (Cambridge: Cambridge University Press, 2006); Lucy Newlyn (ed.), *The Cambridge Companion to Coleridge* (Cambridge: Cambridge University Press, 2002); Michael O'Neill (ed.) *Shelley* (Harlow: Longman, 1993); Kelvin Everest, *Coleridge's Secret Ministry* (Hassocks: Harvester, 1979); Nicholas Roe (ed.) *Keats and History* (Cambridge: Cambridge University Press, 1995); Jane Stabler, *Byron: Poetics and History* (Cambridge: Cambridge University Press, 2003); Earl Wasserman, *Shelley: A Critical Reading* (Baltimore: Johns Hopkins,1971); Susan Wolfson (ed.), *The Cambridge Companion to Keats* (Cambridge: Cambridge University Press, 2001); Jonathan Wordsworth, *The Music of Humanity* (London: Thomas Nelson, 1969); *The Borders of Vision* (Oxford: Oxford University Press, 1982).

2
Solitude and Sociability

For many modern readers, the very idea of a 'Romantic poet' conjures up images of a solitary young man, afflicted by unmanageable emotions, communing with an empty landscape or even collapsing upon a forlorn deathbed. Henry Wallis's well known Victorian painting of 'The Death of Chatterton' depicted the poet stretched out in his lonely garret room, white shirt open to reveal an almost equally pale chest, smooth face framed by unruly red hair, eyes closed for ever and, on the floor by his simple bed, a pile of torn up manuscripts. Thomas Chatterton, the young genius from Bristol, who had created an elaborate body of pseudo-medieval poetry before apparently being driven to suicide at the age of seventeen, rapidly came to symbolize Romantic solitude at its most extreme. One of Coleridge's earliest poems was a 'Monody on the Death of Chatterton', while Keats's first long poem, *Endymion*, published in 1818, was dedicated to his memory. Within three years of *Endymion*'s publication, the popular image of the poet as a young genius, misunderstood by the world and prematurely blasted, was painfully confirmed by the death of its author, at the age of twenty five. Keats might not be remembered as a self-destructive genius in a lonely attic room, but youth, solitude and extreme sensitivity long seemed inseparable from his poetic legacy. When Victorian artists turned their hands to posthumous portraits of Shelley or Keats, they would place their young subjects alone amidst the ruins of Ancient Rome or beneath the moonlit trees of a very unspoiled Hampstead Heath.

Recent scholarly interest in historical contexts has done much to qualify Victorian images of Romantic despair or solitary reverie, since strong

Reading Romantic Poetry, First Edition. Fiona Stafford.
© 2014 Fiona Stafford. Published 2014 by John Wiley & Sons, Ltd.

political connotations have been discovered in many poems that were traditionally admired principally for aesthetic and formal qualities. The numerous poems that explicitly address contemporary issues have also received more critical attention, with satire re-emerging as an important genre in this period, often seen in the context of contemporary prints and cartoons. Though an emphasis on alienation has continued (the views of poets not always being in close accord with prevailing Government policy), the marginality of the political radical is rather different in kind from the Victorian image of the over-sensitive artist. Interest in contexts has also given a fresh impetus to biographical approaches, often turning attention to the poets' letters and their correspondents. Since the 1980s, Romantic poets have increasingly been portrayed at the centre of writing circles, significant groups and coteries, sharing their work and defining ideas against those of their contemporaries. Sociability and conversation, no longer confined to eighteenth-century Club and coffee-house culture have come to be seen as a vital part of the Romantic period, too.

The very idea of the 'Solitary Genius' has been exposed as a myth by scholars such as Jack Stillinger, whose careful work on the manuscripts of Keats and Coleridge has led to an understanding of Romantic composition as a collective activity, involving not just the poet, but often friends, family, editors, publishers and typesetters as well. The new periodical culture that gave such prominence to literary reviews meant that anonymous critics could also have considerable influence, prompting minor revisions to a text or even a wholesale rethinking of poetic style. John Clare's texts were heavily edited, excised, and, at times, rewritten by his publisher, John Taylor, so the popular image of the lonely poet in the garret is often wide of the mark. Whether writing circles and energetic editors necessarily prevent feelings of isolation or whether the removal of a stanza or addition of a comma really constitutes composition, however, are matters for further consideration. Issues of revision and editing will be addressed later in the book, but this chapter explores Romantic solitaries, resistance to solitude and the role of poetic friendships.

Romantic Solitude

The endurance of the Romantic solitary is not very surprising, given that much of the poetry initially appears to substantiate the myth of misunderstood genius inherited from the Victorian era. Many of the shorter lyric poems of the period adopt the first person and present an isolated speaker expressing a personal response to some natural phenomenon – a river, a songbird, a flower, a mouse. What is perhaps Wordsworth's most famous poem begins 'I wandered lonely as a cloud', thus inadvertently fixing the popular idea of the solitary poet, at once wanderer and wonderer. 'The Solitary Reaper', published in the same volume as 'The Daffodils', records the poet's response to a figure of complete self-sufficiency, whose striking isolation makes a similarly powerful impression on the reader's imagination,

> Behold her, single in the field,
> Yon solitary Highland Lass!
> Reaping and singing by herself
> (1–3; O'Neill and Mahoney, 169)

The poem, of course, represents an encounter with another human being, so the isolation portrayed here is really a celebration of human presence and of poetry's power to sustain the singer and delight others. Nevertheless, the abiding image is of a single figure, alone in a remote, northern landscape.

In Wordsworth's poems, Nature generally offers a means to recovery and reintegration, but many works of the later eighteenth century depicted a poet in despair, often culminating in a lonely death in lovely surroundings. European readers had become attuned to the voice of the isolated poet by a lonely seashore or remote mountain in the 1760s when the melancholy poems of James Macpherson's ancient bard, Ossian, had enjoyed such spectacular success. In the decades that followed, the tropes of melancholy and isolation remained, but the poet at the centre became much younger. In 1774, just four years after Chatterton's death, the German poet, Johann Wolfgang von Goethe, published *The Sorrows of Werther*, a massively popular novel which did much to establish the figure of a young man, too brilliant, too sensitive, too idealistic to survive in an uncaring world, as a recognized type for the poet.

For the generation who grew up with images of Chatterton and Werther, writing poetry often seemed fatally linked to solitude, despair and early death. In several of her elegiac sonnets, Charlotte Smith adapted passages from Goethe's novel to create poems 'Supposed to be written by Werther', who is depicted hiding amidst 'wild woods and untrodden glades' in an address to 'Solitude' ('Sonnet XXII', 5; Wu, 94). The next sonnet in the sequence shows the tormented Werther gaining momentary relief from watching the North Star appearing through the stormy night sky, only to lapse into melancholy reflection:

> So o'er my soul short rays of reason fly,
> Then fade – and leave me to despair and die!
> ('Sonnet XXIII', 13–14; Wu, 94)

The title poem in Shelley's first major collection, published some thirty years later in 1815, was 'Alastor. Or the Spirit of Solitude', an elaborate tale about the restless idealism and premature death of a young poet: 'He lived, he died, he sung, in solitude' (60; O'Neill and Mahoney, 322). Shelley's young poet ends his days not in a squalid garret, but in an evergreen recess, high on a mountainside, visited only by winds and dead leaves. He was a Chatterton figure for a generation who had come to envisage the poet in natural surroundings, soothed by beautiful scenery even as he despaired of society. Youth, isolation, misery and early death remained a compelling imaginative cocktail for modern poets.

Although the lonely wanderings of Shelley's doomed poet owed much to the melancholy figures of the later eighteenth century, they also gained from more recent creations. In 1812, Byron had eclipsed all earlier poetic solitaries in his dazzlingly successful narrative poem, *Childe Harold's Pilgrimage*. The strange, semi-archaic tale of a young nobleman abandoning the halls of his father, and bidding farewell to his native land, 'Which seem'd to him more lone than Eremite's sad cell' (I, 36) entranced Regency audiences. Byron became a celebrity overnight, as readers thrilled to the restless, world-weary hero, sharing his long journey around the Spanish peninsula to the Mediterranean, in languid Spenserian stanzas, driven and impeded by a brooding melancholy. At times, Harold's voice breaks through the narrative in a pithier ballad meter, but only to darken the gloom with self-loathing:

> And now I'm in the world alone,
>   Upon the wide, wide sea:
> But why should I for others groan,
>   When none will sigh for me?
> Perchance my dog will whine in vain,
>   Till fed by stranger's hands;
> But long ere I come back again
>   He'd tear me where he stands.
>   (*Childe Harold*, I, 182–9)

Harold's uncompromising distance from his fellow countrymen, sustained through two cantos over a journey stretching as far as Istanbul, was to prove especially congenial to his creator in 1816, when Byron left Britain for ever, and with it his wife, his daughter, his half-sister and his ancestral home. 'Self-exiled Harold' wandered forth again in Canto III, across the empty battlefield of Waterloo to the bleak, pine-clad wastes of Switzerland, before finishing his travels in a fourth Canto, composed two years later in Venice, in 1818.

Ironically, the mass appeal of the most popular poet of the Romantic age depended on the elusive, misanthropic character of his young protagonist –

> Is it not better then to be alone,
> And love earth only for its earthly sake?
> By the blue rushing of the arrowy Rhone
> Or the pure bosom of its nursing lake,
> Which feeds it as a mother who doth make
> A fair but forward infant her own care
> Kissing its cries away as these awake?
> Is it not better thus our lives to wear
> Than join the crushing crowd, doomed to inflict or bear?
> (*Childe Harold*, Canto III, 671–9)

For Harold, the crowd was crushing and so the bleak choice of life was either to endure suffering or to inflict it on others. The only refuge from such a dilemma was to be found in nature, the eternal mother with her 'pure bosom', where restless 'wanderers o'er eternity' might still find some temporary relief (*Chile Harold*, III, 671, 689).

This was the image of Byron that Shelley evoked, when he described 'the Pilgrim of Eternity' coming to mourn at the shrine of one who would rapidly become the best known poetic victim of the cruel world – John Keats. In 'Adonais', his formal pastoral elegy on Keats, Shelley introduced Byron in stanza 30, 'veiling all the lightnings of his song in sorrow' over the untimely death of their young contemporary ('Adonais', 267–8; O'Neill and Mahoney, 392). In the following stanzas, Shelley portrayed himself as a

> frail form,
> A phantom among men, companionless
> As the last cloud of an expiring storm
> ('Adonais', 271–3)

This succession of melancholy images culminated with the elegist himself, the last in the procession, 'neglected and apart – / A herd-abandoned deer struck by the hunter's dart' (296–7), which made the mourner a mirror-image of his subject – and vice versa. As with many formal poetic tributes, from Milton's 'Lycidas' to Tennyson's *In Memoriam*, the elegy is often concerned as much with the elegist as the deceased.

In this passage, Shelley was recalling not just Keats, nor his own unhappiness, however, but also a moment from Cowper's *The Task*, where the poet-speaker memorably cast himself as 'a stricken deer, that left the herd / Long since' (*Task*, III, 108–9). Cowper had continued this metaphor with gratitude for his personal redemption through Christ, who had similarly 'Been hurt by the archers' (*Task*, III, 112–3), but Shelley carefully presented his own 'branded and ensanguined brow' as being 'like Cain's or Christ's' ('Adonais', 306). The allusion is characteristic of Shelley's poetry, in that it draws on Christian tradition while eschewing Christian consolation. His equation of Christ the redeemer, with Cain, the original outsider, permanently marked out from other men, is a rejection of both Cowper's answer to alienation and the comfort offered by religion in the face of death. For Shelley, who had been sent down from Oxford for writing a pamphlet entitled *The Necessity of Atheism*, Christianity could neither resolve the problems of the world nor alleviate the human condition. Not only was Shelley presenting the modern poet as an isolated sufferer, he was also suggesting that Christ had been similarly abandoned.

Shelley's fusion of Christian and classical traditions continues throughout 'Adonais' until the closing image of the 'spirit's bark' being 'borne darkly, fearfully, afar' (492). Here Biblical metaphor joins with classical apotheosis, to render Keats as the Evening Star, a beacon in 'the abode where the Eternal are' ('Adonais', 495). Whether or not 'Adonais' offers any hope of a spiritual afterlife is a matter for individual interpretation, but it certainly expresses faith in the immortality of poetry, drawing its own confirmation from the enduring presence of the greatest literature. If the Romantic poet wished to seek his true company, the poem seems to suggest, then more hope may be derived from the memory of departed writers than from religion or the unfeeling crowd.

The very fact that Shelley was writing an elegy for Keats, however, demonstrates that images of isolation did not constitute his entire imaginative landscape. Indeed, the very consciousness of loneliness depends on a powerful sense of love and community. 'Adonais' was prefaced by an attack on the hostility of contemporary reviewers, 'wretched men' who, like those condemning Christ to the cross, 'know not what they do' (Preface to 'Adonais'). Shelley's indignation over the negative reception of Keats's *Endymion* burst out in his prefatory condemnation of the reviewers' indifference over where their 'poisoned shaft' might land. This opposition between pack and prey not only informs the poetic lament for Keats, 'pierced by the shaft which flies in darkness' ('Adonais', 11–12), but also prepares readers for the alignment of the victim with his elegist, 'struck by the hunter's dart' ('Adonais', 297). If Shelley's haunting elegy contributed to Victorian perceptions of the Romantic poet's excessive fragility, it also revealed an acute awareness of the literary circles of the period and the saving strength of poetic friendships.

Shelley was never a close companion of Keats, but they had met and enjoyed evenings of lively conversation and sonnet-writing at Leigh Hunt's house before the Shelleys' departure for Italy in 1818. 'Adonais' may emphasize the alienation of the young poet, representing Keats as an over-sensitive artist struck down by an unfeeling reception, but it shows him being mourned by a dazzling host of well-wishers as well. Keats's death is lamented by Byron, Moore, Hunt and Shelley, who evokes, in turn, the spirits of Plato, Dante, Milton, Chatterton, Sidney and Lucan. This is a portrait of the poet not as a solitary, but as part of a select band of the like-minded, who are at once mutually affirmative and sustained by a sense of their eventual far-reaching influence. The companions of Adonais were not all personal friends of Keats: they join together, nevertheless, to recognise one of their own. Though equally stylized, 'Adonais' is, in many ways, a much truer representation of the experience of most poets of the Romantic period than Wallis's dramatic image of the dead Chatterton. For it acknowledges the common fear of alienation, while affirming the vital existence of sympathetic friends.

Shelley admitted in the preface to 'Adonais' that if the details of Keats's last illness had been available to him, he would have included a tribute to Joseph Severn, who accompanied Keats to Italy and remained at his side until death. Had Shelley known Keats better, he might also have introduced into the funeral procession many more of the real friends who had sustained the young poet throughout his short writing life – George Felton Mathews, Benjamin Bailey, John Hamilton Reynolds, Charles Armitage Brown, Benjamin Robert Haydon, John Taylor – as well as members of his family – George and Georgiana Keats, his younger sister, Fanny - and last of all, his fiancée, Fanny Brawne. Such a party of supportive family and friends would have been at odds, of course, with the conventions of pastoral elegy, which demand that the dead poet be mourned by other poet-shepherds, and it would also have blunted Shelley's attack on hostile critics. As a formal elegy, 'Adonais' serves more purposes than a simple obituary, but it conveys a sense of lamentation among sympathetic companions nonetheless. This is not after all an Alastor poet, dying alone and unmourned in a hidden mountain recess.

For later generations of readers, privileged with access to Keats's own, wonderful, letters, the strength of his capacity for friendship is evident on every page of the correspondence. Keats himself emerges almost like a character in an epistolary novel, offering his latest thoughts, testing ideas, entertaining his correspondents, sending love and, through the process of affectionate exchanges, defining himself. Since the surviving correspondence spans only eight years, we are able to trace his growth from the first glimpse of the caring elder brother, sending his eleven-year old sister a skipping rope to encourage her to 'jump and skip about, to avoid those nasty Chilblanes', to the final, moving letter to Charles Brown, written on his deathbed in Rome, 'I always made an awkward bow' (Keats, *Letters*, I, 99; II, 360). Through the letters, we gain an understanding of Keats's personality, relationships and opinions, including the host of literary ideas about 'beauty', 'the truth of imagination', 'Negative capability', 'the chameleon poet', 'the Mansion of many Apartments' or 'the vale of soul-making', not to mention his shifting responses to Shakespeare, Milton, Wordsworth, Byron, Shelley.

The body of correspondence has had such a strong influence on critical understandings of Keats that it also helps to make sense of the secondary literature almost as much as the primary. It is always worth bearing in mind, however, that Keats's voice often alters according to his correspondent, that the most-quoted passages are generally part of a longer, more complicated train of thought, and that each letter is really a text in its own right. In spite of all this, the letters offer invaluable insights into the mind of the poet. What they demonstrate, as well, is Keats's perpetual dialogue with friends and family: he may have sat quietly in the garden for three hours composing the 'Ode to a Nightingale', but this was after a memorable walk with Coleridge when nightingales had been among the topics of conversation. In January, 1818, Keats wrote to his younger brother, George, that he was 'in the habit of taking my papers to Dilkes & copying there; so I chat & proceed at the same time' (*Letters*, I, 215); the survival of this and many other letters allows the modern reader privileged access to a poet for whom literary progress was twinned with chatting. Though

Keats followed literary fashions in writing sonnets to 'Solitude' and 'Sleep', and his odes suggest a solitary, meditative and often melancholy speaker, the letters reveal very different aspects of the poet and his relationships.

Despite Shelley's self-portrayal in 'Adonais' of the elegist as 'companionless', his career was similarly bound up with those closest to him – the men and women who inspired his poems, supplied intellectual challenges, emotional support, professional esteem and who would, eventually, be faced with the practical task of editing and arranging his surviving manuscripts. Shelley met his future wife, Mary, when paying homage to one of his intellectual idols – the radical philosopher, William Godwin. Indeed, the satisfaction Godwin took from the adulatory visit was somewhat tarnished when the young poet – already a married man – eloped with his sixteen-year-old daughter. Mary Shelley was a writer and the daughter of writers, being the child of Godwin and Mary Wollstonecraft. Her mother, the political polemicist and educationalist, was well known for both her essay on *The Rights of Woman* and her scandalous life, made public after her untimely death from postnatal complications in a frank *Memoir* by the bereaved Godwin. In the Shelleys' immediate circle, lives and letters were inextricably entwined, the exchange of ideas and manuscripts part of their everyday existence.

Some of Shelley's greatest poems were written in response to Byron, who became a close friend in the summer of 1816, which both poets spent in Switzerland, with Mary Shelley and her half-sister, Claire Clairmont. In the stunning Alpine surroundings, conversation ran on literary, religious, philosophical, political, scientific and personal topics, feeding into poems such as Shelley's 'Mont Blanc', where the mountain inspires profound exploration of the human mind and its relationship to the universe. The foundations of later work such as *Prometheus Unbound* were also being laid, in response to the image of Prometheus created by Byron at this time. Poems were pouring out of Byron during this remarkable summer, which saw not only Childe Harold among the Alps, but also new creations such as 'Prometheus' or 'The Prisoner of Chillon' (inspired by the Castle of Chillon on Lake Geneva), the experimental mental drama, *Manfred*, 'Darkness' and a series of fine lyrics expressing his longing for his half-sister, Augusta Leigh. Byron may have felt exiled from his native land, but he was eager to retain his fans through new publications, and benefiting from the more immediate responses of the Shelley entourage.

For Shelley, inspiration was coming not just from the unpredictable visitations of the poetic spirit or the loving presence of Mary, but also from the volcanic creativity of Byron. This was the intellectual and artistic dialogue imaginatively recreated by Shelley in 'Julian and Maddalo', once they had each moved south to Italy. And it was to be memorialized all too soon in the recollections, notes and biographies written by mutual friends such as Edward Trelawney, Leigh Hunt, Thomas Moore and Thomas Medwin. In his 'Letter to Maria Gisborne', Shelley paid warm tribute to the friends he had left behind in London, portraying Leigh Hunt, for example, surrounded by 'dozens / Of female friends, sisters-in-law and cousins' (218; *Poems and Prose*, 225). Though far from many of his old literary companions, in the 'Paradise of Exiles, Italy' ('Julian and Maddalo', 57; *Poems and Prose*, 90), Shelley still derived comfort from thoughts of 'those hearts which must remember me' ('Letter to Maria Gisborne', 13, *Poems and Prose*, 220). After moving to Italy, Shelley became acutely conscious of the important of long-lasting poetic friendships and he was eagerly awaiting a visit from Leigh Hunt when he drowned during the storm that capsized his sailing boat in July 1821.

The creative inspiration afforded by literary conversation is nowhere more apparent than in the writings of Mary Shelley, who worked closely with her husband and also acted as an amanuensis for Byron. Her early novels drew creative energy from their shared ideas, actions, conversations, her later work from memories of a life enriched by mutual intellectual and emotional experience. When she reflected on the origins of *Frankenstein* for the new edition of 1831, she recalled the Swiss summer of 1816 which she spent with Shelley, Claire and Byron. The powerful experiences and alpine scenes that fed *Childe Harold* and 'Mont Blanc' nourished her imagination just as much as theirs, but it was Byron's challenge, 'We will each write a ghost story', that prompted the composition of *Frankenstein*. Though a novel rather than a poem, Mary Shelley's version of the Prometheus myth makes fascinating reading in relation to the poetry composed during the summer in which it was first conceived, demonstrating the effects of one kind of Romantic sociability, even as it explores Romantic solitude. Extensive analysis is not appropriate in a book devoted to Romantic poetry, but some consideration of Mary Shelley's work sheds valuable light on the crucial relationship between solitude and companionship in the period.

Like her protagonist's creation, Mary Shelley's first novel was created from a mass of disparate elements – conversations, personal memories, European folktales, Greek mythology, English literature, travel books, modern science, political ideologies, landscapes of the mind and the eye.

At the heart of this strange amalgamation, however, was an acute concern for individual well-being and the dangers of damaging the human capacity for sympathy. The book is narrated by an arctic explorer, Robert Walton, whose obsessive pursuit of the unconquered North takes him further and further from home and family. Walton is characterized from the beginning as a man without friends, and his loneliness makes him especially receptive to Frankenstein's extraordinary entry into the narrative on a floating block of ice in the deserted landscape. But if Frankenstein's cautionary tale of unholy creation is addressed to Walton, its real warning is directed to anyone whose single-minded ambitions might lead to the neglect of loved ones. At the novel's center is the towering figure of monstrous creation – huge, powerful, highly articulate, but driven by a desperate sense of isolation:

> am I not alone, miserably alone? You, my creator, abhor me; what hope can I gather from your fellow-creatures, who owe me nothing? They spurn and hate me. The desert mountains are my refuge. I have wandered here many days; the caves of ice, which I only do not fear, are a dwelling place to me'.
> (*Frankenstein*, vol II, chap.2; *Novels*, I, 78)

The creature, formed by Frankenstein from body parts stolen from crypts and mortuaries and brought to life in the laboratory, startles readers of the novel as much as much as the characters he encounters because of his eloquent speeches and profound loneliness. Like Goethe's Werther, he is a Romantic solitary, in search of a sympathetic soul-mate, and his language echoes with literary allusion – to Milton, Shelley, Byron, Coleridge and Wordsworth. The creature's frustrated desire for companionship leads not to his own destruction, however, but to that of all those connected to his creator, until both Frankenstein and his monster-child are locked in mutual flight and pursuit through an empty, frozen wasteland. Rather than celebrate the creative power and psychological support inherent in loving relationships directly, *Frankenstein* dwelled on the horrors attendant on their absence. As a critique of Romantic solitude and visionary pursuit, it is hard to find a more uncompromising example.

In the years following the shock of Shelley's shipwreck, Mary worked hard to piece together his surviving manuscripts for a volume of *Posthumous Poems*, annotating each poem with details about its composition. In her gloomy novel, *The Last Man*, she drew a series of fictional portraits, revisiting imaginatively the places she had lived with Shelley, as well as conjuring up a

Byronic character, Raymond, to express some of the complex feelings provoked by Byron's own premature death in Greece in 1824. *The Last Man* represented Romantic solitude at its most extreme, but it was a horrifying image of enforced isolation, not a state to be sought voluntarily. Lionel Verney's predicament is even more desperate than that of Frankenstein's shunned creature, because he is tormented by the traumatic experience of losing his wife, sister, and children in painful, prolonged succession, as well as the entire human race. Mary Shelley was revisiting one of the bleakest poems to emerge from the memorable summer of 1816 – Byron's 'Darkness' – but by treating her secular apocalypse in a novel, she was able to dwell on the prolonged suffering of the last survivor of the human race.

Romantic Resistance to Solitude

The Last Man was published in 1826, two years after Byron's death, but Mary Shelley's critique of the myth of solitary genius was just as much part of the Romantic movement as *Childe Harold*. If the figure of the solitary haunted much Romantic poetry, it often provoked resistance, or at least, qualification, more readily than emulation. Few writers expressed as deep a horror of alienation as Mary Shelley in *The Last Man*, but the need to counter melancholic loneliness was often in evidence. Charlotte Smith's adaptations of Goethe's suicidal young Werther, for example, provoked an eloquent riposte from Anna Seward, when she read the third edition of Smith's *Elegiac Sonnets* in 1786:

> Ah, never let thy lyre superior dwell
> On themes thy better judgement must disdain!
> It ill befits that verse like thine should tell
> Of Petrarch's love, or Werther's frantic pain!
>   ('Advice to Mrs Smith', 5–8)

What especially alarmed Seward were Smith's sympathetic renderings of Goethe's self-destructive hero, and she urged her friend not to let 'the dark dreams of suicide obtain / Deceitful lustre from such tones as thine' (11–12). The responsibility of poets to their readers had been brought home by a wave of suicides across Europe in the 1770s, apparently inspired by *The Sorrows of Werther*. Melancholy solitude not only had a dangerous appeal to creative writers of the period – but also to those who admired the sensibility spilling from their tender lines. The 'friendship' of Romantic poets was not necessarily a question of sympathising with fellow writers, but often involved recalling them from the perils of their own highly-wrought personalities. For if solitude was a recurrent motif in Romantic poetry, so was the desire to rescue the solitary.

The potential dangers inherent in the poet's character were addressed directly in Wordsworth's 'Resolution and Independence', which begins in cheerful enough mood, celebrating the special pleasure of a sunny morning after a night of storms:

> All things that love the sun are out of doors;
> The sky rejoices in the morning's birth,
> The grass is bright with rain-drops; on the moors
> The Hare is running races in her mirth;
> And with her feet she from the plashy earth
> Raises a mist; which, glittering in the sun,
> Runs with her all the way, wherever she doth run.
>
> I was a Traveller then upon the moor;
> I saw the Hare that rac'd about with joy;
> I heard the woods, and distant waters, roar;
> Or heard them not, as happy as a Boy;
> The pleasant season did my heart employ:
> My old remembrances went from me wholly;
> And all the ways of men, so vain and melancholy.
> (8–21; O'Neill and Mahoney, 157)

The joy of the early stanzas is almost instantly deflated, however, by sudden, inexplicable anxieties: 'fears, and fancies, thick upon me came; / Dim sadness, and blind thoughts I knew nor could not name' (27–8). As the young speaker grapples with his fears, the happiness derived from his sense of hare-like freedom rapidly becomes a torment, aggravated by fears of 'Solitude, pain of heart, distress, and poverty' (35). Dark thoughts of poets such as Chatterton or Burns, whose promising lives had been suddenly cut short, could blacken the sunniest moment:

> We Poets in our youth begin in gladness,
> But thereof comes in the end despondency and madness.
> (48–9)

Memories of Chatterton and Burns prompted a very different response in Wordsworth from Shelley's indignation at the death of 'Adonais': though similarly prey to an uncaring world, their examples were as likely to provoke despair as inspiration in the rising generation of poets. What was even more chilling was the thought that their suffering might even be self-generated – a consequence of the kind of creative personality capable of composing the greatest poetry.

'Resolution and Independence' does not dwell on the memory of prematurely dead poets in the same way as 'Adonais', however, but is bent instead on the recovery of the young speaker from any self-destructive tendencies. The young speaker's horror of 'solitude, pain of heart, distress, and poverty' is countered by an unlikely meeting with a very different kind of solitary. The old Leech gatherer who rouses the young poet from his sudden gloom is a figure of utter isolation, standing single in a 'lonely place', but despite his apparently desperate situation – forced to make a living from gathering leeches from the ponds – his words are 'Cheerfully uttered' (53, 142) Though a most improbable agent of salvation, the uncomplaining old man, who trusts in his own future 'with God's good help, by choice or chance' (111), provides the troubled speaker with such a bracing example that he is able to banish the despondency of the preceding stanzas. The old man's unexpected strength and redemptive words rescue the speaker from the 'fear that kills' (120) by revealing its source: in the mind. The young poet continues to be haunted by the figure of the old man, 'Wandering about alone and silently', but he has been recalled from his own, more isolating, condition by the old man's unintentional 'admonishment' (138, 119). Wordsworth, perhaps, understood better than anyone how solitude might bring its own dangers and salvation.

Although the poem has a timeless quality that seems oddly removed from daily life, its composition was partly a result of Wordsworth's immediate concerns for his close friend and collaborator, Coleridge. 'Resolution and Independence' is cast as a poem of self-rebuke, but it was also a reply to Coleridge's recent verse letter to Sara Hutchinson, originally composed in April 1802 and subsequently published in the *Morning Post* as 'Dejection: An Ode', on Wordsworth's wedding day in October, 1802. The speaker's sudden despondency in 'Resolution and Independence' is associated explicitly with thoughts of Chatterton and Burns, but beneath the public images of sudden decline lay private memories of Coleridge's stricken confession, 'I am not the buoyant thing I was of yore' ('Letter to Sara Hutchinson', 227; Wu, 669). Coleridge's lacerating verse epistle was in itself a response to the opening stanzas of the Ode Wordsworth had begun in March 1802, which contained a haunting confession,

> It is not now as it has been of yore; -
> Turn wheresoe'er I may,
> By night or day,
> The things which I have seen I now can see no more.
> ('Ode. Intimations of Immortality, 6–9;
> O'Neill and Mahoney, 163)

Wordsworth's wistful meditation on the disappearance of 'the visionary gleam' had been answered by his friend's much more anguished expression of despair over his own creative paralysis. Paradoxically, the fears associated with solitude that Wordsworth addressed in 'Resolution and Independence' were part of a painful, unfolding poetic dialogue between close friends: as so often, images of Romantic solitude were also signs of companionship.

As Wordsworth's poem described the young speaker rescued by his mysterious encounter, then, it was engaged in a private attempt to reach the dear friend and fellow poet whose current state of mind seemed dangerously reminiscent of Chatterton and Burns. Wordsworth knew from personal experience that sensitive, creative minds were especially susceptible to depression and fully recognized his own massive psychological and spiritual debt to Coleridge. The prospect of his brilliant friend being afflicted by 'despondency and madness' was horrifying, and yet Coleridge's evident despair over his unhappy marriage, his hopeless love for Sara Hutchinson, his poor health, troubled sleep and fears of declining poetic ability, was impossible to ignore and very difficult to dispel. 'Resolution and Independence' is a courageous affirmation of the tenacity of hope and, therefore, a moving reaffirmation of unshaken devotion to his closest friend as well.

As Wordsworth portrays the volatile young man upset by thoughts of 'the sleepless soul who perished in his pride', he was not only recalling Chatterton, but also Coleridge's 'Monody on the Death of Chatterton' and one of his own poems, published in their joint collection, *Lyrical Ballads*. The volume originally published in 1798 opened with what is probably the period's most terrifying narrative of isolation, 'The Rime of the Ancyent Marinere', with its image of the principal speaker

> Alone, alone, all all alone,
> Alone on the wide wide sea,
> And Christ would take no pity on
> My soul in agony.
> (224–7; Wu, 338)

By the end of his ordeal, the Mariner is driven by a compulsion to address strangers, but, despite his hard-won wisdom, he remains a figure of restless alienation, passing from land to land with strange power of speech.

The first poem by Wordsworth in the 1798 volume of *Lyrical Ballads* was less instantly memorable than 'The Ancient Mariner', but it was equally concerned with solitude and carried an even more explicit warning against the attendant dangers. 'The Lines left upon a seat in a Yew-tree, which stands near the Lake of Esthwaite, on a desolate part of the shore, yet commanding a beautiful prospect', offers a sensitive understanding of the lure of loneliness for a young idealist, disappointed by his experience of the world, who bears a strong resemblance to Goethe's Werther and provides a model for the later youthful solitaries of Shelley's 'Alastor', Keats's *Endymion* and Byron's *Childe Harold*. Wordsworth presents a solitary, who has abandoned his idealism and spends his days alone in lovely surroundings, dwelling on unfulfilled hopes, 'Till his eyes streamed with tears' ('Lines left upon a seat in a Yew Tree', 42; Wu, 353). Despite the obvious sympathy for the recluse, the poem nevertheless delivers its own strong admonishment,

> that pride,
> Howe'er disguised in its own majesty,
> Is littleness; that he, who feels contempt
> For any living thing, hath faculties
> Which he has never used; that thought with him
> Is in its infancy.
> (46–51)

Visionary solitude is exposed in this poem as a form of 'pride' – the very word that would later be chosen to evoke Chatterton in 'Resolution and Independence'.

In the 'Lines left upon a Seat in a Yew-Tree', society's neglect is devastating to the young visionary, but his reaction is shown to be every bit as misguided as 'the world' itself:

> and so, his spirit damped
> At once, with rash disdain he turned away,
> And with the food of pride sustained his soul
> In solitude.
> (18–21)

In the light of this description, Wordsworth's subsequent summary of Chatterton as 'the sleepless soul that perished in his pride' ('Resolution and Independence', 44) seems more complicated than straightforward indignation over the failure of society to recognise contemporary genius. That the poet might be his own worst enemy was a fear that Wordsworth explored again and again, but the chilling possibility offered in 'The Yew Tree Lines' was that the beauty of nature might sometimes contribute to the self-destructive cycle by offering such a soothing alternative to human company.

It is an illuminating poem to read beside 'Lines Written a few Miles above Tintern Abbey', which recalls an earlier self, now lost, for whom Nature 'was all in all' (76; O'Neill and Mahoney, 107). The passionate younger figure, bounding over mountains and beside lonely streams, has strong appeal, but his growth into one attuned to the 'still sad, music of humanity' and sustained by a new awareness of both divine and human presences is ultimately a matter for celebration not lament. In many of Wordsworth's poems, hope for salvation emerges through an encounter with a human being, rather than through the ministrations of nature alone. *Lyrical Ballads* is full of human voices, demonstrating the poet's need for those able to 'chasten and subdue' his more wayward tendencies ('Tintern Abbey', 94). The final poem of the collection, 'Lines written a few miles above Tintern Abbey', extols nature as the 'nurse, / The guide and the guardian' of the poet, but this celebration is prompted by the loving companionship of the poet's 'dear, dear Sister!' (110–11; 122). Far from being a hymn to seclusion, it is a paean of praise for feelings powerful enough to combat 'solitude, or fear, or pain, or grief' (144). Wordsworth and Coleridge were poets of love in its widest sense: not of sexual passion alone, but of affection, loyalty, companionship, parental feeling and friendship. The volume that they planned and published together is filled with moments in which isolation is countered and, at times, triumphantly overcome, and it was born from the heady mutual discovery of loving like minds.

This was the joyful time recalled fondly by Wordsworth in *The Prelude*, after painful examination of his own turmoil in the wake of the French Revolution and outbreak of War. *The Prelude* records his gradual recovery, paying tribute to 'those two dear ones', Mary Hutchinson and Dorothy Wordsworth, and to the 'Friend' who is such a crucial presence throughout the massive poem:

> beloved Friend,
> When, looking back thou seest, in clearer view
> Than any sweetest sight of yesterday,
> That summer when on Quantock's grassy Hills

> Far ranging, and among the sylvan Coombs,
> Thou in delicious words, with happy heart,
> Didst speak the Vision of that Ancient Man,
> The bright-eyed Mariner, and rueful woes
> Didst utter of Lady Christabel;
> And I, associate in such labour, walked
> Murmuring of him who, joyous hap! was found,
> After the perils of his moonlight ride
> Near the loud Waterfall; or her who sate
> In misery near the miserable Thorn;
> When thou dost to that summer turn thy thoughts,
> And hast before thee all which we then were,
> To thee, in memory of that happiness
> It will be known, by thee at least, my Friend,
> Felt, that the history of a Poet's mind
> Is labour not unworthy of regard:
> To thee the work shall justify itself.
> (*Prelude*, XIII, 390–410;
> *William Wordsworth*, 514–5)

As Wordsworth reached the end of his great meditation on the growth of the poet's mind, he turned directly to address Coleridge, comforted by the vivid memories of their earlier collaboration and the knowledge that at least one reader would understand the purpose of his great labor. The passage recalled their conversations about 'The Idiot Boy', 'The Thorn', 'Christabel' and other poems being written for *Lyrical Ballads*, though here the Ancient Mariner is remembered as being as 'bright-eyed' as his creator, and the product of a happy rather than lonely heart. Coleridge had offered sympathetic encouragement and professional esteem just when Wordsworth needed it most and now, eight years later, Wordsworth was instinctively seeking corroboration for his latest work. Their relationship had always been a complicated mutual dialogue and, in *The Prelude* (known to the immediate circle as 'The Poem to Coleridge'), Wordsworth was at once soliciting reassurance and offering hope to his friend.

The long passage of fond recollection above is followed by reflections on the deep unhappiness that Coleridge had experienced in the interim, before sealing hopes for 'renovated health', with the gift of the poem itself as 'an Offering of my love' (*The Prelude*, XIII, 424, 427). *The Prelude* is, perhaps, the most generous 'Get Well' greeting ever. When Wordsworth read the complete thirteen-book poem to his friend in January 1807, Coleridge rose to the occasion by rallying his own reluctant powers into a poetic response. 'To William Wordsworth' describes 'such sense of wings uplifting' at the realization of Wordsworth's 'faithful hopes / Thy hopes of me, dear friend', uttered with 'heights and depths of harmony' (57–60; Wu, 687), that despair must now be abandoned. He could not have paid a more appropriate tribute to Wordsworth's great imaginative achievement, nor to the vital importance of poetic friendship.

The Public and Private Friendships of Poets

Although Wordsworth's greatest tribute to poetic friendship, *The Prelude*, remained private throughout his life, many of the poems he published included references to close companions, friends and acquaintances. In the second edition of *Lyrical Ballads*, for example, the 'Poems on the Naming of Places' described local spots that had special meaning for the poet and his family because of the little incidents which had occurred there. The pastoral poems in the volume, too, suggested a poet who knew the family histories of everyone in the neighborhood, while poems written during trips elsewhere often featured people encountered on the journey as well as the 'dear companion' or friend who went with him. Coleridge, too, published poems not only to Wordsworth, to Sara Hutchinson, to his son, to his wife, to his brother, to his friends, Charles Lamb, Charles Lloyd and Robert Southey, but also to numerous well known figures, literary and political, including Edmund Burke, William Godwin, Lord Stanhope, Richard Brinsley Sheridan, Horne Tooke and William Bowles. Poetry provided a means of making political comment through direct address to a public figure, or of making public a more personal tribute to a friend or family member.

Verse epistles had become an established form in the early eighteenth century, often used for satiric or comic purposes; but as fellow-feeling became a moral imperative, so poems 'To a Friend' tended to offer heartfelt expressions of private affection or public concern, taking the form of sonnets as readily as longer verse. The verse epistle nevertheless continued to attract poets, offering, like their prose letters, a forum for exchanging ideas, exploring feelings and testing convictions. The very idea of a correspondent, or better still, a circle of different correspondents, seemed to offer helpful boundaries through which to define the multi-faceted, fluid and inherently elusive self. The literary fraternity, or sorority, became widely recognised in the period – both by critics who liked to label poets according to 'Schools' or 'Circles' ('Blue Stocking', 'Della Cruscan',

'Lake', 'Cockney', 'Satanic') and by poets who liked to present themselves in lively, creative company. What may sometimes appear to be a simple aspect of biographical context can often turn out to be a careful rhetorical construct, promoted by either the poets themselves, by their friends and admirers, or by those hostile to their work.

Robert Burns, for example, though figured along with Chatterton in 'Resolution and Independence', presented himself to the reading public as part of a group of 'brither bards'. His debut volume, *Poems, Chiefly in the Scottish Dialect*, 1786, was full of poems addressed to friends and fellow poets, which gave the impression that the author was perpetually engaged in literary exchanges with equally talented local figures. In fact, the poems published by the local recipients of Burns's epistles were rather less proficient in the art than Burns suggested, but the lively series of poems places the author at the centre of a thriving independent, contemporary culture. Through his verse epistles, Burns constructed an image of the poet as a sociable, often self-ironizing figure, equally fond of whisky and women. The voice that emerges from the 'Epistle to James Smith' could hardly have been less like that of the intensely melancholic poets who wrote in the shadow of Ossian, Chatterton or Werther, as he summarizes his own motive for composition – 'I rhyme for *fun*' (30; *Poems and Songs*, I, 179).

In the epistles to David Sillar, Willie Simson and John Lapraik, Burns presented his poems as spontaneous overflowings of a 'tinder' heart – at once tender to the feelings of others and quick to ignite. In the preface to the *Poems, Chiefly in the Scottish Dialect*, he acknowledged his desire to 'kindle at the flame' of his Scottish predecessors, Allan Ramsay and Robert Fergusson, but the poems that followed showed that Burns's imagination was just as apt to light up in response to the smallest experience or encounter (*Poems and Songs*, III, 972). 'Epistle to Davie' celebrates the creative power of both love and friendship, as the poem reaches its climax with an apostrophe to 'tender feelings', in particular those associated with 'My Davie or my Jean!':

> O, how that *name* inspires my style!
> The words come skelpan rank an' file
>   Amaist before I ken!
>   (141–3; *Poems and Songs*, I, 69)

Poem after poem in his first collection upheld the values of the heart over those of the world, and 'joys that riches ne'er could buy' ('Epistle to Davie', 103).

Burns's epistles were pre-eminently poems of friendship, for through the comically inebriated pose of the sentimental bard at the bar, he reached out to embrace anyone who came within reach of his words. The invitation to 'Come to my bowl, come to my arms, / My friends, my brothers!' ('Epistle to J. L****k', 125–6; Wu, 265) might have been directed towards the fellow poet, John Lapraik, but the sentiments spread far beyond the notional recipient of the verse letter. Since the 'Epistle to J. L****k' begins as an offer of friendship to an unknown poet, whose song has been performed at a recent party, it enacts a gesture of goodwill towards the stranger reading his letter. Though the reader of Burns's volume might not even recognize the local references to Muirkirk or Mauchline, the prevailing tone of generous amiability is unmistakeable. Only the frostiest reader could resist the unassuming pledge of friendship, offered so freely by the author of the verse letter:

> Now, Sir, if ye hae friends enow,
> Tho' *real friends* I b'lieve are few;
> Yet, if your catalogue be fow,
>   I'se no insist;
> But gif ye want a friend that's true,
>   I'm on your list.
>   (85–90)

As so often, the 'friend' named in the poem is a surrogate for the reader, who seems redeemed from the anonymity of modern print culture by the personal invitation of the poet.

It is not surprising that the Romantic period witnessed the beginnings of modern 'fan' culture, once the poetry had developed ways of creating an illusion of intimate companionship amongst strangers. Burns himself received a number of admiring verse epistles in response to *Poems, Chiefly in the Scottish Dialect*, including the accomplished rhyming couplets from Elizabeth Scot of Jedburgh, beginning

> My canty, witty rhyming ploughman
> I hafflins doubt, it is na' true man,
> That ye between the stilts was bred,
> Wi' ploughman school'd, wi' ploughman fed.
>   (1–4; *Poems and Songs*, I, 324)

Whether it was her scepticism about Burns's supposed lack of education or her offer of a 'marled plaid' or the skill of her verse epistle that caught Burns's attention is uncertain, but her effort elicited a spirited reply:

> For you, na bred to barn and byre,
> Wha sweetly tune the Scottish lyre,
>   Thanks to you for your line.
> The marled plaid ye kindly spare,
> By me should gratefully be ware;
>   'Twad please me to the Nine.
>   (57–62; *Poems and Songs*, I, 327)

(Not all Burns's admirers received such warm replies: a verse epistle by Janet Little, who worked as a dairymaid before being talent-spotted by Burns's friend, Frances Dunlop, elicited nothing in return.)

To cast unknown readers as friends might run the risk of unwanted adulation, but in general, it was a useful strategy for pre-empting adverse comment on the poems. The 'Epistle to J. L***k' deftly binds the author and reader of the verse letter together, in defiance of 'Your Critic-folk' (55), whose inability to discern true poetry is made only too clear. Even a reader who might pride himself on his educated taste would hesitate to be classed with 'A set o' dull, conceited Hashes' who 'Confuse their brains in *Colledge-classes*!' (67–8) Far preferable was the role of the new friend, invited to swap 'rhymin-ware' over a drink with this engaging author and joining those whose hearts 'the *tide of kindness* warms' (107, 122). The affectionate tone of Burns's verse epistles was highly effective for disarming anyone who might find fault with his verse: his poems emerged remarkably unscathed even in the savage reviewing culture of the early nineteenth century.

The skilful opposition of poetic friendships to unfeeling critical opinion runs throughout the Romantic period, even though the tone of the poems can be as different as Burns's verse epistles are from 'Adonais'. As early as 1782, Hannah More's 'Sensibility' included an impressive parade of talented friends, before lamenting David Garrick, the literary friend and mentor who had fostered her own talent:

> If harsher critics were compelled to blame,
> I gained in friendship what I lost in fame
> And friendship's fostering smiles can well repay
> What critic rigour justly takes away.
>   ('Sensibility', 91–4; Wu, 59)

More is not adopting the wholesale dismissal of 'critic folk' that Burns recommended to Lapraik, but rather distinguishing the careful acumen of a friend, who, though quite capable of recognizing defects, might still 'detect a happy line' (99). The poet's acknowledgement of her own faults in a passage expressing gratitude for the kindness of the friendliest readers is another way of pre-empting negative responses, while avoiding any unkindness to the unnamed critics. Since her poem is a celebration of 'Sweet sensibility' or 'sympathy divine', it could not descend to expressing uncharitable sentiments, even when considering the harshest critics. As a woman poet, too, a certain politeness was necessary – to follow Burns in calling critics 'asses' would hardly have seemed ladylike.

More did, nevertheless, allow herself to reject certain kinds of readership:

> Let not the vulgar read this pensive strain,
> Their jests the tender anguish would profane.
> (151–2)

Her poem was addressed to a particular friend, Frances Boscawen, and appears to move through a catalogue of illustrious companions to embrace the whole of humankind. More was nevertheless constructing an ideal reader in the process, who would be a sympathetic friend and share the delicate feelings of 'Sensibility':

> Sweet sensibility, thou keen delight!
> Thou hasty moral, sudden sense of right!
> Thou untaught goodness! Virtue's precious seed!
> Thou sweet precursor of the generous deed!
> Beauty's quick relish! Reason's radiant morn,
> Which dawns soft light before Reflection's born!
> (245–50)

Friendship went hand in hand with sensibility and both reached out appealingly – and improvingly – to contemporary readers.

The poetic emphasis on friendship was not just a consequence of the contemporary elevation of sympathy, nor of the fashion for expressive kinds of literature that dominated later eighteenth-century British culture. Very often, affectionate addresses were rhetorical strategies to construct a particular kind of reader and, by casting that reader as a personal friend, poets were not merely pre-empting hostile criticism or lifting unknown hearts. Often their purposes were political. An appeal to like-minds might win sympathy for the poet, but it could also direct attention towards social and political issues. Henry Mackenzie had revealed the benefits of sympathy, for example, when he presented scenes of contemporary distress to his tearful hero, the Man of Feeling, in his 1771 novel of the same name. When More reflected on proper responses to the world's ills in 'Sensibility', she evoked Mackenzie's model of 'blessed Compassion', as distinguished from the false men of feeling who might make a parade of pity for a 'dying fawn', and yet 'persecute a wife or wrong a friend' (290–97). Sympathy, if properly directed, should bring about an improvement to the moral condition of society, as Adam Smith had argued (see above, Chapter 1). Better understanding of the self and others might also lead from individual acts of charity to major reforms in wider social attitudes, which made the cultivation of friendship a public as well as private benefit.

The ideal of true friendship often informed poems concerned with humanitarian issues, as evident in Anna Barbauld's angry response to the initial failure of the Bill proposing the abolition of the Slave Trade in 1791. Her address to William Wilberforce, the leader of the Abolition movement, takes the form of a verse epistle which, after exposing the unhealthy, uncaring, materialistic values of those content to allow the iniquitous trade to continue, concludes with praise of both William Wilberforce and the prison reformer, John Howard:

> Friends of the Friendless – hail, ye generous band
> Whose efforts yet arrest Heaven's lifted hand,
> Around whose steady brows in union bright
> The civic wreath and Christian's palm unite!
> ('Epistle to Wilberforce', 110–14; Wu, 41)

To be 'Friends of the friendless' was the highest praise, and the rhetoric of the poem, with its careful plural, 'Friends' invited readers to emulate the great examples of Wilberforce and Howard. Barbauld was promoting an ideal of befriending the friendless – the disempowered African slaves, the prisoners held in dreadful conditions – and by publishing a verse epistle, she encouraged readers to recognize shared sympathies and become virtual friends, in the hope that they might also become supporters of the cause.

Disappointment over the Abolition Bill of 1791 also contributed to Helen Maria Williams's departure for revolutionary France, where freedom seemed more in the ascendancy, as she made clear in a poem published when she left, 'A Farewell, for Two years, to England'. Again, the poem made careful use of the motif of 'Friendship', as Williams emphasized the different kinds of chains that linked her to her 'dear land' and would keep her attached to England despite the sense of national guilt (52; Wu, 302). The poem treads a careful path between criticism and affection for England, but crucial to its persuasion is the recurrent emphasis on friends, emerging most clearly in the closing lines, looking forward to her return from France:

> But may that moment to my eyes restore
> The friends whose love endears my native shore!
> Ah, long may Friendship, like the western rays,
> Cheer the sad evening of a stormy day,
> And gild my shadowy path with ling'ring light,
> The last dear beam that slowly sinks in sight.
> (211–16)

The patient loyalty of friends is a perennial prompt to personal gratitude, but in the context of a poem so concerned with political issues, Williams's friends are also sympathizers in whom she is placing her hopes for national redemption. Her 'shadowy path' may have been temporarily overcast by political disappointments in England, but some light still lingers, emanating from those who shared her radical commitments. The closing lines of her poem are, in effect, a plea to readers to keep the flame alight whatever the prevailing political climate.

Friendships Tested and Tried

The Romantic ideal of sociability extended beyond the personal to moral, philosophical, political and social concerns and print was a vital medium for reaching those who might be sympathetic to the writer's opinions. When Coleridge launched his own periodical in 1809, as a vehicle for regular essays on all manner of subjects, he attracted sufficient subscribers to finance the venture, thanking them in his choice of title: *The Friend*. Unlike his predecessors in the previous century, Coleridge avoided the authorial stance of a 'Spectator', 'Tatler', 'Idler' or 'Rambler', and opted for a persona more in keeping with the sentiments of his age. It soon became apparent, however, that not everyone would be likely to persevere with Coleridge's *Friend*, given its somewhat elaborate prose style and challenging philosophical approach. Once again, the author's presentation of himself as a friend was a rhetorical device to ensure a sympathetic response to his new work.

One friend, however, who was drawn to the new journal was Wordsworth, whose first 'Essays upon Epitaphs' as well as some passages from the unpublished *Prelude* appeared in its pages. What might initially have seemed a reaffirmation of the old collaboration was really, however, its swansong, for by 1811, the two poets had fallen out. Relations between Wordsworth and Coleridge had been strained for some years, but the difficulties that had given rise to the poetic dialogue of 'The Immortality Ode', 'Dejection' and 'Resolution and Independence' gradually deepened into a serious breach. Their lives had become less and less alike, as Coleridge left his wife and children behind to travel to Malta and eventually settled in London, while Wordsworth remained firmly fixed in the Lakes. As Coleridge's opium habit hardened, aggravating the associated problems, Wordsworth, struggling to support his own growing family, became less tolerant of his friend's behavior and worried by its effects on others. When he offered advice about Coleridge to their mutual friend, Basil Montagu, who had invited him to stay in London, Montagu passed on a version of their conversation to Coleridge, who was mortified. In a notebook entry of 3 November 1810, Coleridge's sense of loss is palpable: 'No one on earth has ever LOVED me' (Coleridge, *Notebooks*, III, entry 4006). It is almost as if Frankenstein's creature had taken up a pen.

Broken friendships are always painful, and especially if the friendship has been close. For poets who had done so much to elevate an ideal of friendship, however, and had expressed their mutual attachment in published poems, the breach was devastating For Coleridge, the thought that the relationship he had valued so highly might have been only a 'Semblance of Friendship' was almost too much to bear (Coleridge, *Notebooks*, III, entry 4006). When Wordsworth learned of Coleridge's distress, he felt deeply aggrieved, but despite efforts to retrieve their old mutual affection, things were never the same again. The hard-hitting assessment of Wordsworth's preface to *Lyrical Ballads* made by Coleridge a few years later in *Biographia Literaria* was rather more heartfelt than might be expected of an objective critical analysis.

The obverse of the Romantic elevation of friendship was the profound sense of loss sustained by a breach. Wordsworth and Coleridge's writing partnership was probably the most high profile friendship of the period, embodied as it was in *Lyrical Ballads* and pilloried by Francis Jeffrey in his attacks on the Lake School, so their quarrel seems especially significant. The Romantic period, however, saw a number of important poetic friendships being made and then unmade again. Since the poets involved were given to celebrating their fellow-feeling in verse, biographical detail often sheds helpful light on what might otherwise seem rather puzzling poems. Ann Yearsley's 'Address to Friendship', for example, was informed by both the contemporary ideal of true friendship and the painful awareness that it could be denied. She had enjoyed the unexpected friendship of Hannah More, who discovered Yearsley's talent while she was working as a dairymaid and struggling to support her family. More's patronage enabled Yearsley to publish her *Poems on Several Occasions* and win instant fame as the Milkwoman of Bristol. Things rapidly turned rather sour, however, when More and other well-meaning supporters decided that Yearsley was not quite capable of managing her own affairs and took steps to ensure that she only had partial control of her finances. Yearsley was not at all pleased and the friendship of the two women poets was at an end.

The well-publicized antagonism that had so rapidly developed between Yearsley and her patron, Hannah More, was only too obvious in Yearsley's 'Addressed to Sensibility', which was directed not just towards an abstract ideal of sensibility but also to More's poem of that name. Passages such as this, though not explicitly referring to Hannah More, possessed a strong personal dimension, easily recognisable after their unhappy breach:

> Pensive I rove,
> More wounded than the hart whose side yet holds
> The deadly arrow. Friendship, boast no more
> Thy hoard of joys o'er which my soul oft hung
> Like the too anxious miser o'er his gold.
> My treasures all are wrecked; I quit the scene
> Where haughty Insult cut the sacred ties
> Which long had held us.
> ('Addressed to Sensibility', 23–30; Wu, 23–30)

The arrow sent by a friend was even more deadly than those hurled at later poets by unthinking critics. If Yearsley was wounded by More's controlling attitude, however, she was quite capable of firing arrows of her own, such as the 'Autobiographical Narrative' which prefaced the fourth edition of her *Poems* and gave her account of More's behavior.

The painful saga also raises questions about literary patronage in the period, since the social inequality between More and Yearsley seems to have rendered the foundations of their 'friendship' unstable. Though an

extreme example of the way in which gratitude could rapidly become resentment, or patronage a form of control, the relationship between working class poets and those who helped them into print was often far from easy. James Hogg and Walter Scott, for example, remained on very good terms, but there was little sense on either side that their friendship was one of equals. Burns was able to play on the assumptions underlying such relationships by suggesting in his witty 'A Dedication to G**** H******* Esq.' that if ever misfortune befell his patron, making him 'as poor a dog as' the poet, then he would be there to help – 'If friendless, low, we meet together, / Then, Sir, your hand – my FRIEND and BROTHER' (124, 133–4; *Poems and Songs*, I, 246). Not all poets of the period, however, found the situation quite so amenable to comedy. When a poem of the Romantic period proclaims its author's friendship with a patron, then, it is often a mask for something more complicated.

Yearsley's broken friendship with More was abundantly evident to readers, but often the more painful aspects of poetic friendships remained largely hidden from view. Moments of rivalry, disapproval and hurt can be traced in private correspondence or memoirs of most of the poets mentioned in this chapter, but this does not undermine the warm feeling embodied in their verse. Poetry, as Shelley argued, can capture the best moments of human experience; the knowledge that not all experience is equally positive only heightens the importance of what has been caught in words. Biographical evidence often reveals relationships that were more complicated, scratchy and uneven than the depictions in the poems they inspired, but it does not diminish the poetry itself. To read a volume of John Lapraik's poems reveals at once that the image created by Burns was far from being an accurate representation of reality, but this does not make Burns's verse epistle any less powerful.

Poems that offered the hand of friendship could appeal to anyone suffering from feelings of loneliness, of being misunderstood, or to those merely conscious of some difference from the rest of the world. For many poets, poems were themselves, friends, reassuring, constant and inspiring. When Letitia Landon wrote her 'Stanzas on the death of Mrs Hemans' in 1835, her tribute emphasized the way in which poets became inseparable from their poems, making them the friend of countless unknown readers:

> How many loved and honoured thee
> Who only knew thy name;
> Which o'er the weary working world

> Like starry music came!
> With what still hours of calm delight
> Thy songs and image blend;
> I cannot choose but think thou wert
> An old familiar friend.
> (89–96; Wu, 1452)

Many of the friendships informing the poems discussed in this chapter had a biographical basis, but Landon's poem underlines the importance of poetry for those who were not personally acquainted with the poet or part of a literary circle – in other words, for the majority if readers in the period. In a society undergoing rapid urbanization, the consciousness of isolation was often especially strong, but through the print culture that expanded along with towns and industry, readers could find congenial voices to combat feelings of alienation. When Keats told the Grecian Urn, 'Thou shalt remain, in midst of other woe / Than ours, a friend to man', he was at once acknowledging the power of art to provide enduring friendship and creating a new friend for future generations.

Further Reading

Influential books with an emphasis on the isolation of the Romantic poet include M. H. Abrams, *Natural Supernaturalism* (New York: Oxford University Press, 1971); Frances Ferguson, *Solitude and the Sublime* (New York and London: Routledge, 1992); Robert Gleckner, *Byron and the Ruins of Paradise* (Baltimore: Johns Hopkins University Press, 1967); Geoffrey Hartman, *Wordsworth's Poetry 1787–1814* (New Haven and London: Yale University Press, 1964); Frank Kermode, *Romantic Image* (London: Routledge, 1957); Mario Praz, *The Romantic Agony* (1933, rev. edn., London: Oxford University Press, 1970).

Books more concerned with the social interactions influencing poets of the period include Stephen Behrendt, *British Women Poets and the Romantic Writing Community* (Baltimore: John Hopkins University Press, 2009); Marilyn Butler, *Romantics, Rebels and Reactionaries* (London and New York: Oxford University Press, 1981); William Christmas, *The Lab'ring Muses* (Newark, De., University of Delaware Press, 2001); Elizabeth Eger, *The Brilliant Women: Eighteenth-Century Blue Stockings* (New Haven and London: Yale University Press, 2008);

Timothy Fulford, *Coleridge's Figurative Language* (Basingstoke: Palgrave Macmillan,1991); Iain MacCalman (ed.) *The Oxford Companion to the Romantic Age* (Oxford: Oxford University Press, 1999); Thomas Mcfarland, *Romanticism and the Forms of Ruin* (Princeton: Princeton University Press, 1981); Jerome McGann, *The Romantic Ideology* (Chicago: University of Chicago Press, 1983); Richard Matlak, *The Poetry of Relationship: The Wordsworths and Coleridge, 1797–1800* (New York: St Martin's Press,1997); Jon Mee, *Dangerous Enthusiasm: William Blake and the Culture of Radicalism in the 1790s* (Oxford: Clarendon Press, 1992); Nicholas Roe, *Wordsworth and Coleridge: The Radical Years* (Oxford: Oxford University Press, 1988); Gillian Russell and Clara Tuite (eds.), *Romantic Sociability* (Cambridge: Cambridge University Press, 2002); Jack Stillinger, *Multiple Authorship and the Myth of the Solitary Genius* (Oxford: Oxford University Press, 1991).

In addition to the letters, journals and notebooks written by the poets, major modern biographies provide invaluable insight into the writing relationships of the period. See for example, Rosemary Ashton, *The Life of Samuel Taylor Coleridge* (Oxford: Blackwell, 1996); Jonathan Bate, *John Clare* (London: Picador, 2003); Robert Crawford, *The Bard: A Biography of Robert Burns* (London: Cape, 2009); Stephen Gill, *William Wordsworth: A Life* (Oxford: Oxford University Press, 1989); Robert Gittings, *John Keats* (London: 1968); Richard Holmes, *Shelley: The Pursuit* (London: Quartet,1974); *Coleridge: Early Visions* (London: Hodder and Stoughton, 1989); Fiona MacCarthy, *Byron: Life and Legend* (London: Faber, 2002); Andrew Motion, *Keats* (London: Faber,1997); Michael O'Neill, *Shelley. A Literary Life* (London and Basingstoke: Macmillan, 1990); Anne Stott, *Hannah More: The First Victorian* (Oxford: Oxford University Press, 2003); Mary Waldron, *Lactilla, Milkwoman of Clifton* (Athens and London: University of Georgia Press, 1996).

For influences on and images of Keats see Hyder Rollins (ed.) *The Keats Circle*, 2 vols (Boston, Ma., : Harvard University Press,1948); Jeffrey Cox, *Poetry and Politics in the Cockney School: Keats, Shelley, Hunt and their Circle* (Cambridge: Cambridge University Press, 1998); Nicholas Roe (ed.) *Keats and History* (Oxford: Oxford University Press, 1995); *Keats and the Culture of Dissent* (Oxford: Oxford University Press, 1997); Wolfson, Susan, 'Keats the Letter-Writer: Epistolary Poetics', *Romanticism Past and present*, 6 (1982), 43–61.

On the Shelley/Godwin Circle and the Swiss summer of 1816, see Kenneth Cameron (ed.), *Romantic Rebels: Essays on Shelley and His Circle* (Cambridge, Mass.: Harvard University Press, 1973); David Ellis, *Byron in Geneva* (Liverpool: Liverpool University Press, 2011); Daisy Hay, *The Young Romantics* (London: Bloomsbury, 2010); Anne K. Mellor, *Mary Shelley: Her Life, Her Fiction and Her Monsters* (London: Routledge, 1989); Charles Robinson, *Shelley and Byron: The Snake and the Eagle Wreathed in Flight* (Baltimore: Johns Hopkins University Press, 1976); William St Clair, *The Godwins and the Shelleys* (London: Faber, 1989); Fiona Stafford, *The Last of the Race* (Oxford: Clarendon Press, 1994).

Several books have examined the poetic dialogue between Wordsworth and Coleridge of 1802, including Stephen Parrish (ed.), *Coleridge's Dejection* (Ithaca: Cornell University Press, 1988); William Heath, *Wordsworth and Coleridge: A Study of their Literary Relations in 1802* (Oxford: Clarendon Press,1970); Lucy Newlyn, *Coleridge, Wordsworth and the Language of Allusion* (Oxford: Clarendon Press, 1986); Gene Ruoff, *Wordsworth and Coleridge: The Making of the Major Lyrics, 1802–4* (New Brunswick, NJ.: Rutgers University Press, 1989).

3
Common Concerns and Cultural Connections

The close literary relationships that flourished in the Romantic period often led to poems with strikingly similar features. That Keats and Leigh Hunt each composed poems 'On the Grasshopper and the Cricket', might seem surprising until it becomes clear that both were written at the same sonnet-writing party. Links between poems are not always so obvious, however, and often become visible only through allusive lines and recurrent images or from clues in contemporary letters, journals and memoirs. The private dialogue that continues through the poems written by Wordsworth and Coleridge in the spring of 1802, for example, would not have been immediately evident to those reading 'Ode: There was a time', 'Dejection' and 'Resolution and Independence' on first publication. For though 'Dejection' was printed in a newspaper later the same year, Wordsworth's poems were not published until 1807, when they appeared at opposite ends of his *Poems, in Two Volumes.* Modern readers, benefiting from careful literary scholarship, can now trace the unfolding dialogue, revision and development of the three poems; when encountered in separate volumes of each poet's selected works, however, their original connections may nevertheless remain as obscure as on first publication.

If some poetic dialogues are difficult to spot, other texts may appear to be mutually engaged when in fact they were written quite independently of each other. What may initially appear to be an exchange between writers can turn out to result from a particular historical moment, when numerous creative imaginations were warming to prevailing trends or memorable events rather than each other's poems. Ideas spread rapidly in the print culture of the period, and so numerous writers were simultaneously

Reading Romantic Poetry, First Edition. Fiona Stafford.
© 2014 Fiona Stafford. Published 2014 by John Wiley & Sons, Ltd.

inspired, often without realizing that their subject was not quite as new as it seemed. When Mary Shelley and Thomas Lovell Beddoes turned their attention to the figure of the 'Last Man' in the 1820s, for example, they appear to have been unaware of each other's interest in the subject, though reviewers were quick to point to the dark fashion for apocalyptic fictions. Public events and political causes prompted writers to express opinions, whether or not they were consciously adding their voices to a sense of collective outrage, anxiety or celebration. The rapid succession of major events and contested issues during the Romantic period led to an outpouring of literature relating to America, the French Revolution, the Rights of Man, the Rights of Woman, the Slave Trade, Ireland, Napoleon, Waterloo, Peterloo, Greek Independence, Catholic Emancipation and Political Reform. Some texts responded directly to a particular event, others were contributions to an ongoing debate or collective cause.

Key events generated key images that accrued power as they appeared in new poems or pictures. The pioneering work of critics such as Ronald Paulson and Olivia Smith has helped to direct attention to some of the recurrent motifs of the 1790s – the idea of revolution and related images of storms, crowds, prisons, bursting light or violent destruction – as well as stylistic features, such as the use of antitheses, organic metaphors, chivalric language, Roman iconography, classical myths or Biblical references. A rich common culture emerged rapidly, offering possibilities for radical and conservative writers alike. Images of trees and planting, for example, could suggest continuity and resistance to change, as Edmund Burke demonstrated in 1790 in his eloquent *Reflections on the Revolution in France*. The tree was also a symbol for radical hopes, however, as Thomas Paine showed in his vigorous reply, *Rights of Man*, with its stirring image of the Tree of Liberty, springing up in America and throughout Europe.

In the later part of the period, greater awareness of larger historical movements often led to different kinds of imagery, as James Chandler has argued in a book that takes its name from Shelley's sonnet, 'England in 1819'. Here the 'old, mad, blind, despised, and dying King', 'leech-like' Rulers, 'people starved and stabbed', a 'two-edged' army, 'sanguine laws' and 'unrepealed' Parliament, are conceived as the graves from which the 'glorious Phantom' of Liberty 'may burst' (Wu, 1180). Shelley's elaborate metaphor is both idealistic and tentative, perhaps reflecting the complicated perspective of the younger radical writer who looked back on the French Revolution rather than having witnessed its course unfolding unpredictably during the 1790s. *Prometheus Unbound* also looks forward to the eventual demise of tyranny, imagining Jupiter overthrown by Demogorgon, who celebrates both the 'patient power' of Love and Hope's capacity to create 'from its own wreck the thing it contemplates' (Wu, 1164). Keats's 'Hyperion', too, which similarly adapts the classical myth of the Titans and the overthrow of apparently all-powerful gods, can be read in relation to the new awareness of shifting imperial powers post Waterloo. Where writers of the 1790s were responding to a rapidly shifting sequence of unprecedented public events, those writing in the aftermath of Waterloo saw current affairs against the background of three decades of tumultuous political change. Their poems were at once individual works of art and self-conscious details in a much larger canvas.

Not all poems with similar features were inspired by contemporary politics, of course. The Romantic period was heir to new scientific, medical, educational and philosophical theories, as well as discoveries in natural history, geography, astronomy and anthropology. New knowledge inspired new writing, and often demanded a readjustment of old, inherited assumptions. Traditional images of the human body, for example, often acquired different associations as medical advances altered perceptions of the blood, lungs or nervous system. The remarkable discovery of electricity sparked new images and vocabulary for writers, while exploration of areas of the world still little known to Europeans opened up untold creative possibilities. When images of idyllic islands appear in Romantic poetry, they might derive from classical mythology or from recent accounts of Pacific voyages, while lightning strikes could evoke divine or natural power. Often poems drew on a range of sources, ancient and modern, literary and scientific, reanimating worn-out images or infusing new ideas with rich traditional associations.

In a culture bursting with so many creative possibilities, poets were likely to alight on similar images and ideas, whether or not they intended to be responding to the work of their contemporaries. Since originality was increasingly prized as the mark of great art, inadvertent resemblances were not always welcome to writers. At the same time, originality often lay in the treatment rather than the subject, and so poets might turn their hands to major issues or prevailing ideas without necessarily incurring charges of mere imitativeness. What constituted 'originality' was one of the common concerns of the age. Though tracing dominant themes and connections in Romantic poetry can sometimes founder, it is generally worth considering whether an apparent connection between poems reveals direct literary influence or is merely an analogy. If there is a direct influence, is the later poem an imitation, a tribute, a creative engagement or a parody?

Careful consideration of the links between Romantic poems can help to deepen our understanding of their meaning by illuminating specific literary associations as well as their place in the wider culture. Since this is a large area to explore, the discussion below focuses on one major political concern – the Abolition Movement; and one major image – the Rainbow. Analysis of a selection of poems on the Slave Trade, followed by a consideration of Romantic rainbows, is designed to illuminate both individual works and their interconnections, and the collective concerns of the Romantic period.

Common Causes: The Abolition

Few causes inspired more passionate poems of protest in the late eighteenth century than the Abolition movement. Poets of the period were quick to add their eloquent voices to the humanitarian outcry against the barbaric trade in human beings, and while each of their poems stands as an independent statement, together they acquire a cumulative force indicative of the general turn in British opinion which led, at last, to the Act of Abolition in 1807. Concern over slavery erupts in many of the major long poems of the period, from *The Task* and *The Prelude* to *Prometheus Unbound* and *Don Juan*, but it is even more apparent in the direct responses to key moments in the campaign. When Sir William Dolben brought a Bill to Parliament proposing restrictions on the numbers of slaves being transported to the British colonies in 1788, for example, William Cowper, Hannah More and Ann Yearsley each composed poems in support of his proposal, even though the measures proposed seemed to fall far short of their shared ideal of complete abolition. Cowper's 'Sweet Meat has Sour Sauce, or The Slave-Trader in the Dumps' satirised the greed of the merchants who objected to the Bill on economic grounds, by adopting the voice of the disgruntled trader, singing about a rich source of income that was 'like to be o'er' (2; Wu, 21). The hard-hitting parody of a sea shanty combines horrifying details about the conditions on board with a jaunty tone that seems to invite readers to join in the chorus:

> 'Tis a curious assortment of dainty regales,
> To tickle the Negroes with when the ship sails –
> Fine chains for the neck, and a cat with nine tails,
>   Which nobody can deny.
>
>   (10–13; Wu, 22)

The traditional refrain, 'which nobody can deny', conveys all the coercive mirth of the drinking song, while also reminding readers of the awful truth being exposed in successive verses. The speaker certainly sounds jolly, but he is hardly a jolly good fellow. Cowper's careful choice emphasizes the collective responsibility for the evils of the slave trade, his inviting song a match for contemporary 'sweetmeats' – at once tempting and utterly repellent. The details in his poem reveal his own horror at what went on in the transatlantic slave ships, but the culinary title and sing-song chorus bring the horrifying practices uncomfortably close to home. What Cowper was pointing out in his ironic monologue was that any British reader who enjoyed puddings, cakes or sweets, was inadvertently supporting the speaker, whose trade supplied the labour for European sugar colonies in the West Indies. It was the same point that Coleridge would later make in a lecture given in 1795 in Bristol, the centre of the British Slave Trade, using almost Gothic imagery of to remind his audience that their food was 'sweetened with the Blood of the Murdered.' (Coleridge, *Lectures*, 248).

Despite the laudable sentiments conveyed in Abolitionist poems, modern readers often find the tone of these poetic protests difficult. Though never intended as soothing verses, the choice of language and implied attitudes can grate on twenty-first century sensibilities differently from the ways in which they affected their original audiences. Hannah More, for example, was as opposed to the Slave Trade as Cowper, demonstrating her distaste for unwitting consumerism by the symbolic abolition of sugar from her own tea-table and, for those more obviously culpable, by the composition of a poem entitled 'Slavery'. The tone adopted by More for addressing the slave-traders is at once more direct and rather less winning than Cowper's:

> Barbarians, hold! Th'opprobrious commerce spare,
> Respect His sacred image which they bear.
> Though dark and savage, ignorant and blind,
> They claim the common privilege of kind;
> Let malice still strip them of each other plea,
> They still are men, and men should still be free.
>   (135–40; Wu, 69)

Although her unquestioned sense of superiority to the unfortunate Africans is almost as unpalatable to modern readers as the slave-merchants themselves, these lines nevertheless help to shed light on the longevity of what now seems such an astonishing abuse of human rights. For if even those most sympathetic to the plight of slaves regarded them as 'dark and savage, ignorant and blind', how were they viewed by less imaginative members of British society, especially those with strong vested interests in keeping up the trade? The very question posed in the Abolitionist motto, 'Am I not a man and a brother?' makes clear that the answer to this rhetorical question was still not universally agreed.

More's reference to the African captives as 'dark and savage' was a reflection of attitudes used to justify an unjustifiable practice rather than necessarily being a statement of personal opinion, but the line between sympathetic indignation and patronizing racism was, at times, thin. The question is complicated, too, by changing linguistic usage, for in the later eighteenth century, the 'savage' was often described as 'noble' – in contrast to the corruptions inherent in modern commercial society. For the influential thinker, Jean-Jacques Rousseau, man was born free, but everywhere he was in the 'chains' imposed by human society, which meant that slavery had a metaphorical as well as literal meaning for Romantic writers. Eighteenth-century philosophers in France and Scotland were exercised by the so-called 'progress' of Civil Society and attempted to identify distinct 'stages' in the history of mankind. In some Enlightenment theories of progress, the stage of 'savagery' was understood to be the innocent beginning of human society, which preceded a descent into 'barbarism' – the violent condition from which civilised society would eventually emerge. For More to alert greedy 'Barbarians' to the feelings of the 'savage' was not necessarily a sign, then, that she regarded the traders as in any way superior to their victims. Her own tone and language, however, still convey a clear sense of distance from both the 'savage' and the 'barbarian'.

Poetry, in all its variety and flexibility, nevertheless offered a relatively open space for reflection on contemporary concerns, especially before the outbreak of War in 1793, when the Government rapidly began to clamp down on anything deemed seditious. Through poetry's engaging forms, readers were often exposed to truths that might not be very palatable, but which demanded wider recognition. For intelligent women with a strong sense of social injustice, especially, poetry offered a means to put forward strongly held opinions and, if their words were effective enough, to influence others. Unlike women in the twenty-first century, those living in this period had no political voice, being denied not only careers as Members of Parliament, but even the right to vote. For Ann Yearsley, who had to overcome the double difficulties of gender and class in order to have her opinions taken seriously, poetry offered a public platform which would otherwise have been unattainable. Abolition was a topic of urgent – and local – concern for her, and so she used her newly found fame as a poet to express her opposition to slavery. Since she had been presented to the public as the remarkable 'Milkwoman of Bristol', discovered by Hannah More in a lowly cowshed, Yearsley's name was inextricably associated with Britain's chief slaving port. Her own response to Dolben's Bill, 'A Poem on the inhumanity of the Slave-Trade', began accordingly with a direct address to 'Bristol' – at whose 'glory' slaves had 'gazed /With wonder and amazement' (Wu, 160).

Yearsley's indignant blank verse included reference to the immediate and the familiar, accusing first 'Bristol' and then the 'Christian' merchant, who happily fed his family on the profits of human suffering. She brought home the evils of the trade by suggesting that the prosperous local businessman might like to put his own family up for sale:

> Away, thou seller of mankind! Bring on
> Thy daughter to this market, bring thy wife,
> Thine aged mother (though of little worth),
> With all thy ruddy boys.
>
> (83–6)

Such direct appeals to universal human experience were often more effective than the fanciful evocations of the pre-captivity life of a slave ('For her he strained the bow, for her he stripped / The bird of beauteous plumage', 150–1). An inherent difficulty of the Abolitionist poem was the gulf dividing British poets from the objects of their pity, which meant that the most fervent attempts at sympathy were often those mostly likely to recoil. For Ann Yearsley, already highly sensitive to her own unelevated place in a hierarchical society and bitter about the behavior of patrons such as More, the plight of slaves provoked special sympathy – but also a desire for distance. While fully conscious of the lottery of birth, Yearsley was keen to establish her own presence in British culture as an intelligent, independent citizen. Her poem ends with an apostrophe to 'social love' and a renewed plea to Bristol to recognize this as the true principle of the city's soul. Universal equality was especially appealing to a poet whose own poverty had been so publicly displayed, and yet her poem still adopted the voice of an educated lady, dispensing wisdom to those less enlightened than herself. Yearsley was promoting equality for all mankind, but driven in part by the desire to prove herself the equal of her patrons.

Despite these impassioned attempts at political intervention, the Abolition movement was not very rapid. Three years after More and Yearsley published their poems, Anna Barbauld was faced with writing an 'Epistle to William Wilberforce, Esq., on the rejection of the Bill for Abolishing the Slave Trade'. As she reflected on this disappointing turn of events in 1791, Barbauld had to admit that 'The Muse, too soon awaked' had 'in vain foretold' the new age of universal liberty (11–13; Wu, 39). Conscious of the efforts of her friend, Hannah More, to bring about a more sympathetic attitude to the victims of the lucrative trade, Barbauld added her voice to renewed calls for compassion. As she addressed Wilberforce on the urgent political issue, she was also recalling recent poems such as Cowper's *The Task*, which had included a heartfelt denunciation of the slave trade as part of his wider, personal meditation on the individual's relationship to the world and to God. As Barbauld described how the preacher, poet and senator had each displayed the suffering of the slave before their contemporaries, forcing England's 'averted eyes his stripes to scan' (7), she was recalling Cowper's horror over human nature's 'foulest blot':

> Thus man devotes his brother, and destroys;
> And worse than all, and most to be deplored
> As human nature's broadest, foulest blot,
> Chains him, and tasks him, and exacts his sweat
> With stripes that Mercy with a bleeding heart
> Weeps when she sees inflicted on a beast.
> (*The Task*, II, 20–5; Wu, 19)

In their choice of the already archaic word, 'stripes', to describe the lashes inflicted on slaves, or the marks they left behind, both Barbauld and Cowper implied that slavery should be consigned to the past. 'Stripes' also carried the more familiar, modern meaning during this period, and thus the word emphasized the distressing visual impact of the suffering body on 'England' (in Barbauld's poem) or 'Mercy' (in *The Task*). At the same time, the Biblical associations of 'stripes', which evoked both the suffering of Job and the crucifixion, rendered the innocent victims Christ-like. In his highly influential poem, *Paradise Regained*, Milton had described Satan taunting the Son of God with a vision of 'scorns, reproaches, injuries / Violence and stripes, and lastly cruel death' (IV, 386–8), and so the use of similar language for suffering slaves had special potency in a Christian country. The transformation of patient suffering into triumphant liberation was a pattern very familiar to readers in eighteenth-century Britain, but for Dissenting poets in this period, the desire to follow Christ and reclaim those who had erred far from his teachings was also a powerful impulse to composition. What's more, the recollection of other poems motivated by similar Christian and humanitarian impulses gave additional weight to each new contribution: cumulative images accrued power with each recurrence.

Reading different poems relating to the Abolition thus sheds light on each individual utterance. Cowper's condemnation of the Slave Trade, for example, is explicit in the opening of the second book of *The Task*, but knowledge of his other poems – and those by poets he influenced – reveals that the concern expressed in this passage was far from being a mere passing thought in the longer meditation. Reading Barbauld's 'Epistle to Wilberforce', as we have seen already, casts light not only on the political issues of her day, but also backwards onto Cowper's poem. As she directed disapproval at 'pale Beauty… / Diffused on sofas of voluptuous ease' (57–8), contemporary readers would have been likely to remember *The Task*, published six years earlier and beginning with its surprising mock-epic invocation, 'I sing the Sofa' (*Task*, I,1). Barbauld's diatribe against the effects of foreign luxury on domestic tastes is reminiscent of numerous lines from Cowper's long poem, as she describes how corruption 'infects each limb', while 'Simplicity, most dear of rural maids / Weeping resigns her violated shades' (99–101). Barbauld's poem thus reiterates the point made in Cowper's prose 'Argument of the second book' that the shameful trade in human flesh is inseparable from the dismaying excesses of modern, British society. *The Task* may begin as gentle mock-heroic on the progress of human convenience, from simple stool to luxurious sofa, but it turns into a powerful lament for lost simplicity and a critique of the iniquitous practices underpinning fashionable life. And once *The Task* is read alongside poems that focused exclusively on the slave trade, its pervasive political concerns emerge with even greater clarity.

The dialogue between Barbauld's 'Epistle to Wilberforce' and *The Task* illustrates the way in which attentive readers might come to understand an apparently innocuous word such as 'sofa' as a codeword for exploitation, with particular reference to slavery. Jane Austen's comic portrayal of Lady Bertram, reclining indolently on her sofa in *Mansfield Park*, for example, takes on a rather darker tone when the novel is read in relation to *The Task*. When she dispatches Lady Bertram's husband, Sir Thomas, to visit his plantations in Antigua, Austen effectively underlines the point made by

Cowper and other Romantic writers – that the luxurious lifestyles of many English ladies was supported by slavery. For contemporary Abolitionists, the very name of the Bertram mansion, which is also the title of the novel, would have had a special irony, since the landmark ruling over the illegality of slavery in Britain had been made in 1772 by Lord Chief Justice Mansfield. *The Task*, one of Austen's favourite poems, is quoted directly by the downtrodden heroine of her novel, Fanny Price, herself a victim of the tyrannical Aunt Norris. By transposing the abuses of the plantations to the genteel world of the English upper classes, Austen was not only following the Abolitionist's insistence on collective responsibility for the Slave Trade, but also exploring the different kinds of slavery flourishing in contemporary society. Slavery is mentioned explicitly only once in the novel, but the abuse of power in social situations and the essential lack of freedom enjoyed by young women in contemporary society are exposed throughout. Such implicit connections brought Abolitionist arguments into the very homes of her readers, while also suggesting that the Slave Trade was an extreme example of inequalities endemic in contemporary society.

In this respect, Austen's work bears illuminating comparison with those poets of the period whose indignation over the Slave Trade was part of a general humanitarian concern with social injustice. Their poetry not only contributed to the growing revulsion over the traffic in human beings, but also to awareness of other contemporary injustices. Since many of the voices raised against slavery were female, their work was effectively drawing attention to the intelligence and abilities of women as well as to their cause. The language of slavery, initially employed in arguments over actual slaves, gradually became part of the wider discourse of human rights and especially the situation of women in what was still a largely patriarchal society. When Mary Wollstonecraft composed her passionate *Vindication of the Rights of Woman* in 1792, she adopted the highly charged language of the Abolition debate to expose the subjugation of women in contemporary Britain:

> The duty expected from them is, like all duties arbitrarily imposed on women, more from a sense of propriety, or out of respect for decorum, than reason; and thus taught slavishly to submit to their parents, they are prepared for the slavery of marriage.
> (Wollstonecraft, *Vindication*, 237)

When William Blake turned his attention to the plight of women, he accordingly introduced his *Visions of the Daughters of Albion* with an image of enslavement and presented the oppressive male tyrant, Bromion, as a slave owner, stamping his sygnet on 'the swarthy children of the sun' (21; O'Neill and Mahoney, 43).

Blake's more obvious 'Abolition' poem, 'The Little Black Boy', on the other hand, has more in common with its companion pieces in *Songs of Innocence and Experience*, 'The Chimney Sweeper' or 'Holy Thursday', than with More's 'Slavery' or Barbauld's 'Epistle'. Instead of dwelling on the physical suffering inflicted by slave merchants on other human beings, Blake's poem exposes the kinds of conditioning that perpetuate social injustice. The innocent attitude of the poem's speaker, taught by his own mother to see himself as 'black as if bereaved of light' reveals the effects of 'mind-forged manacles' just as unbreakable as those denounced by the voice of experience in Blake's 'London' (O'Neill and Mahoney, 38). The Little Black Boy's desire for release from earthly experience into a heaven of imagined equality is similar to the Chimney Sweep's vision of escape from the 'coffins of black' – in both poems, the opposition between black and white has physical and metaphorical significance, while the desire to be free from darkness is at once sincerely conveyed and heavily ironized.

Although Blake was responding to the same political cause as the poets who supported the Abolition, his approach was highly individual. Unlike poems by More, Cowper, Yearsley or Barbauld, Blake's 'The Little Black Boy' does not refer explicitly to slavery, though knowledge of the contemporary suffering of African families and their descendants in the West Indies gives a powerful charge to the innocence of the young speaker. By introducing into his collection of *Songs* a poem so evidently inspired by the Abolition movement, Blake was able to condemn not only the Slave Trade but also the appalling abuses rife in contemporary England. For while the Little Black Boy makes no direct reference to the trade in human beings, the Chimney Sweeper declares, 'my Father sold me while yet my tongue / Could scarcely cry weep weep weep weep' (2–3; O'Neill and Mahoney, 28). Like More, Cowper, Barbauld, and Coleridge, Blake was well aware of the human cost demanded by wealthy British lifestyles. Rather than offer explicit condemnation of the slave merchants in his *Songs*, however, he pointed to the overwhelming scale of human injustice and questioned the traditional Christian promise of consolation for suffering endured on earth. If evangelical poets were inspired by their faith to urge an end to the Slave Trade, Blake was driven by anger over the irony of an innocent child's assumption that only when he had shed his own distinctive body could there be any chance of an English 'angel' loving him. His poem was part of the cumulative poetic argument against the Slave Trade, but it was also bent on challenging the larger body of apparently enlightened opinion.

Blake's complicated response to slavery helps to demonstrate the benefits of comparative criticism within the Romantic period because so many of his poems are interlinked and, collectively, engaged in dialogue with the work of his contemporaries and predecessors. His evocation of Christian ideas of ultimate freedom in *Songs of Innocence* is both a retort to the oppressors of children *and* a comment on the well-meaning writers who sought to encourage sympathy for the oppressed through their poetry. For Blake, poetry was not so much a tool for single-issue political opinion, but a vital means to recover the visionary potential in everyone, obscured as it inevitably was by conventional habits of mind. His contribution to the poetry of the Abolition was thus as critical and contrary as it was collaborative.

Blake's scepticism about the beneficial effects of organized religion was by no means unique. When Shelley turned to the ancient myth of Prometheus, seeing him as the suffering Champion of mankind, he too was drawing on the literature of the Abolition Movement, but vigorously rejecting the approach of religious writers. Responsibility for Prometheus's centuries of torture, chained to a rock with a vulture preying on his vital organs, is laid at the feet of the tyrannical Jupiter, 'multitudinous with thy slaves, whom thou requitest for knee-worship, prayer, and praise, / And toil' (5–7; Wu, 1095). For Shelley, slavery was the universal condition of mankind, as long as human beings remained in thrall to what he regarded as outmoded systems of belief and conventional thinking. Like Blake, Shelley saw poets as 'the companions and forerunners of some unimagined change in our social condition or the opinions which cement it' and his own lyrical drama as a contribution to the great 'awakening of the public mind' (Preface to *Prometheus Unbound* Wu, 1093). The unbinding of Prometheus was not a simple political allegory of the successful Abolition of slavery, but of the all-encompassing liberation of humanity still to come. The lyrical chorus of spirits in the fourth book is a celebration of the great power of the human mind to enact its own liberation:

> We come from the mind
> Of humankind,
> Which was late so dusk, and obscene, and blind;
> Now 'tis an ocean
> Of clear emotion,
> A Heaven of serene and mighty motion.
> (93–8; Wu, 1151)

At the same time, however, the visionary nature of the poem makes it clear to readers that this joyful condition has yet to come into being, and so the world remains in a state 'dusk, and obscene and blind'.

In the wake of the 1807 Act abolishing the Slave Trade, the rising generation of poets, including Shelley and Byron, were free to reflect on the general condition of mankind. While there were those who regarded the Act as a great symbolic step forward in the necessary progress towards universal liberation, others remained more sceptical. Byron's 'Prometheus', for example, offered no prospect of release from man's 'funereal destiny' (50), because it focused on the hero in chains, not on his eventual triumph: his heroic attempt to 'render...less / The sum of human wretchedness' had been 'baffled' (36–9; Wu, 888). Byron's lyric was not, of course, representative of his entire world-view, nor was it explicitly concerned with the Abolition, but it does offer an important counter to the idealism that infused Shelley's treatment of the myth. If some writers of the period looked forward with high hopes to a better state of society, others remained deeply sceptical about the realization of political and moral hopes.

In 1816, when he wrote 'Prometheus', Byron dwelled on a classical myth of eternal enslavement to explore the human condition, but four years later he adopted a much jauntier tone for his treatment of slavery in the fifth Canto of *Don Juan*. Rather than drawing directly on classical mythology, Byron's tongue-in-cheek epic presented a hapless modern hero whose adventures provided an opportunity for observations on a dazzling range of contemporary questions as well as more perennial human experience. The flexibility of the narrative meant that Byron was able to consider the topic of slavery from unexpected angles, putting Juan up for sale in a Turkish market in order to show that despite the British celebrations over the 1807 Abolition, traffic in human beings was still widespread:

> A crowd of shivering slaves of every nation
>   And age, and sex, were in the market ranged;
> Each bevy with the merchant in his station:
>   Poor creatures! Their good looks were sadly changed.
> All save the blacks seem'd jaded with vexation,
>   From friends, and home, and freedom far estranged;
> The negroes more philosophy display'd,
> Used to it, no doubt, as eels are to be flay'd.
>   (*Don Juan*, V, 49–56)

Byron's flippant tone was evidently designed to shock the sensibilities of contemporary readers for whom the Slave Trade was such an emotive issue, but his underlying points were, nevertheless, very serious. The sardonic description could hardly have been further removed from the tone of Barbauld's exhortations to sympathy, and yet its very matter-of-factness carries great conviction. This is the voice of a poet who seems to see through the rhetoric of optimism to a world in which humans continue to abuse those less powerful than themselves. The 'vexation' of those unaccustomed to being enslaved is especially hard-hitting and, in the next stanza, Byron focuses on the shock to Juan's youthful hopes of finding himself 'up for auction'. The complacent attitudes of the liberal-minded British Christians, whose faith in their own native liberties made slavery something which happened to other unfortunate races, are given a further jolt when Juan is purchased by a black Muslim, who advises him to convert to Islam.

Byron's objection to the kinds of optimism that gave people a sense of living in the best of all possible worlds made him suspicious of anything generally regarded as a universal improvement. By transporting Juan across different countries and cultures, Byron was able to show that many 'truths' were culturally specific and that what might be greeted by British readers as a great victory could be viewed very differently by other nations. Instead of joining in the congratulations of Wilberforce, the narrator of *Don Juan* drily points out that the British Abolition Act had merely put up the prices of slaves across the world:

> Twelve negresses from Nubia brought a price
>   Which the West Indian market scarce would bring;
> Though Wilberforce, at last, has made it twice
>   What 'twas ere Abolition.
>   (*Don Juan*, IV, 913–16)

Far from presenting the Abolition as a step towards the universal liberation, Byron's caustic narrator reveals that the world had continued in much the same way, driven by economics and the will to power. If he was making a contribution to the literature of Abolition, it was in issuing a warning that support of good causes might often be little more than cant – soothing to the well-meaning humanitarian, but not necessarily doing much to solve the world's deep-rooted problems. The effect of *Don Juan* was nevertheless dependent on the reader's awareness of the attitudes being satirized, for without prior knowledge of poems such as Barbauld's

'Epistle to Wilberforce', Byron's stanza addressing the great Abolitionist loses much of its force. As in so much of the literature of the period, direct treatment of a topical issue also meant engagement with the earlier responses it had provoked. Reading Romantic poetry, then, is greatly enriched by some awareness of the cumulative discourse of the age.

Common Culture: Romantic Rainbows

Poems associated with the Abolition demonstrate the ways in which Romantic writers built on each other's work, even when apparently writing in direct response to a political issue, but their creative practices can be illuminated equally well by tracing a single poetic image in a number of different texts. The Romantic period has sometimes been characterized by the use of telling metaphors, such as the 'correspondent breeze', 'the eolian harp', 'the lava flow', 'the river', 'the nightingale' or 'the sensitive plant', which were not primarily responses to current events or political ideas. The recurrence of such images can reveal much about an individual poet's perception of the world and his or her place within it, as well as about the literary influences on the poem. Once images become part of the general culture, however, it seems neither possible nor necessary to trace their origins to a single text, since they exist almost like a natural resource on which poets draw freely. Exploration of particular examples, however, quickly reveals that what might seem commonplace is often open to a variety of possible interpretations – recurrent metaphors are not the same as recurrent meanings.

Even when an image is ultimately Biblical in origin, it may be modified through centuries of literary tradition, or transformed by cultural innovation or scientific discovery. The permanent truths handed down through the ages continued to inform writers of the Romantic period, but this did not mean that they were impervious to new interpretation and refashioning. The legend of Noah, for example, was radically recast by Byron in his drama, *Heaven and Earth,* which focused on the experience of those abandoned to the flood waters, rather than on those divinely selected for survival. The image of the rainbow, which symbolised the end of the storm and God's new Covenant with mankind, nevertheless continued to retain its Biblical associations with hope, appearing and disappearing in many other poems of the period. Its fascination for Romantic writers and artists derived not just from the Christian tradition, however, but also from the modernization of understanding brought about by eighteenth-century science. In addition to the great texts of the past, poets of the Romantic period inherited modified versions of ancient stories and images, which in turn enabled their own adaptations of rich cultural symbols.

At the beginning of the eighteenth century, Isaac Newton's *Opticks* had revealed that the colors of the rainbow were caused by the refraction of light through water. His famous experiments with the prism demonstrated to an amazed reading public that shining white light through glass changed the direction of the beam to produce a multi-coloured spectrum. Suddenly, the rainbow ceased to be a mysterious sign from the heavens and became evidence of the wonders of the physical world, now gradually being comprehended by enlightened men of science. For a natural philosopher such as Newton, the physical world was evidence of God's astonishing plenitude: through studying the most remarkable phenomena, man might therefore learn to come closer to the divine. The rainbow, especially, caught the imagination of devotional poets seeking God through his works, as is evident in James Thomson's description of a spring shower in his hugely popular poem, *The Seasons*, first published in 1730, and reprinted throughout the century:

> Meantime, refracted from yon eastern cloud,
> Bestriding earth, the grand ethereal bow
> Shoots up immense; and every hue unfolds,
> In fair proportion running from the red
> To where the violet fades into the sky.
> Here, awful Newton, the dissolving clouds
> Form, fronting on the sun, thy showery prism;
> And to the sage-instructed eye unfold
> The various twine of light, by thee disclosed
> From the white mingling maze.
> ('Spring', 203–12; Thomson, 10–11)

Thomson's admiration for 'awful' Newton (by which he meant 'awe-inspiring') is evident in his image of the rain-cloud forming his 'showery prism' – the tribute to Newton's explanation of physical phenomena makes the scientist seem almost godlike. The language of the passage, too, has a scientific precision in its vocabulary of 'refraction' and 'proportion', as well as in its detail of the spectrum from red to violet, untwined from the sun's white light. The superior understanding of the modern, 'sage-instructed eye' is underlined by the contrast that follows:

> Not so the swain;
> He wondering views the bright enchantment bend
> Delightful o'er the radiant fields, and runs
> To catch the falling glory; but amazed
> Beholds the amusive arch before him fly,
> Then vanish quite away.
>
> ('Spring', 212–17)

If the ignorant 'swain' continued to be baffled by his failure to catch up with a rainbow, any educated, modern man would know that the phenomenon was caused by the passage of light through rain. There was, however, still something compelling about the idea of 'bright enchantment' and in much Romantic poetry the instinctive wonder of the uninformed eye began to command admiration.

In *The Seasons* there is no tension between scientific understanding and religious belief, since the natural world is seen as the Book of God, just as surely as the Bible. Thomson's poem frequently recalls both the Bible and *Paradise Lost*, but the scientific accuracy of his descriptions reveals a widely-felt gratitude for the advances made by enlightened man in understanding God's gift. Milton's image of the rainbow had after all been imagined with only 'three listed colours gay' (*Paradise Lost*, XI, 866), because his great epic was informed by Renaissance theories of light and vision. The prism experiment, like the invention of the telescope and microscope, had enabled people to see so much more in the world than had hitherto been visible, and so the modern scientist assumed an almost prophetic stature, revealing God's ways to those who had been walking in darkness. As Pope put it pithily in his epitaph for the Westminster Abbey monument to Newton, 'Nature, and Nature's Laws lay hid in Night / God said, *Let Newton Be*! and All was *Light*.'

The Seasons continued to be one of the most popular poems in the English language during the Romantic period, so when poets wrote of rainbows they were following not just the Bible, but also a much more recent tradition of scientific poetry and in particular Thomson's set-piece description of the 'grand ethereal bow.' The very passage in *The Seasons*, however, though celebrating Newtonian science as a revelation of God's creation, offered potential challenges to traditional religious belief. For questions rapidly began to arise over whether the Book of Nature could be as easily reconciled with the Bible as many eighteenth-century scientists had assumed. If the swain's wonder at the 'bright enchantment' turned out to result from ignorance, it was also possible that Noah's interpretation of the rainbow as a symbol of God's care might have been similarly misguided. Once something that seemed miraculous had been explained by science, the possibility that the entire world ran according to mechanistic principles rather than being evidence of divine bounty began to dawn. And though the majority continued to thank God for a creation that seemed ever more plentiful, there were those who started to question the need for a benevolent God to superintend such a well-orchestrated creation. If God had made a world that worked as perfectly as a great clock, surely he did not need to be winding it up or interfering with the mechanism? The necessity for God's presence in a mechanical universe was beginning to strike some philosophers as rather doubtful. As more sceptical writers, such as Byron, created their own storms and rainbows, they also contributed to the long-running debate over whether evidence from the natural world could ever prove the existence of a benevolent Creator – as we shall see.

Even without the great theological argument from Design, the image of the rainbow provoked questions about the effects of modern science on the creative imagination. In *The Seasons*, the swain's view of the world is set against that of the 'sage-instructed eye' to demonstrate modern understanding, but by the early nineteenth century a new longing for 'bright enchantment' was widely felt. For Keats, the truths of science carried a heavy cost, as suggested in his narrative poem, 'Lamia':

> Do not all charms fly
> At the mere touch of cold philosophy?
> There was an awful rainbow once in heaven:
> We know her woof, her texture; she is given
> In the dull catalogue of common things.
> Philosophy will clip an Angel's wings,
> Conquer all mysteries by rule and line,
> Empty the haunted air, and gnomèd mine –
> Unweave a rainbow, as it erewhile made
> The tender-personed Lamia melt into a shade.
> ('Lamia', II, 229–38; *Complete Poems*, 431)

Where Thomson had referred to Newton as 'awful', Keats was redirecting attention to the 'awful rainbow once in heaven' – which was now nothing more than a part of the ordinary material world. For Thomson the modern scientist's unraveling of the 'various twine of light' was a cause for celebration, but by the following century Keats was questioning the benefits of unweaving the rainbow. Keats's education and subsequent medical studies meant that he was well informed about modern scientific advances and given to expressing a generally positive view of the collective progress made since the Renaissance – the 'grand march of intellect' as he termed it in a letter to his friend John Hamilton Reynolds (Keats, *Letters*, I, 282). Nevertheless, the potential effects of reducing everything to fact and reason were troubling. The objections expressed in 'Lamia' to scientific explanations of natural phenomena were not religious, but rather aesthetic, imaginative and psychological. For Keats understood the deep human need for the marvellous and sought to create in his own art a kind of beauty so intense that it 'obliterates all consideration' (*Letters*, I, 194). This was something achieved by Shakespeare not Newton. That modern scientific experiments and taxonomies were making the aesthetic achievement any easier was becoming increasingly doubtful: 'the dull catalogue of common things' was not the stuff of great art.

Not all Romantic poets shared Keats's misgivings about 'cold philosophy', however. Shelley, for example, was an enthusiastic amateur scientist, whose excitement over the physical world inspired much of his poetry. There is no sense of philosophy clipping an angel's wing in poems such as 'The Cloud', where understanding of the natural world launches the poet skywards. Here Shelley adopted the cloud's perspective rather than the 'sage-instructed eye' of a human observer, to create a beautiful, innovative lyric, celebrating nature's capacity for perpetual change through a dazzling shower of images. The rainbow, in Shelley's poem, is neither a sign of divine power, nor of bright enchantment, but part of the endlessly shifting energy of the atmosphere:

> The triumphal arch through which I march
>   With hurricane, fire, and snow,
> When the powers of the air are chained to my chair,
>   Is the million-coloured bow;
> The sphere-fire above its soft colours wove,
>   While the moist earth was laughing below.
> ('The Cloud', 67–72; Shelley, *Poems and Prose*, 191)

Far from seeing the rainbow being unwoven by cold Philosophy, Shelley used his understanding of the phenomenon to create verse acoustically satisfying and visually intriguing. The marching cloud is as fluid and mercurial as the human imagination and, by choosing a cloud as the speaker, Shelley emphasized the connection rather than opposition between the natural world and the creative mind of the poet.

Shelley's acute awareness of nature's capacity for perpetual change was not always so positively expressed, however. In 'When the Lamp is shattered', for example, the rainbow's dependence on the cloud is recalled as part of a melancholy reflection on the inevitable transience of love:

> When the lamp is shattered,
> The light in the dust lies dead –
> When the cloud is scattered
> The rainbow's glory is shed.
> When the lute is broken,
> Sweet tones are remembered not;
> When the lips have spoken,
> Loved accents are soon forgot.
> (1–8; Shelley, *Poems*, 667–8)

If rainbows still delighted people by their sudden appearances after a storm, they were equally given to disappearing just as rapidly. Science might offer physical explanations, but this did not give modern man any real power over the elements: rainbows still came and went as unpredictably as ever before.

The inherent elusiveness of rainbows made them oddly resistant to consistent symbolic meaning – Shelley could adopt the rainbow for a pang of longing just as readily as for a moment of triumphant happiness. In either case, the emotion being conveyed was intensified by the fleeting nature of its beauty rather than by any physical analysis of its light. The tendency of the rainbow to 'vanish quite away' had been just as visible in *The Seasons*, but where Thomson presented its elusiveness as an image of limited understanding, poets in the Romantic period often dwelled on the nature of momentary delight. Wordsworth summed up its fascination very concisely in his 'Ode, There was Time', with its short, memorable couplet: 'The Rainbow comes and goes / And lovely is the Rose' (10–11; O'Neill and Mahoney, 163). The rainbow was a herald of the poem's gathering questions – 'Whither is fled the visionary gleam? / Where is it now, the glory and the dream?' (56–7). Visionary power, so prominent in childhood, seemed destined to 'fade into the light of common day' (76) and although the recompense is there - 'in the years that bring the philosophic mind' (189) – the note of lament continues to resound. As discussed in Chapter 1, the strength of human sympathy and faith in eternal life offer adequate consolation, but the 'radiance which was once so bright' is never forgotten or negated.

When Wordsworth included the Ode in his substantial collection of *Poems*, 1815, he gave it a new title, 'Ode. Intimations of Immortality' and added an epigraph:

> The Child is Father of the Man;
> And I could wish my days to be
> Bound each to each by natural piety.

For many readers in 1815, including Byron, Shelley and Keats, the lines would have been instantly recognizable as part of the short poem, 'My heart leaps up when I behold / A Rainbow in the sky' ('The Rainbow', 1–2; Wu, 528), originally published in 1807 in the same volume as the Ode. Though readers were soon reminded that the Rainbow comes and goes, they were now primed by the earlier lyric to associate its appearance with a spontaneous, childlike joy that could still lift the heart even in old age. Wordsworth was celebrating the visionary capacity of 'simple childhood' in his Ode and through his carefully pared-down language, he reaffirmed the ancient promise of the rainbow. At the same time, its evanescent qualities were fully acknowledged, along with the likelihood of vanishing vision and impending shades. There was none of the easy optimism that maintained hope merely by ignoring despair: instead the cheerfulness advocated in Wordsworth's poems was a conscious choice made in the full knowledge of human decline and misery. Seeing the world was largely a matter of individual perception – the heart continued to leap up because it always had in childhood, gaining in age from the powerful memories of a less self-conscious stage of life.

Wordsworth's celebration of youthful perception was effectively elevating the response of 'the swain' over that of Thomson's 'sage-instructed eye'. Rather than regarding 'bright enchantment' as an illusion, Wordsworth was using rainbow imagery to convey a sense that glimpses of the divine were visible to everyone at the start of life, and might still inform the adult imagination. The Child was in fact 'father of the man', and had much to teach those who regarded themselves as infinitely superior in knowledge and understanding. It was a view informed by older traditions and modern advances – but one that challenged the literal-mindedness of some scientific analyses and reasserted the claims of hope, faith and imaginative experience.

Wordsworth's affirmations struck a special chord with some readers of *Poems*, 1815, published in the year of Waterloo; for Byron, however, the hopefulness of both Romantic rainbows and children would prove an irresistible target for satire. The notorious second Canto of *Don Juan* accordingly sees Juan adrift in a longboat, with a crew of starving sailors and a host of literary allusions, ancient and modern. After Juan's tutor, Pedrillo, has been eaten by the shipwrecked men, the crew become further depleted by illness, starvation and despair, until the nadir is reached in the image of two desperate fathers witnessing the death of their young sons. The first boy dies and is unceremoniously thrown overboard, but the other survives a little longer and seems almost on the point of being saved:

> And o'er him bent his sire, and never raised
>   His eyes from off his face, but wiped the foam
> From his pale lips, and ever on him gazed,
>   And when the wish'd-for shower at length was come,
> And the boy's eyes, which the dull film half-glazed,
>   Brighten'd, and for a moment seem'd to roam,
> He squeezed from out a rag some drops of rain
> Into his dying child's mouth – but in vain.
>   (*Don* Juan, II, 705–12)

There is little chance for a child in these circumstances to become father of the man. As if to underline the irony at this point, Byron introduces a strikingly beautiful natural image:

> Now overhead a rainbow, bursting through
>   The scattering clouds, shone, spanning the dark sea,
> Resting its dark base on the quivering blue;
>   And all within its arch appear'd to be
> Clearer than that without, and its wide hue
>   Wax'd broad and waving, like a banner free,
> Then changed like to a bow that's bent, and then
> Forsook the dim eyes of these shipwreck'd men.
>   (*Don* Juan, II, 721–8)

The rhythm of the lines and the movement of the participles, 'bursting', 'scattering', 'spanning', 'Resting', 'quivering', 'waving', suggests that perhaps at last, the sailors' ordeal is over and that, despite their losses, the battered boat might be moving towards better fortune.

Byron continues to suspend his comic genius for this breathtaking stanza, adopting simple rhymes that propel rather than interrupt the movement of the lines, and unifying the long sentence with alliteration and assonance. The visual detail arrests the reader with the force of firsthand observation, while also gathering momentum indirectly from the less visible eighteenth-century tradition of scientific poetry with its set-piece rainbows. For a moment, readers can visualize the great colorful arch bursting across the dark sea. The striking contrast with what has come before accentuates a sense of change, as if to indicate that the worst is over and a new phase in the narrative is beginning.

Almost before there has been time to breathe a sigh of relief, however, the poem reverts to its more characteristic strategies of undermining conventional poetic beauty in stanza 92:

> It changed, of course; a heavenly cameleon,
>   The airy child of vapour and the sun,
> Brought forth in purple, cradled in vermilion,
>   Baptized in molten gold, and swathed in dun,
> Glittering like crescents o'er a Turk's pavilion,
>   And blending every colour into one,
> Just like a black eye in a recent scuffle,
> (For sometimes we must box without the muffle).
>
> Our shipwreck'd seamen thought it a good omen –
>   It is as well to think so, now and then;
> 'Twas an old custom of the Greek and Roman,
>   And may become of great advantage when
> Folks are discouraged; and most surely no men
>   Had greater need to nerve themselves again
> Than these, and so this rainbow look'd like hope,
> Quite a celestial kaleidoscope.
>   (*Don* Juan, II, 729–44)

The description expands as elaborately as a traditional epic simile, but only to be deflated by the concluding comparison with a black eye. Unlike the previous stanza, where readers are encouraged to share the pleasure of the vibrant rainbow, suspension of disbelief is rendered impossible by such a simile and such unignorable rhymes. The very human image of a colourful bruise, acquired in a scuffle without a muffle, is a far cry from the grateful reverence of Thomson or from Wordsworth's sensitive reflections. Stanza 92 reminds us that the poem is the construction of a very clever poet, whose knowledge of the world is equally obvious in his references to the effects of 'vapour and the sun', the 'Turk's pavilion', or the sport of boxing. Byron's authority, however, is consolidated most effectively by the kaleidoscope – a particularly eye-catching detail because of its novelty. Sir David Brewster invented the kaleidoscope in 1816 and two years later, Byron's friend, Hanson, had brought one with him to Venice. Within a month, it was featuring in *Don Juan*. The kaleidoscope was not only a highly effective visual simile for the rainbow, but also a sign that though the author might be out of town, he was quite up-to-date with the latest scientific gadgets.

The choice of 'kaleidoscope' was determined partly by the rhyme, of course, because of the rainbow's traditional association with hope. As Milton had stated unequivocally in *Paradise Lost*, when the great Flood began to recede at last, a rainbow appeared, 'Betok'ning peace from God' (*Paradise Lost*, XI, 867). For Byron's narrator to suggest that the rainbow 'looked like hope' was at once to evoke the Biblical paradigm and to introduce doubt, since his phrase resists the absolute assurance of the Christian symbol. 'Looking like' is not the same as being. Indeed, the entire passage, shifting between simile and metaphor, was exploring the religious, psychological and aesthetic functions of imagery. At every stage, readers are presented with new ideas to convey the scene, but the more resemblances are invoked, the less persuasive each appears. Since the passage is drawing overtly on the Bible, its facetiousness over the failure of language to sustain truth can be read as an expression not just of irreverence, but of profound scepticism. The difficulty, however, lies in judging the tone. How seriously are we to take a passage that includes black eyes and kaleidoscopes?

The Biblical resonances are re-affirmed in stanzas 94 and 95, with the arrival of a 'beautiful white bird, / Webfooted, not unlike a dove' (*Don Juan*, II, 745–6). Once again, however, any thought that *Don Juan* might be conforming to the Christian pattern of salvation is very rapidly exploded:

> And had it been the dove from Noah's ark,
>   Returning there from her successful search,
> Which in their way that moment chanced to fall,
> They would have eat her, olive-branch and all.
>   (*Don* Juan, II, 757–60)

Even as the stanza makes us laugh out loud, it also renders the human condition somewhat rueful. For just as God's rainbow had been levelled to the colors of a bruise, so the dove of peace is reduced to a potential dinner for starving men. Byron fully acknowledged the human propensity to hope and the related impulse to discover a 'good omen', but his representation simultaneously undercuts the sailor's beliefs, by showing how the demands of the body were always likely to override those of the spirit.

Once the kaleidoscope, which only looks 'like hope', is seen as part of a sceptical onslaught, its changing shapes and colors may take on a darker hue. Where the Biblical rainbow brought the promise of God's ultimate care for the human race, the new invention offered an image of arbitrary, mechanistic change for change's sake. This interpretation is carefully prepared in the preceding stanzas, with their sequence of fleeting images – an arch, a banner, an archer's bow, a chameleon, a baby, a Turkish crescent, and a black eye. The kaleidoscope is undermined by coming last, even as its own character is embodied in this bewildering list: 'It changed of course.' As Byron deconstructed his own similes, however, he was also posing the possibility that the world consisted of ever-changing surfaces and that any search for divine meaning was therefore futile. The narrator's observation of the 'dim eyes of these shipwrecked men' suggests that the men's limitations are as much intellectual as visual, given their propensity to finding superstitious signs of hope in natural phenomena. Echoes of Thomson's ignorant swain, left bewildered as the bright enchantment vanishes from the sky are never far away.

The wit and wordplay mean, however, that it is also possible to read the passage as part of Byron's ongoing parody of contemporary Romantic poetry. For, as he poked fun at the sailors' attitudes, he was evoking not just the Biblical legend of Noah, nor Thomson's ignorant rustic, but also Coleridge's 'The Ancient Mariner'. Like the shipwrecked men in *Don Juan*, the crew of the Mariner's vessel had been followed very memorably by a bird, which also met an unfortunate fate. As in Byron's narrative, Coleridge had recorded the sailors' reactions to the albatross, initially hailed as a Christian soul, subsequently mourned, and then despised:

> And I had done an hellish thing,
>   And it would work 'em woe:
> For all averred I had killed the bird
>   That made the breeze to blow.
>
> Ne dim ne red, like God's own head
>   The glorious sun uprist:
> Then all averred I had killed the bird
>   That brought the fog and mist.
> "'Twas right", said they, "such birds to slay,
>   That bring the fog and mist".
>   ('The Ancyent Marinere', 93–8; Wu, 335)

In this version of the ballad, first published in *Lyrical Ballads* in 1798, the Mariner's shooting seems random and inexplicable, the reaction it provokes, inconsistent and contradictory. When Coleridge reissued his poem in *Sibylline Leaves* in 1817, however, he revised the spelling, expanded the lines and added marginal explanatory glosses: 'His shipmates cry out against the ancient mariner, for killing the bird of good luck. But when the fog cleared off, they justify the same – and thus make themselves accomplices to the crime' (Wu, 697). Coleridge had introduced an editorial voice, which seemed to rationalize the arbitrariness of the men's behavior, as if to make sense of the Mariner's story and control the reader's interpretation. The voice in the margins is a Christian commentator, who subsequently refers to 'God's creatures' and 'the holy Mother', subtly encouraging readers to find a religious moral in the tale.

Byron's recollection of 'The Ancient Mariner' in *Don Juan* is evident not only in the appearance of the bird after the rain, but also in the crew's determination to see the rainbow as a 'good omen' and the seabird as an even 'better' one (stanzas 93–4). The 'good omen' is a direct quotation from Coleridge, because according to the marginal glosses, 'the albatross proveth a bird of good omen', while the narrator's actions are condemned: 'The ancient Mariner, inhospitably killeth the pious bird of good omen.' Byron's stanzas can thus be seen as a gloss on Coleridge's glosses, since his irreverent treatment of the plump, dove-like bird makes plain that the sailors' assessment of the relative good of the omens is determined by their ravenous hunger. He is, in a sense, explaining Coleridge's explanation – just as he had recommended to Coleridge in the Dedication to *Don Juan*.

What might seem a somewhat cynical allusion to Genesis is also, therefore, a subtle renewal of the hostilities launched in the Dedication to *Don Juan*, which took the Lake poets to task for their abandonment of the radical ideals of *Lyrical Ballads*. In the Dedication, Byron had ridiculed Coleridge for his narrowness, obscurity and self-obsession, but his harshest criticism was levelled at the Lakers' turn towards the Establishment – Church and State. It was Robert Southey, in particular, whose recent elevation to Poet Laureate most provoked Byron's caustic pen, but the practice of turning 'Tory at / Last' was presented as 'a common case' among the poets associated with the English Lake District – namely Southey, Wordsworth and Coleridge (Dedication, 3–4). The image of Coleridge, 'like a hawk encumbered with his hood' (14) suggests a taming and blindfolding of a poet who had once been the champion of liberty, and Byron's attack on the obscurity of his philosophy is part of his disquiet over the general move towards conservatism. The new glosses that surrounded 'The Ancient Mariner' were hooding the poem, just as effectively as Coleridge's earlier radicalism was being masked in *Biographia Literaria*. Coleridge's 'metaphysics' – as set out in *Biographia Literaria* and the *Lay Sermons* – now seemed to be affecting even the poems he had written years before, as the enchanting, inexplicable 'Rime' was suddenly framed by Christian allegorising. The mysterious afterlife of the Mariner, passing 'like night from land to land', was now being rationalized as a life of 'penance' (Wu, 710), following the Hermit's shriving, while any passages that did not so easily conform to a Christian pattern of sin and expiation were silently passed over.

When Byron observed that the rainbow in *Don Juan* 'looked like hope' he may have been mocking the credulity of shipwrecked men, but he was also reflecting indirectly on Wordsworth and Coleridge's faith in the redemptive power of the imagination and the subjectivity of human perception. His mockery nevertheless rested on the awareness that his readers had already shared Childe Harold's soul-bearing declarations of feeling for nature. The despair of his earlier protagonist, Harold, had been eased only by his love of the natural world, and so while Byron had rejected the eighteenth-century readiness to seek God in the works of nature, he had still acknowledged a deep love of the earth 'for its earthly sake' (*Childe Harold*, III, 672). When the narrator of *Don Juan* eyes the wretched sailors with lofty derision, he is therefore making fun, also, of his creator's earlier creation.

The way in which the narrator of *Don Juan* offers glosses on the action may also indicate a different kind of debt to Coleridge, unacknowledged but not insignificant. The addition of marginal glosses to 'The Ancient Mariner' was, after all, a way of drawing attention to questions of story-telling and interpretation just as much as to the morality of the poem. *Don Juan* was therefore paying a quiet tribute to the revised 'Ancient Mariner', even as it offered a critique. Byron's continuing admiration for Coleridge is evident in the role he played in bringing 'Christabel' and 'Kubla Khan' into print in 1816, as discussed in Chapter 7 of this book, and his ability to parody 'The Ancient Mariner' reveals his close knowledge of the poem. By criticising the voice of the marginal glosses in *Don Juan*, he also drew attention to Coleridge's self-reflexive techniques in a poem that drew much of its interest from the varying distances between the action of the story and the narrator's commentary. Some of Byron's overt mockery of Coleridge may have been a rhetorical strategy to deflect readers from spotting his debts.

The complexity of the conversation between Byron's poem and those of his immediate predecessors in the generation before shows just how much can be gained from reading Romantic poems with other poems in mind. Though passages such as the shipwreck in Canto II work brilliantly on a purely narrative level, they prove even more rewarding once the layers of allusion and intertextual play become apparent. Byron's rainbow is explicitly likened to many different things, but the passage finds further resemblances in a host of earlier texts. It is, of course, possible and enormously rewarding to read *Don Juan* as an entertaining narrative, packed with different kinds of humour, engaging reflection and arresting dramatic scenes. The full depth of Byron's comic masterpiece, however, becomes apparent only when it is viewed as part of the rich, literary culture of his day, which was open to influences from religious, political, scientific, and philosophical discourses. The single instance of the rainbow demonstrates the complicated ways in which Romantic poems engaged with other texts, consciously evoking, or unconsciously resembling, elements of existing poems. The image of hope even links the rainbow to the poetry of the Abolition, since it could be read as a sign of a better world to come. In *Prometheus Unbound*, for example, future liberty is heralded in Asia's vision by the 'rainbow-winged steeds / Which trample the dim winds' (II, 130–1; Wu, 1132), while earth's revival is nurtured by the 'rainbow-skirted showers' (III, 118). Romantic poems were linked by the same contemporary issues and general familiarity with prominent texts, which combined to create a common culture. For modern readers, placing such poems beside other poems of the period helps to illuminate the individual text through contrast and comparison. The best poems can always be read and enjoyed independently, but they benefit, too, from being seen in good company.

Further Reading

The language and imagery associated with the French Revolution has been analyzed in books such as Ronald Paulson, *Representations of Revolution* (New Haven and London: Yale University Press, 1983); Stephen Prickett, *England and the French Revolution* (Basingstoke: Macmillan, 1989); Olivia Smith, *The Politics of Language* (Oxford: Oxford University Press, 1984); Kevin Whelan, *The Tree of Liberty* (Cork: Cork University Press, 1999). Useful anthologies of prose relating to the

Revolution controversy include Marilyn Butler (ed.), *Burke, Paine, Godwin and the Revolution Controversy* (Cambridge: Cambridge University Press, 1984); Jon Mee and David Fallon (eds.), *Romanticism and Revolution* (Oxford: Wiley-Blackwell, 2011). Simon Bainbridge's books, *Napoleon and English Romanticism* (Cambridge: Cambridge University Press, 1995) and *British Poetry and the Revolutionary and Napoleonic Wars* (Oxford: Oxford University Press, 2003) are also very informative. For the post-Napoleonic period, see also James Chandler, *England in 1819* (Chicago: University of Chicago Press, 1998); Richard Cronin, *Paper Pellets: British Literary Culture After Waterloo* (Oxford: Oxford University Press, 2010); Roger Sales, *Jane Austen and Representations of the Regency* (London: Routledge, 1994). Iain MacCalman (ed.) *The Oxford Companion to the Romantic Age* (Oxford: Oxford University Press, 1999) is a mine of useful information and commentary on the period.

The literature associated with the Abolition has received a great deal of critical attention in the last two decades, with the rise of post-colonial studies. Edward Said's *Culture and Imperialism* (London: Vintage, 1993), for example, prompted considerable debate and further research into post-colonial issues in the Romantic period. More recently, the Bicentenary of the 1807 Act, together with the establishment of new museums concerned with the Slave Trade, has encouraged further research into the related literature. Marcus Walsh (ed.), *The Poetry of Slavery* (Oxford: Oxford University Press, 2003) provides a useful collection, together with a substantial introduction, and see also James Basker (ed.), *Amazing Grace: An Anthology of Poems about Slavery, 1680–1810* (Yale: Yale University Press, 2002); Jane Austen, *Mansfield Park*, ed. Kathryn Sutherland (London: Penguin, 2003). For historical and critical studies, see Roger Anstey, *The Atlantic Slave Trade and the British Abolition, 1760–1810* (Basingstoke: Macmillan, 1975); Joan Baum, *Mind-Forg'd Manacles: Slavery and The Romantic Poets* (Archon Books, 1994); Stuart Curran, 'The Political Prometheus', *Studies in Romanticism*, 25 (1986), 430–55; David Fairer, *English Poetry of the Eighteenth Century, 1800–1789* (Harlow: Pearson, 2003); Moira Ferguson, *Subjected to Others: British Women Writers and Colonial Slavery* (London: Routledge, 1992); Timothy Fulford and Peter Kitson (eds.), *Romanticism and Colonialism: Writing and Empire* (Cambridge: Cambridge University Press, 1998); Timothy Morton, *The Poetics of Spice* (Cambridge: Cambridge University Press, 1994); James Walvin (ed.) *Slavery and British Society 1776–1846* (Basingstoke: Macmillan, 1982).

On the significance of the Rainbow for Romantic poets, see Stephen Prickett, *Coleridge and Wordsworth: The Poetry of Growth*, new edn. (Cambridge: Cambridge University Press, 1980); M. H. Nicolson, *Newton Demands the Muse* (Princeton: Princeton University Press, 1946); Patricia Spacks, *The Poetry of Vision* (Cambridge Mass.: Harvard University Press, 1967).

For Romantic literature and science more generally, see H. Almeida, *Romantic Medicine and John Keats* (New York: Oxford University Press, 1991); A. Cunningham and N. Jardine (eds.). *Romanticism and the Sciences* (Cambridge: Cambridge University Press, 1990); Timothy Fulford, Debbie Lee and Peter Kitson (eds.) *Literature, Science and Exploration in the Romantic* Era (Cambridge: Cambridge University Press, 2004); Carl Grabo, *A Newton Among Poets: Shelley's Use of Science on Prometheus Unbound* (Chapel Hill, NC, University of North Carolina Press, 1930); Desmond King-Hele, *Shelley: His Mind and Thought* (London: Macmillan, 1971); Trevor Levere, *Poetry Realized in Nature: Samuel Taylor Coleridge and Early Nineteenth-Century Science* (Cambridge: Cambridge University Press, 1981).

4
Traditions and Transformations: Poets as Readers

For John Keats, *the* Man of Achievement in literature was Shakespeare. As a poet possessed of 'negative capability', Shakespeare had a unique capacity for being 'in uncertainties, Mysteries, doubts, without any irritable reaching after fact or reason' and this, for Keats, was the essence of his power. Keats wrote excitedly to his brothers on a cold, December night in 1817, after watching Edmund Kean's astonishing performance as Richard III, that in Shakespeare's work, 'the sense of Beauty overcomes every other consideration, or rather obliterates all consideration' (Keats, *Letters*, I, 194). Reading Shakespeare was not a matter of searching for the message of his work, nor of analyzing the plot, nor of paraphrasing the language, nor of considering the political and social contexts: for Keats, it was a powerful, all-consuming experience that momentarily obliterated all rational thought. 'The excellence of every Art is its intensity, capable of making all disagreeables evaporate, from their being in close relationship with Beauty & Truth', he wrote, adding as evidence for his claim, 'Examine King Lear & you will find this exemplified throughout' (Keats, *Letters*, I, 192). For Keats, true art was distinguished by 'intensity', an overwhelming beauty such as that of Shakespeare's great tragedy.

In his own sonnet, 'On Sitting Down to Read *King Lear* Once Again', the experience of Shakespeare's tragedy is, accordingly, something to be braced for rather than embraced. The alluring pages of 'Romance' have to be reluctantly put aside, as the speaker girds himself to 'burn through' the play, knowing that in the process, he will be 'consumed in the fire'. Far from seeming a pleasant pastime for a winter afternoon, reading *Lear* is an active, harrowing experience, with the poet-reader cast as a kind of mental

Reading Romantic Poetry, First Edition. Fiona Stafford.
© 2014 Fiona Stafford. Published 2014 by John Wiley & Sons, Ltd.

knight, daring Hell for the promise of new wings. The image of the Phoenix, reborn from the flames, is an image of the Romantic poet, utterly altered by his encounters with great literature, chastened and renewed for his own creative quest.

Even as Keats paid this deeply felt tribute to Shakespeare, however, he was still asserting his own independence from the great Master by choosing for the octave of his sonnet a Petrarchan (*abbaabba*), rather than Shakespearean (*ababcdcd*) rhyme-scheme:

> Oh golden-tongued Romance, with serene lute!
>   Fair plumed siren, queen of far away!
> Leave melodizing on this wintry day,
> Shut up thine olden pages, and be mute.
> Adieu! For, once again, the fierce dispute
>   Betwixt damnation and impassioned clay
> Must I burn through; once more humbly assay
> The bitter-sweet of this Shakespearean fruit.
>   (1–8; Wu, 1351)

Shakespeare's choice is nevertheless recalled in the closing couplet, as if to embody formally the very pursuit it sets out as a goal:

> But, when I am consumed in the fire
> Give me new Phoenix wings to fly at my desire.

Just as Keats seemed to be bowing to Shakespearean authority, he found an image of personal renewal, as a poet not so much reborn, but re-launched through his encounter. Ultimately inspirational rather than intimidating, Shakespeare provided Keats with an endless source of beauty, which, if temporarily obliterating, proved steadily empowering.

For Keats, reading was a passionate, all-consuming activity, from which his own poems drew inspiration. After reading the fifth canto of Dante's *Inferno*, Keats had a dream which he described to his brother as 'one of the most delightful enjoyments I ever had in my life – I floated about the whirling atmosphere as it is described with a beautiful figure to whose lips mine were joined at it seem'd for an age – and in the midst of all this cold and darkness I was warm' (Keats, *Letters*, II, 91). Memory of the Dantean dream survives in the sonnet Keats wrote the morning afterwards, which concludes,

> Pale were the sweet lips I saw,
> Pale were the lips I kissed, and fair the form

I floated with, about that melancholy storm.
('A Dream, after reading Dante's Episode of Paolo and
Francesca', 12–14; Keats, *Complete Poems*, 334)

Poetry opened the way into a world of intense, unrestricted pleasure, which in turn prompted fresh creation. Again and again, Keats attempted to recreate the sense of wonder inspired by great art, comparing himself when reading Chapman's Homer to an astronomer, discovering a new planet, or an explorer, staring out across the Pacific for the first time.

So great was his admiration for certain writers that the sight of a lock of Milton's hair produced both an overwhelmingly physical reaction and an Ode:

> For many years my offering must be hushed;
>   When I do speak, I'll think upon this hour,
> Because I feel my forehead hot and flushed,
>   Even at the simplest vassal of thy power –
>   A lock of thy bright hair.
>   Sudden it came,
> And I was startled, when I caught thy name
>   Coupled so unaware;
> Yet at that moment, temperate was my blood.
> Methought I had beheld it from the Flood.
>   ('On Seeing a Lock of Milton's Hair. Ode',
>   33–42; Keats, *Complete Poems*, 220)

Although the discovery of a surviving part of Milton's body stuns the living poet, it also offers a pledge for the future – 'when I do speak, I'll think upon this hour'. Great poets were guarantors of a living tradition, for whom the newcomer felt an energizing gratitude as well as a momentarily paralysing awe.

Keats may have been exceptional in the intensity of his reading experience, but his desire to learn from the greatest practitioners of his art in order to achieve independent greatness was typical of his age. Romantic poets were great writers, but they were great readers, too, and so, to understand their innovations, it is helpful to remember their passionate enthusiasm for great literature. Awareness of earlier poetry was heightened by its sudden availability. Keats's interest in Dante, like that of Shelley, Byron and Leigh Hunt, was largely stimulated by Henry Cary's translation of the *Divine Comedy*, which was completed in 1814. Cary's Dante was only one of numerous editions of older literature to be found in contemporary bookshops and libraries by readers eager to expand their knowledge and taste the pleasures of earlier ages. Johnson's magisterial *Lives of the Poets*, which had appeared in 1777–1781, was commissioned by a group of London publishers, who recognized the demand for a new multi-volume edition of English poetry. From the 1780s onwards, in the wake of a new legal ruling over copyright in 1774, massive editions of poetry began to appear in Edinburgh and London, opening the eyes of British readers to the wealth of their own national literature, as well as that of the classical world and Renaissance Europe. Wordsworth, Coleridge and Southey were all able to read Elizabethan and Jacobean poets in the pages of Robert Anderson's thirteen volume edition of *The Works of the British Poets*, published between 1792 and 1795. Here they encountered the work of John Donne and Michael Drayton, Samuel Daniel and Philip Sidney, along with a vast number of other lyricists, sonneteers, elegists and devotional writers. For the generation brought up on the heroic couplets of the Restoration, the modern recovery of earlier Renaissance poetry was an opening into an uncharted world. No wonder Keats felt like Cortez, when he first encountered George Chapman's version of Homer.

Would-be travellers in the realms of gold also had the guidance of a new understanding of literary history, pioneered by scholars such as Richard Hurd and Thomas Warton in the 1770s and developed more recently by William Hazlitt, Coleridge and Leigh Hunt, as well as by German critics such as Gottfried Lessing and the Schlegel brothers, Friedrich and August Wilhelm. Writers of the sixteenth and early seventeenth centuries were increasingly seen as forming a 'Golden Age' of English literature, on which modern poets could gaze with admiration and draw fresh inspiration. When Leigh Hunt published Keats's sonnet 'On Reading Chapman's Homer' in *The Examiner*, he paid him a very high compliment by suggesting that this new, young writer might recover the natural strength of the Renaissance for English poetry. Hunt's attitude was characteristic of an age that began to idolize early modern literature and to place Shakespeare and Milton at the centre of the literary pantheon. For Hazlitt, 'the four greatest names in English poetry' were Chaucer, Spenser, Shakespeare and Milton, but 'the great distinction' of Shakespeare was that his genius virtually included 'the genius of all the great men of his age', (*Lectures on the English Poets*, 1818, Hazlitt, *Works*, V, 46–7). Coleridge, on the other hand, saw Shakespeare and Milton seated 'on the two glory-smitten summits of the poetic mountain', complementary in their genius because, 'the former darts himself forth, and passes into all the forms of human character and passion, the one Proteus of the fire and the flood; the other attracts all forms and things to himself, into the unity of his own IDEAL' (*Biographia Literaria*, II, 27–8). For Coleridge, as for many readers of the Romantic period, reflection on these mighty poets stirred feelings of patriotic pride in the nation that had produced such men: 'O what great men hast thou not produced, England! my country!' (*Biographia Literaria*, II, 28).

Intense admiration for Shakespeare and Milton was prompted in part, however, by a desire to distinguish modern literature from its immediate predecessors – from the critical judgments of Dr Johnson and the neoclassical aesthetics that had prevailed in the early eighteenth century. The Romantic revival of interest in Milton's early poems, which had been languishing in relative obscurity for a century, was part of a growing confidence in the superiority of modern taste and critical understanding. Keats's dual purpose – to fly after Shakespeare *and* to find new forms and language for modern poetry – seems less contradictory once the Romantic admiration for the Renaissance is seen as a deliberate rejection of more recent predecessors. In 1815, Hazlitt published an essay in *The Examiner* which made disparaging comment on the literary tastes of Johnson and Pope, whose views on versification would have meant converting Milton's 'vaulting Pegasus into a rocking-horse' (Hazlitt, 'On Milton's Versification', *Works*, IV, 40) The following year, in 'Sleep and Poetry', Keats expressed a similar disdain for the heroic couplets of his Augustan predecessors, who 'swayed about upon a rocking horse, / And thought it Pegasus' (186–7). For ambitious young poets of a new century, it was time to fly with Pegasus once again.

The elevation of earlier literature was not, however, without difficulties. How were the Moderns to live up to their Elizabethan forefathers? If Shakespeare's genius had been marked by its startling originality, then mere imitation of his work could never lead to equal achievement. The bardolatry of the later eighteenth century had resulted in part from new aesthetic ideas, developed by poets such as Edward Young and Scottish theorists such as William Duff and Alexander Gerard, which prized originality, individuality and process rather than the attainment of perfection according to recognised standards. The critical turn towards great innovators such as Shakespeare and Milton, also gave rise to what Harold Bloom memorably termed 'the anxiety of influence' and which W. J. Bate analyzed in somewhat different terms as 'the burden of the past': in other words, the problems afflicting Romantic poets who began to look back in anguish at their mighty predecessors. Although Keats eventually laid

'Hyperion' aside, because of an excess of 'Miltonic inversions in it', however, he was questioning Milton's grand style as much as admitting his own defeat (Keats, *Letters*, II, 167). Despite the potentially intimidating examples of the great poets of the past and the pressure to create something unique and unprecedented, Romantic poets still picked up their pens and wrote.

To be a worthy successor meant finding an independent voice, creating beauty of a kind that measured up to the modern world, even as it drew inspiration from the great models of the past. In 'The Nightingale', Coleridge urged modern poets to respond directly to the natural world, rather than relying on books for their ideas, but his new poem still revealed his own wide reading and his knowledge of Milton's influence on eighteenth-century poetry. Romantic poetry is often characterized in terms of the return to nature, but it was a self-conscious return, its celebrations of the immediate deepened by knowing uses of the past.

The Romantic period was an age of experimentation as well as revival, of intensely forward-looking, visionary writings and of almost obsessive returns to earlier centuries. The very term, 'Romantic' was evocative of a lost age of fantastic narrative, but in its new incarnation, it came to signify radical politics and revolutionary ambition. Poets of the period read past masters and revived forms long since fallen from favor, but they did so with an energy and ambition that rendered the old kinds almost unrecognizable from their original traditions. Many of the poetic forms we associate most readily with the Romantic period had histories that long predated the poets who adapted them. And yet the late eighteenth and early nineteenth-century examples seem vital, new creations, as forward-looking as they are retrospective. Even when poets revisited Milton's remarkable legacy, with its exemplary odes, hymns, elegies, songs, sonnets, poetic drama and blank verse epic, their versions of the same kinds were deliberately differentiated from the great model. Wordsworth regarded 'Lines written a few miles above Tintern Abbey' as an 'ode', even though its meditative, blank verse looked very different from the elaborate stanzas of Milton's 'Ode on the Morning of Christ's Nativity', or indeed, of any Ode by Marvell, Cowley, Dryden, Gray or Collins. The narrator of *Don Juan* underlined the poem's genre by discussing epic tradition in the opening Canto, but what followed is also quite unlike any previous example of the form. In 'Hyperion', Keats followed Milton's choice of verse in *Paradise Lost*, but published it as an unfinished 'Fragment' before going on to recast it as the more Dantean 'The Fall of Hyperion'.

Often past masterpieces were recalled only to be transformed into something new – folded into different registers, filled out with contemporary references, or fused with other poetic kinds. This chapter considers the ways in which Romantic poets signalled their connection to the past through formal choices and direct allusions, while simultaneously asserting their own modernity. Since the topic is a large one, it considers only one major form – the sonnet – and one major precursor text – *Paradise Lost*. It concludes with a brief consideration of another major and multifaceted cultural revival, which was in itself responding to the Italian and classical heritage of the Renaissance – the rediscovery of native traditions within Britain. These discussions are inevitably selective but will help to draw attention to the significance of generic choices made by Romantic poets and to the variety of literary traditions that flourished in the period.

The Sonnet Revival

Keats's sonnets on Shakespeare, Dante or Homer, were part of a newly revived tradition of literary-inspired sonnets, self-consciously situated in relation to the greatest practitioners of the form. As modern poets called on their mighty predecessors for inspiration, they also asserted their own independent voices, whether through formal experimentation, personal tone, or through the choice of insistently contemporary subject matter. Keats clearly felt the Shakespearean couplet to be appropriate to a sonnet in praise of *King Lear*, but in a letter written in the following spring, he expressed his dissatisfaction with the standard form: 'I have been endeavouring to discover a better sonnet stanza than we have. The legitimate [Italian] does not suit the language over-well from the pouncing rhymes – the other kind [English] appears too elegiac – and the couplet at the end of it has seldom a pleasing effect' (O'Neill and Mahoney, 442). To make his point, he composed 'If by dull rhymes', with its own unique variation on the traditional sonnet schemes: *abcabdcabdede*.

Keats's new composition was explicitly concerned with its own form, drawing attention to its innovative rhymes by expressing frustration with conventional schemes and the difficulties of importing Italian forms into English literary tradition:

> If by dull rhymes our English must be chain'd
> And, like Andromeda, the Sonnet sweet,

> Fetter'd in spite of pained Loveliness;
> Let us find out, if we must be constrain'd
> Sandals more interwoven and complete
> To fit the naked foot of Poesy.
> (1–6; O'Neill and Mahoney, 442)

So vivid was Keats's imagination that he could present the technical restrictions governing sonnets in the shape of Andromeda, the beautiful young woman from Greek mythology, who was chained to a rock until eventually freed by Perseus. The new rhyme-scheme devised for Andromeda, avoiding the mini-sections of traditional sonnets (the quatrains and concluding couplet, the decisive break between the octave and the sestet), showed that Keats had indeed found a 'more interwoven and complete' form for his metrical feet. He understood the beauty of rhymes and the benefits of tight forms, but also capitalized on the pleasure of something slightly unexpected, closing his sonnet with the assertion that 'if we may not let the Muse be free / She will be bound with garlands of her own' (13–14). His poem might not conform to the old rules, but still self-consciously asserted its existence as a sonnet.

The adventurous resistance of Keats's new sonnet was also a statement of faith in the creative possibilities of the English language, a confidence that distinguished the Romantic writer from his great Elizabethan predecessors. When the sonnet form was imported from Italy into sixteenth-century Britain, it marked a fairly late stage of the great European Renaissance of classical civilisation. Since then, however, Shakespeare and Milton had shown what English writers could achieve in their native tongue, while the eighteenth century had seen the more general growth of a powerful sense of British identity. For Romantic poets, there was no longer any need to regard their language as inferior to classical or European languages, for Britain had a great culture and rich language of her own. The desire to tackle complicated poetic forms nevertheless meant engaging with linguistic differences, which in turn increased awareness of the distinct character of the English language.

Keats's dissatisfaction with the 'legitimate' sonnet may suggest an interest in the history of the form, but it also points to more recent influences. In 1796, Mary Robinson, for example, had published *Sappho and Phaon, in a Series of Legitimate Sonnets*, which were presented as a deliberate corrective to the looseness with which the word 'sonnet' was applied in contemporary magazines. Robinson was by no means the first to revive the Petrarchan sonnet for Romantic readers, however. Thomas

Gray had been moved to write a sonnet in 1742, after the death of his friend, Richard West, and Thomas Warton included some of his experiments with the form in a collection of *Poems* published in 1777. These, in turn, provided inspiration for Warton's student, William Bowles, whose volume entitled simply *Fourteen Sonnets* was an immediate success when it appeared in 1789. As the work of Stuart Curran, Stephen Behrendt and others has shown, however, the pioneering sonneteer of the period was Charlotte Smith, whose *Elegiac Sonnets* went into a seventh edition in the year before *Sappho and Phaon* appeared. In the third edition of her popular collection, published in 1786, Smith had drawn attention to some of the new poems she had added, using 'the Italian model', though she added modestly, 'with what success I know not' (Wu, 84). As a way of advertising the inclusion of new poems and fending off potential criticism, the rhetorical trope of false modesty was skilfully deployed, but it also raised awareness of the different sonnet traditions. Readers were being reminded that though her poems might seem to be spontaneous utterances from an overflowing heart, they were also the work of a serious artist. The preface was also prompting further debate over what might be the best form for the modern sonnet – Italian or English?

Long before Keats expressed his reservations about the 'pouncing rhymes' of the Petrarchan sonnet, Charlotte Smith was considering the challenges of adapting Italian forms into English. In her note to the seventeenth sonnet, 'The Thirteenth Cantata of Metastasio', she explained that it was not, strictly speaking, a translation, because she had reduced the length and omitted any images unsuitable for a sonnet, on the grounds that 'some of them, though very beautiful in Italian, would I believe not appear to advantage in an English dress' (Wu, 91). Smith, like many of her contemporaries, felt free to invoke Italian masters, but this did not preclude her from asserting her artistic independence and adapting the material to suit her own tastes and purposes. If Metastasio's images were unsuitable for the English language, they could be rejected in favor of more attractive ideas: admiration by no means led to uncritical imitation.

For a woman poet to draw explicitly on Petrarch, as Smith did for several of her *Elegiac Sonnets*, was after all a bold statement in itself, since the classic Italian sonnet sequence had been addressed by the love-struck male sonneteer to his idealized Laura. Although she based her poems on Petrarch's, thereby implicitly elevating her own sequence, Smith freely transformed her sources with Shakespearean rhymes and varied meters. 'Sonnet XIII. From Petrarch', for example, adopts a shorter, tetrameter line in place of the usual pentameter, and replaces the Petrarchan octave (abbaabba) with Shakespearean quatrains (ababcdcd):

> Oh place me where the burning noon
>   Forbids the withered flower to blow;
> Or place me in the frigid zone
>   On mountains of eternal snow;
> Let me pursue the steps of fame,
>   Or poverty's more tranquil road;
> Let youth's warm tide my veins inflame,
>   Or sixty winters chill my blood:
>   (1–8; Wu, 90)

The shorter line and unexpected shift in lines 5–6 suits the impatient hyperbole of the poem, which seems bent on encompassing the entire world in its expression of devotion to the unattainable object of love. For a woman poet in this period, the expression of such passion was likely to attract charges of impropriety, but translation from an Italian master allowed greater freedom of subject and style. The female voice that mingled with that of the classic male sonneteer also added a fresh dimension to imagery of withering and poverty, since Smith, aged thirty seven and the survivor of twelve pregnancies, was only too aware of the struggle to support her large family.

Although Smith drew attention to the Italian tradition, she employed the sonnet just as readily for English subjects. 'Sonnet XXX. To the River Arun', for example, upheld the attractions of the small river that ran through her home in Sussex in preference to those of the better known:

> Be the proud Thames of trade the busy mart!
>   Arun, to thee will other praise belong;
> Dear to the lover's and the mourner's heart.
>   And ever sacred to the sons of song!
>   (1–4; Wu, 97)

The local river might not be the centre of the nation, nor offer the economic advantages of the great Thames, but its personal value was incalculable. The Arun had its own claim to national fame, as Smith's notes pointed out, since both the successful dramatist, Thomas Otway, and the poet, William Collins, who also lived in Sussex, had written poems in which it featured. Warm, personal celebration of the local area is therefore an opportunity for raising questions about contemporary attitudes, because Smith is effectively presenting the literary heritage as a challenge to the pre-eminence of trade. Her address to the Arun, like Thomas Warton's sonnet 'To the Lodon' and William Bowles 'To the Itchin', also helped unloose a positive flood of Romantic river poems, flowing on towards Wordsworth's *The River Duddon* and *Yarrow Revisited*.

Smith's *Elegiac Sonnets* did much to revive Romantic interest in the sonnet form itself, by revealing rich possibilities in the Renaissance form for the expression of modern feelings and ideas. As a young man, Wordsworth admired her work so much that he called to visit Smith on his way to France in 1791. If Petrarch and Shakespeare had offered the most important models for Smith, however, it was Milton who most inspired Wordsworth to reconsider the possibilities of the modern sonnet. Wordsworth had come to realize by 1802 that the Miltonic sonnet had 'an energetic and varied flow of sound crowding into narrow room more of the combined effect of rhyme and blank verse than can be done by any other kind of verse I know of' (Wordsworth, *Letters: Early Years*, I, 379). In the sequence written at the same time, he called explicitly on his great English predecessor: 'Milton, thou shouldst be living at this hour / England hath need of thee!' ('London 1802'; Wu, 537). By choosing short rhyme-words and varying the stresses, Wordsworth attempted to recover the Miltonic effects of mingled rhyme and blank verse he so admired:

> Thy soul was like a star and dwelt apart;
> Thou hadst a voice, whose sound was like the sea;
> Pure as the naked heavens, majestic, free –
> So didst thou travel on life's common way,
> In cheerful godliness; and yet thy heart
> The lowliest duties on itself did lay.
> ('London, 1802', 9–14; Wu, 537)

In the sestet, Wordsworth took the basic pentameter, but by combining enjambment with mid-sentence line breaks, he too succeeded in creating verse 'whose sound was like the sea; / Pure as the naked heavens, majestic, free –'. The absence of a closing couplet, and intermingling of long vowels with short, unstressed syllables to vary the iambic measure, mean that the lines of the sestet seem to swell and flow towards the end of the poem, like great waves. Wordsworth was attracted to the conciseness of the sonnet form, just as Keats would be, but within the 'narrow rooms' that he explicitly praised in 'Nun's Fret Not', his aim was artistic freedom.

For Wordsworth, Milton's sonnets were admirable for their conciseness, lack of false ornament, and clear purpose, but equally important was their association with liberty. In *Poems, in Two Volumes*, which he published in 1807, Wordsworth included an entire sequence of Sonnets 'dedicated to Liberty'. The technical choices of Romantic poets were often guided by social and political concerns as much as aesthetic preferences and when Wordsworth invoked Milton ('thou shouldst be living at this hour') he was not merely in search of a formal model. 'London, 1802', with its image of England as a 'fen of stagnant waters', was evidently not presented as a stylistic experiment as much as an urgent appeal to a nation in crisis. The invocation of Milton was a clear political gesture, reiterated in companion pieces such as 'Great Men have been Among Us', where the 'men' in question were writers of the English Republic: Andrew Marvell, Algernon Sidney, James Harrington and Henry Vane (Wu, 537). In a period when the expression of radical sympathies had become liable to prosecution under the new laws on sedition, writers were still able to indicate their commitment to Republican ideals through historical allusion and the choice of literary form.

If Wordsworth invoked Milton in his 'Sonnets dedicated to Liberty', the younger poets who read them regarded Wordsworth himself as a guiding star. After the publication of *The Excursion* in 1814 and *Poems*, 1815, however, there was a growing sense among the rising generation that Wordsworth had abandoned his old commitment to liberty and was becoming a reclusive reactionary. Shelley pointedly chose a sonnet to express his own disillusionment and his address 'To Wordsworth' alluded directly to 'London, 1802':

> Thou wert as a lone star, whose light did shine
> On some frail bark in winter's midnight roar
> (7–8; Wu, 1952)

For Shelley, it was as if Wordsworth had succeeded in reviving Milton's spirit, only to abandon it:

> Deserting these, thou leavest me to grieve,
> Thus having been, that thou shouldst cease to be.
> (13–14)

The great moral responsibility of the poet now seemed to be falling on younger shoulders and, when he composed 'Ode to the West Wind' four years later, Shelley included the plea 'Make me thy lyre, even as the forest is' (O'Neill and Mahoney, 380). Shelley was, in part, taking up the challenge issued by Thomas Gray in his mid-eighteenth-century ode, 'The Progress of Poetry', which asked those who followed Milton's somewhat intimidating example:

> O! lyre divine, what daring spirit
> Wakes thee now?'
> (112–13; *Poems of Gray*, 176)

In his own attempt to seize the lyre, Shelley was also reiterating his sense of the failure of Milton's most obvious contemporary heir, Wordsworth.

By the time Shelley was writing his 'Ode to the West Wind' in 1819, ideas about poetic inspiration had undergone a radical alteration, largely through Wordsworth and Coleridge's desire to bring Gray's 'Aeolian lyre' back into contact with the real breezes blowing in the natural world and, in doing so, to awaken people to a sense of divine possibility. Even as Shelley absorbed the influences of Wordsworth and Coleridge, however, he was also asserting his independence. Coleridge's 'The Eolian Harp' had presented the poet with an 'indolent and passive brain', crossed by thoughts 'As wild and various as the random gales / That swell and flutter on this subject Lute!' (41–3; O'Neill and Mahoney, 177). His later poem, 'Dejection', suggested less passive mental powers, but this in turn rendered their failure all the more painful; the great Wind in Coleridge's ode provokes only a 'scream of agony' from the eolian lute (97–8; O'Neill and Mahoney, 238). In a *Defence of Poetry*, Shelley seized Coleridge's metaphor for the mind, acknowledging that 'man is an instrument over which a series of external and internal impressions are driven, like the alternations of an ever-changing wind over an Aeolian lyre', but his purpose was to argue against either mental passivity or failure: 'there is a principle within the human being...which acts otherwise than in the lyre, and produces not melody alone, but harmony' (Wu, 1185). Rather than being purely passive, humans could control their own creative responses to external stimulation, just as a singer adjusts his voice to musical accompaniment. This innate capacity also meant that whether responding to personal experience or reading, a poet could still create something very different from the source.

In its vivid evocation of the powerful autumn winds of Tuscany, 'Ode to the West Wind' recalled numerous poems by Wordsworth and Coleridge that urged direct response to the natural world, but it was also a formal reply. The benevolence of Wordsworth's divine spirit is replaced by a much more Janus-faced force, a destroyer and preserver, which spreads fear as much as delight. And yet its wild spirit is also contained within a tight form. Both Wordsworth and Coleridge had published remarkable 'Odes', following Pindaric rather than Horatian tradition, with irregular stanzas of varying line lengths. 'Intimations of Immortality' and 'Dejection' each had metrical and rhyming patterns designed to express fluctuating feelings, and each conveyed a distinct movement from stanza to stanza. Shelley's Ode, in contrast, consists of five carefully structured, regular stanzas, which are also sonnets. They were not the Miltonic sonnets favoured by Wordsworth, however, but a new variation, whose use of Dante's *terza rima* and concluding couplet almost disguise the genre:

> O wild West Wind, thou breath of autumn's being,
> Thou, from whose unseen presence the leaves dead
> Are driven, like ghosts from an enchanter fleeing,
>
> Yellow and black, and pale, and hectic red,
> Pestilence stricken multitudes: O, thou,
> Who chariotest to their dark wintry bed
>
> The winged seeds, where they lie cold and low,
> Each like a corpse within its grave, until
> Thine azure sister of the Spring shall blow
>
> Her clarion o'er the dreaming earth, and fill
> (Driving sweet buds like flocks to feed in air)
> With living hues and odours plain and hill:
>
> Wild Spirit, which art moving everywhere;
> Destroyer and Preserver; hear, O, hear!
> (1–14; O'Neill and Mahoney, 378)

This is a poem within a poem, a sonnet masquerading as a lyric, or forming an epode of the larger ode. It is characteristic of the Romantic impulse to experiment with form, creating from old, familiar moulds, something exciting and strange. Like Keats, Shelley was in search of new sandals for the feet of poetry, but instead of loosening the Petrarchan, Shakespearean or Miltonic ties, he wove a new pattern to interlink his Dantean stanzas: *aba bcb cdc ded ee*. As O'Neill points out in his introduction to the poem, Shelley exploited the form's 'ability to look forward, the middle line of each tercet performing the role of a 'winged seed' (7) bearing fruit in the rhymes of the next tercet' (377). In other words, the 'leaves dead' of line

2 grow into the 'hectic red' and 'wintry bed' of the fourth and sixth lines. The effect is to propel the reader along, as if blown by the wild wind, whose power seems manifest in the very length of the opening sentence, which fills the entire sonnet. The absence of end-stops, and the enjambment from stanza to stanza ensures the sense of freedom and energetic movement, even within the tight control of the verse form.

Shelley was showing that dead leaves might live again, as the sheer energy and colour of the opening contributes to the vitality of the poem. This is a wild place, full of uncertainty, with its fleeing ghosts, pestilence-stricken multitudes and winged seeds laid low, and yet utterly compelling. Movement and mortality seem twinned as the wild spirit of autumn breathes disease as well as life. In such startling transformations of familiar Romantic imagery, Shelley was showing how the dead leaves of old books might also be shaken from their customary places, giving room for new growth. Thoughts that might seem to have lost any meaning for modern readers could suddenly be reignited, as the great wind, 'destroyer and preserver', scattered 'sparks' as well as 'ashes.' If Keats imagined himself as a phoenix, reborn through the searing experience of reading *King Lear*, Shelley saw himself in turn as lyre, forest and 'unextinguished hearth', his newly enriched verse springing up to wake mankind. And yet, the terrifying aspect of the West Wind is never fully overcome, its power to destroy as well as to preserve perpetually threatening to break down the confines of Shelley's neat sonnet sequence. The poet's apparently confident command of the elements still ends with a question, 'If winter comes, can spring be far behind?' The closing line can be read most easily as the final triumphal piece of rhetoric – reducing winter's power by making it merely the herald of spring – but it also introduces less optimistic possibilities. For though the prophecy of spring is stirring enough, from an autumnal perspective it might still seem a long way in the future.

While Shelley's exuberant use of Italian elements seems designed to revitalize modern English poetry, his very recourse to Italy could also be seen as a pessimistic comment on the state of his own nation. When Gray envisaged British poets inheriting the lyre in 'The Progress of Poetry', it was as a consequence of the Muses' unhappy departure from conquered Greece, across Europe to England, where political liberty – and therefore the arts – flourished. Shelley might be following Gray in taking up the lyre so overtly, but he was also questioning the idea of 'progress', by returning the Muse to Italy. Other poems written by Shelley in the autumn of 1819, after hearing news of the bloody repression of peaceful protesters at Peterloo Fields in Manchester, such as *The Mask of Anarchy* or 'England in

1819', were not celebrations of British liberty. Indeed, the future of freedom in Britain seemed doubtful enough to make the closing line of the 'Ode' a real rather than rhetorical question.

Despite his deliberate divergence from his older contemporaries, then, Shelley was still following Wordsworth in adapting a religious and personal form such as the sonnet to political ends. 'Ode to the West Wind' is a sonnet sequence, but the object of Shelley's devotion is the whole of humanity rather than an individual. Shelley's desire to awaken mankind also revealed a poetic ambition just as soaring as Keats's urge to fly to Shakespearean heights, or Wordsworth's to equal Milton's achievement. For each of them, thoughts of the mighty dead ignited hopes of artistic excellence and public benefit. Romantic poets were therefore inaugurators of literary tradition as well as inheritors, their vigorous approach to older forms producing new kinds of poetry. And, as they re-formed the past, they also revealed new meanings for future generations.

Paradise Lost

Milton's sonnets inspired a host of fine Romantic poems, but their influence paled beside that of his most famous work, the great epic of *Paradise Lost*. This was the poem that towered over the century following its publication in 1667 and almost all the poets of the Romantic period came under its influence. As Lucy Newlyn and others have shown, Milton was especially attractive to Romantic writers, not only on account of his astonishing literary achievement and generic variety, but also because his poetry could be interpreted in so many different ways. While many readers revered *Paradise Lost* as a quasi-divine text, seeking moral, spiritual and philosophical answers in Milton's profound epic, others pillaged the poem for resonant phrases, classical conventions, memorable images and dramatic moments. Byron, for example, had no qualms about taking what he wanted from Milton throughout his career, turning the rebellious, exiled figure of Satan into the 'Byronic hero' of *Childe Harold*, *Lara*, *The Corsair* and *Manfred*, or adapting the Biblical drama of *Samson Agonistes* for the distinctly sceptical *Cain* and *Heaven and Earth*. Byron's 'Prometheus', characterised by unfailing resistance to 'the inexorable heaven' (18, Wu, 887) owed much to Milton's Satan and, when berating his contemporaries for their political apostasy in *Don Juan*, Byron explicitly recalled Milton's own heroic consistency:

> He deigned not to belie his soul in songs,
> Nor turn his very talent to a crime;
> He did not loathe the sire to laud the son,
> But closed the tyrant hater he begun.
> (*Don Juan*, 'Dedication', 77–80; Wu, 936)

For Byron, Milton represented a more admirable example than the leading poets of his own day, Southey, Wordsworth and Coleridge, who now seemed to have abandoned their Republicanism, despite earlier invocations of England's 'Great Men'. Milton, in contrast, had remained committed to his cause and *Paradise Lost* could be read accordingly as a poem challenging tyrannical power and unjust hierarchy.

Whether Byron's praise was compromised by its place in a poem tracing the sexual adventures of its young hero, is, of course, a question faced by all readers of *Don Juan*, who are presented with a rather different image of Milton in Canto III:

> We're told this great high priest of all the Nine
> Was whipt at College – a harsh sire – odd spouse,
> For the first Mrs Milton left his house.
> (*Don Juan*, III, 817–24)

In an ironic twist, typical of the poem, the grand old poet who had appeared to be a symbol of consistency suddenly becomes an image of human foibles and frailties. This rather unexpected representation of Milton reflects a new fashion for life-writing that had begun to affect Romantic perceptions of past masters. The new fascination with writer's biographies meant that the name of a great poet often referred to the man as much as the work – a development of which Byron, with his scandalous and not very private life, was only too conscious.

If public interest in the private lives of writers was greeted with some trepidation by the major poets of the period, however, biographies of earlier writers often drew attention to the political dimensions of their work, too. Knowledge of Milton's life history and his support for the establishment of an English Republic, for example, had done much to encourage revolutionary readings of his great epic. Byron was not alone in admiring Milton for remaining 'the Tyrant-hater he began', even after the Restoration and Romantic readings of Satan were often coloured by thoughts of Milton's unshaken commitment to the Republican cause. William Godwin, for example, saw heroic fortitude in the charismatic figure of Satan, whose imprisonment at the start of the poem seemed an unjust punishment for the attempted overthrow of an unelected, all-powerful ruler. Shelley, too, who was greatly inspired by his father-in-law's political writings, similarly recalled Satan's 'courage and majesty, and firm and patient opposition to omnipotent force' ('Preface to *Prometheus Unbound*', Wu, 1092) as a model for his own hero, Prometheus. He nevertheless qualified his analogy, by acknowledging that some aspects of Satan's character ('ambition, envy, revenge, and a desire for personal aggrandisement', Wu, 1092) were rather less admirable.

Like many of his contemporaries, Shelley felt free to pick and choose among Milton's characters, forms, images and lines, taking what suited his own purpose and creating effects entirely different from the source. His image of Prometheus, for example, chained to the rock, 'eyeless in hate' (*Prometheus Unbound*, 9) drew as readily on the blind hero of Milton's *Samson Agonistes*, 'eyeless in Gaza' (*Samson Agonistes*, 41), as it did on *Paradise Lost*, while the later lyrical songs in the drama are more reminiscent of those in *Comus*. Romantic writers fused together a variety of elements from the work of earlier poets, sometimes explicitly emphasizing their differences. Shelley was recalling Ancient Greece as much as seventeenth-century England in his poetic drama, but made very clear that what might appear to be a restoration of the lost play by Aeschylus was no such thing: 'I was averse from a catastrophe so feeble as that of reconciling the champion with the oppressor of mankind' ('Preface to *Prometheus Unbound*', Wu, 1092). For Shelley, oppressive tyranny was not to be subject to negotiation and political compromise – it had to be abolished in order for the new world of universal equality to dawn. Milton, 'a republican, and bold enquirer into morals and religion' was, in Shelley's eyes, part of the Protestant Reformation, which by shaking 'to dust the oldest and most oppressive form of the Christian religion' (Wu, 1093) was the forerunner of the Enlightenment and ultimately of the social change sought by European radicals. What might appear contradictory in the atheist poet's invocation of *Paradise Lost*, is explained as a rational choice.

For many poets of the Romantic period, Milton was the champion of liberty, even if they diverged in their understanding of what this meant. Ironically, since Milton's most eloquent fallen angel could be read as an image of the creative individual, throwing off obedience to convention, *Paradise Lost* contained its own justification for a poet's departure from his great model. Milton had, after all, distinguished his own epic from those of his illustrious predecessors, Homer, Virgil and Spenser, on the grounds that his own theme of 'patience and heroic martyrdom' was morally superior (*Paradise Lost*, IX, 32). Blake, too, though rejecting Milton's admiration for patient martyrdom, was happy enough to follow his example in overturning inherited conventions. He famously inverted the pattern of *Paradise Lost* in *The Marriage of Heaven and Hell*, claiming that 'The reason Milton wrote in fetters when he wrote of Angels and God, and at liberty when of devils and Hell, is because he was a true Poet and of the Devil's party without knowing it' (Wu, 208).

In *The Marriage of Heaven and Hell*, the Devil exposes the age-old 'error' of dividing a man's Body from his Soul, arguing that life, the creative impulse, or 'Energy', springs from the Body. Blake was suggesting that the tendency of large, powerful religions had been to restrain mankind's energy to the point of utter passivity, imprisoning the individual within self-imposed mental constraints and encouraging selfishness and fear. He was not writing in opposition to Christ's teaching, however, but to organized religion. The Devil in *The Marriage of Heaven and Hell* announces that 'Jesus was all impulse and acted from impulse, not from rules' and in doing so converts the Angels to his more imaginative point of view (Wu, 216). Similar ideas were later expressed in Blake's much more elaborate illuminated book, *Milton*, only there Satan himself became the authoritarian law-giving God of conventional religious services, who was to be overthrown by the newly awakened poet.

The task of the true Poet, according to Blake, was not to 'justify the ways of God to men', then, but to reveal the divine: 'If the doors of perception were cleansed, everything would appear to Man as it is: Infinite' (*Marriage of Heaven and Hell*, Wu, 212). Blake's startling engagement with Milton's revered text, not to mention the Bible itself, works to melt 'apparent surfaces away' (Wu, 212), thus enabling readers to see things truly rather than conventionally. The 'Proverbs of Hell', for example, use Biblical form for Blakean thoughts: 'The road of excess leads to the palace of wisdom' is hardly in accord with Christian or Miltonic ideas of temperance and self-restraint (Wu, 210). 'Always be ready to speak your mind, and a base man will avoid you' (Wu, 210), on the other hand, has much in common with Milton's emphasis on the power of truth and dangers of deception. Though their language is generally simple, Blake's 'Proverbs' demand the active engagement of a reader, who must test their wisdom against more conventional sayings. Since one of the Proverbs states that 'The eagle never lost so much time as when he submitted to learn of the crow' (Wu, 210), readers are being warned against any kind of unthinking submission – including to the voice of Blake's Devil.

The Marriage of Heaven and Hell was composed in 1790, a year after *Songs of Innocence* and three years before *Songs of Experience*, and it shares a similar concern with the human 'contraries'. Rather than presenting the physical Paradise from which Adam and Eve were expelled after disobeying God, Blake's *Songs* express the contrast between innocent and experienced perspectives – except that throughout the collection, the two states seem inextricably bound together. In *Innocence*, 'The Ecchoing Green', for example, may depict children at play, but the very title, echoing through the poem until it becomes 'darkening', suggests a certain distance from the children, further accentuated by the image of the old folk 'who laugh at our play' (15; O'Neill and Mahoney, 24). The presence of the 'grey-headed beadles' with their 'wands as white as snow' has a similarly chilling effect on 'Holy Thursday' and, throughout *Songs of Innocence*, the voice of experience is never entirely quietened. In the *Songs of Experience*, however, the very existence of innocence seems threatened, in the 'land of poverty' where babies are 'reduced to misery' and hunger ('Holy Thursday', 8, 3; O'Neill and Mahoney, 33). The shared title turns us back to 'Holy Thursday' in *Songs of Innocence* to question the earlier voice that had urged 'Then cherish pity, lest you drive an angel from your door' (12; O'Neill and Mahoney, 29). Readers of *Experience* have come to see that 'Pity would be no more, / If we did not make somebody poor' ('The Human Abstract', 1–2; Wu, 201).

Blake may not have been engaging with *Paradise Lost* as explicitly in the *Songs* as he did in *The Marriage of Heaven and Hell*, but the desire to startle readers into re-examining their conventional assumptions was equally strong. The 'mind-forged manacles' heard everywhere in 'London' (8; O'Neill and Mahoney, 38) are closely linked to the dirty 'doors of perception' and the 'reptiles of the mind' that figure in the *Marriage*. In both books, the poet's purpose is the liberation of mental energy and the renewal of 'fallen fallen light' ('Introduction', 10; Wu, 191). Blake's notion of the Fall may have been personal and even idiosyncratic, but like Milton, he had the capacity to see the world in a grain of sand, the whole of mankind in the individual image. Their ideas about how to renew fallen light and recover paradise on earth were, however, presented very differently. For where Milton offered readers a magnificent image of God creating a world rapidly ruined by man, Blake suggested that Gods had their origins in man's 'enlarged and numerous sense', but became frightening abstractions through the exploitation of power-hungry priests (*Marriage of Heaven and Hell*, Wu, 210).

Despite his emphasis on man's creative potential, Blake was only too conscious of the darker possibilities surrounding mental activity. The capacity of the mind to breed reptiles rather than utter songs of joy is memorably described in 'A Poison Tree' (O'Neill and Mahoney, 40). In this skilful allegory, Blake shows how the repression of negative emotions – in this case 'wrath' – leads first to deceit and eventually to the unhealthy triumph over the enemy – now lying dead beneath the 'poison tree' of mutual hatred. Since the title of the poem was originally 'Christian forbearance', Blake's distance here from Milton's emphasis on patience and quiet obedience could hardly be more marked. The use of garden imagery is reminiscent of Eden, especially as the tree eventually bears forbidden fruit, but rather than follow Milton and Genesis in suggesting that the Fall results from man's theft from the tree of knowledge, Blake's short poem indicates that human malevolence has its roots in repression. The tree is planted not by a generous Creator-God, but grows from the unexpressed anger of the speaker, who waters his poisonous sapling with tears, suns it with smiles and rejoices when it proves fatal to his rival.

When 'The Poison Tree' is read beside a poem such as 'The Clod and the Pebble', it also has the capacity to unsettle what might otherwise seem a poem of fairly clear contrasts. Suddenly, it seems possible that the Clod of Clay's 'Love seeketh not Itself to please' might not after all be so very different from the pebble's 'Love seeketh only Self to please' (O'Neill and Mahoney, 32), if Blake is exposing the Christian ideal of self-sacrifice as a cover for secret resentment and manipulation. For when the words of the apparently selfless 'Clod' are followed by the Pebble's perception of love as self-serving and tyrannical, revelling in 'another's loss of ease' (11), this may be a comment on the Clod's deceit as much as a representation of a contrasting, selfish outlook. The perfect balance and brevity of the lyric make it difficult to arrive at any definite answer. The pebble's view of love as building 'a Hell in Heaven's despite' is strongly reminiscent of the misery experienced by Milton's Satan, 'which way I fly is hell, myself am hell' (*Paradise Lost*, IV, 73), and unless the Song is read according to the inversions of *The Marriage of Heaven and Hell*, it seems a recipe for unhappiness. In the light of some of the other poems in the *Songs of Experience*, however, the Clod of Clay's advice may seem equally unappealing. Readers are therefore faced with a choice between an innocent reading of the Clod of Clay's outlook and that of the more cynical Pebble, but may conclude that contraries such as these are inseparable aspects of human experience.

Through the unassuming genre of 'Songs', then, Blake was taking on Milton's epic themes, forcing his readers to think - and think again - and thereby find liberty. Ironically, in his challenge to Milton's list of 'virtue, patience, temperance... charity' (*Paradise Lost*, XII, 583–4), he was fulfilling the very advice issued by the archangel, Michael, in *Paradise Lost* –

> by small
> Accomplishing great things, by things deemed weak
> Subverting worldly strong, and worldly wise
> By simply meek
> (*Paradise Lost*, XII, 566–8)

Since Blake's work initially appeared only in a handful of hand-printed editions, he was also following Milton in finding a 'fit audience, though few.' Like many Romantic poets, Blake's admiration for Milton was immense, but not uncritical. Perpetual re-engagement with *Paradise Lost* was a sign of his passionate enthusiasm, rather than of rational criticism, but part of his passion meant wrestling with Milton's complicated ideas and wresting new meanings for the new age.

Paradise Lost and The Prelude

The fall from innocence and desire to regain paradise were defining principles for many Romantic poems, none more significant than *The Prelude*. In the aftermath of the French Revolution, struggling to reconcile memories of radical hopes with the subsequent decline into 'times of fear' and the 'melancholy waste of hopes o'erthrown' (*Prelude*, II, 448–9; *William Wordsworth*, 330), Wordsworth explored the Miltonic pattern of the Fall into experience and eventual recovery of paradise within. That Milton's great poem had been composed during the Restoration, when English Republican hopes had been utterly demolished, gave it a new significance for those in the Romantic period who were in despair over what had followed the thrilling dawn of the French Revolution. Wordsworth's own poem was epic in scale and ambition and saturated with Miltonic allusions, but instead of revisiting the creation of the universe, he tried to make sense of the world through the history of an individual mind.

Wordsworth did not present innocence and experience as Blakean 'contraries', but *The Prelude* nevertheless registered a powerful sense of the distance between youth an age. In Book II, for example, as Wordsworth recreated vivid images of his childhood, he paused for a moment of reflection:

> So wide appears
> The vacancy between me and those days,
> Which yet have such self-presence in my mind
> That, sometimes, when I think of them, I seem
> Two consciousnesses, conscious of myself
> And of some other Being.
> (*Prelude* II, 28–33; *William Wordsworth*, 319)

The young boy in the early books of the poem, who delights in snaring birds, skating, swimming or stealing boats, is no sentimental picture of innocence and yet, from the perspective of the older, experienced poet, he seems 'some other being'. Throughout *The Prelude*, images of earlier moments are framed by the voice of experience, which seems at once to suggest that the paradise of childhood is lost, while simultaneously showing its continuing presence in the mind of the creative adult. However vivid the passages recalling youthful experience may be, the perspective of the more mature, reflective speaker is never far from the view, encouraging interpretation just as much as instinctive sympathy.

The Prelude resembles *Paradise Lost* insofar as it is a long poem in blank verse, divided into several books, but its autobiographical focus on personal growth and lack of the classical reference makes it seem less obviously epic in the traditional literary sense. Wordsworth does not begin in Miltonic style, with a Virgilian statement of purpose and a neoclassical invocation to the Muse. Indeed, in the first Book, Wordsworth insists that his poem is just a preparatory exploration of his own suitability for the task of writing – it is a prelude, not the complete work. His very consideration of possible themes for the epic he *might* write nevertheless introduces Milton explicitly:

> Sometimes, mistaking vainly, as I fear,
> Proud spring-tide swellings for a regular sea,
> I settle on some British theme, some old
> Romantic tale, by Milton left unsung.
> (I, 177–180; O'Neill and Mahoney, 145)

Even though all possible subjects are rapidly dismissed by a speaker who berates himself for waywardness and procrastination, they still underline Wordsworth's sense of his own grand potential. Here is a man, who feels himself 'singled out ... For holy services' and preparing for a glorious work' (I, 63–4; 159). No amount of self-recrimination or promise of future success can entirely subdue the epic ambition evident from the start.

Readers familiar with *Paradise Lost* may also notice subtle epic allusions long before Milton is actually named in line 180. The opening sequence captures the heady pleasure of bursting into fresh air and daylight, as depression lifts and hope reappears on the mental horizon. The feeling of the 'gentle breeze' blowing from 'the green fields' and beating against the speaker's cheek is an experience that anyone can imagine, but the language of 'blessing' and the speaker's rapturous greeting, 'O welcome Messenger!' (I, 1–5) imbues it with something more remarkable than an ordinary walk in the country. The entire passage conveys both powerful, physical experience and a sense of the momentousness of the experience. Wordsworth's description of himself as a 'captive .... coming from a house /Of bondage' (I, 6–7), recalls the escape of God's chosen people in the Old Testament, 'from Egypt, from the House of Bondage' (Exodus, 13:3), and thus heightens the significance of his new-found freedom and the expectations of his readers. As the passage continues, the sense of something heaven-sent becomes even more apparent:

> Nay more, if I may trust myself, this hour
> Hath brought a gift that consecrates my joy;
> For I, methought, while the sweet breath of Heaven
> Was blowing on my body, felt within
> A corresponding mild, creative breeze
> A vital breeze which travelled gently on
> O'er things which it had made.
>
> (I, 39–45)

The 'sweet breath of Heaven' is a common metaphor for a light breeze, but in a passage that speaks of consecration, adopts the Miltonic 'methought' and describes a correspondent, creative breeze within the speaker, the memory of God breathing life into Adam seems present, too. As M.H. Abrams suggested many years ago, the 'correspondent breeze' is a key Romantic metaphor, which recovers the etymological origins of inspiration as a 'breathing in' and carries divine resonances from Genesis and *Paradise Lost* (VII, 525–6). Later on, in Book Seven, Wordsworth looks back on the 'glad preamble' (*The Prelude*, VII, 4; William Wordsworth) which opens *The Prelude*, implicitly aligning it with the 'preamble sweet' with which Milton's angels introduce their 'sacred song in *Paradise Lost* (III, 367). The passage celebrating the gentle breeze is thus amplified retrospectively by allusions to divine inspiration and the spontaneous sacred song which accompanied the origin of all things visible and invisible. The spontaneity of the breeze, caught so freshly in Wordsworth's opening lines, might therefore be seen in the light of Coleridge's memorable phrase, as a 'repetition in the finite mind of the eternal act of creation in the infinite I AM' (*Biographia Literaria*, I, 304; Wu, 691).

At the same time, however, the allusiveness of Wordsworth's verse introduces other, less reassuring elements. For although line 14–15 seem to assert an exhilarating self-reliance, 'The earth was all before me – with a heart / Joyous, nor scared at its own liberty', the knowledge that this is a reference to Adam and Eve's departure from paradise ('The world was all before them', *Paradise Lost*, XII, 646) introduces more complicated possibilities. Why does Wordsworth describe his heart as being 'not scared at its own liberty', when he could have found an adjective that avoided any thoughts of fear? To suggest that the allusion to Adam and Eve is ominous would be far too clumsy, but the dim recollection of a moment when an astonishing vista of possibility was seen only through tears of loss and regret must either temper or intensify the joy being conveyed by Wordsworth.

Even more perplexing are the echoes that Lucy Newlyn has pointed out, of Milton's Sin, anticipating her arrival in the fallen world, 'Methinks I feel new strength within me rise' (*Paradise Lost*, X, 243; Newlyn, 86). As Wordsworth announces 'should the guide I chuse / Be nothing better than a wandering cloud, / I cannot miss my way' (17–19), the voice of Sin echoes darkly in the background, 'Nor can I miss the way, so strongly drawn / By this new-felt attraction and instinct' (*Paradise Lost*, X, 262). Perhaps, rather than representing the unfallen Adam or the host of angels, Wordsworth is suggesting that the figure arriving in the paradisial green fields is one who is escaping Hell. Since the 'house of bondage' is also described as 'yon City', thoughts of Satan arriving in Eden having been 'long in populous City pent' (*Paradise Lost*, IX, 445) are just as pertinent as thoughts of Moses. Just as Blake's *Songs of Innocence* are paired with *Experience*, so Wordsworth's allusions to paradise are inseparable from thoughts of the fallen world. For Romantic poets, human beings seemed possessed of both divine and diabolical capabilities and as they struggled to make sense of individual and collective behavior, Milton's great epic offered an invaluable resource.

Wordsworth drew on Milton throughout *The Prelude* and it is possible to see Books 9 and 10, where Wordsworth wrestles with his memories of Revolutionary France as a personal counterpart of the same Books in *Paradise Lost*, recounting the Fall of Man. Since it is clear from the outset, however, that there is no neat match between the poet whose growth is being traced in *The Prelude* and Milton's great archetypal figures, it is wise to treat any overarching parallels between the two poems with care. Wordsworth recalls 'an inner falling off' in the third book, so it is equally possible to trace a gradual decline from the visionary powers of childhood over the course of the poem, rather than attempt to identify a decisive Fall from innocence. Since the poem is overtly charting the 'growth' of the poet's mind, it is also legitimate to play down any ideas of decline and fall, focusing instead on the development of wisdom through cumulative experience. The remarkable climbing of Snowdon in Book Thirteen can nevertheless be read fruitfully in the light of Adam's ascent at the end of *Paradise Lost*, since the ensuing glimpse of a 'paradise within...happier far' (XII, 587) finds a parallel in Wordsworth's conclusion: 'the mind of man becomes / A thousand times more beautiful than the earth / On which he dwells' (XIII, 446–8; *William Wordsworth*, 516). In fact, Wordsworth's celebration of the imaginative power of the human mind is rather different from Milton's concluding emphasis on humility, obedience and faith, but both poems share a movement from an external to internal paradise.

What Milton did offer Wordsworth, indisputably, was a kind of poetic language that enabled him to invest the ordinary with extraordinary significance. The ascent of Snowdon, for example, begins with a matter-of-fact setting of scene and situation:

> In one of those excursions, travelling then
> Through Wales on foot, and with a youthful Friend,
> I left Bethgelert's huts at couching-time
> And westward took my way to see the sun
> Rise from the top of Snowdon.
> (*Prelude*, XIII, 1–5; Wu 566)

The details of the climb in 'fog and damp' and silence, interrupted only by the sheepdog barking when it finds a hedgehog, make this seem the kind of walk that anyone might undertake. The familiar detail of the scene, however, makes the moment when the moon suddenly appears seem all the more startling:

> For instantly a light upon the turf
> Fell like a flash. I looked about, and lo!
> The moon stood naked in the heavens at height
> Immense above my head, and on the shore
> I found myself of a huge sea of mist,
> Which, meek and silent, rested at my feet.
> A hundred hills their dusky backs upheaved
> All over this still ocean
>
> (XIII, 39–46; Wu, 566–7)

Suddenly, there seems nothing ordinary about the experience being described, as the very landscape comes to life. The reference to the hills alludes directly to the scene of God's Creation in *Paradise Lost*, where 'the mountains huge appear / Emergent, and their broad backs upheave / Into the clouds' (VII, 286–7), and so, Wordsworth's choice of language enables him to convey the astonishing surge of power felt in this moment. The idea of a huge sea, 'meek and silent' at his feet, affirms the sense of divinity and turns the Welsh mountain into a site of revelation.

When Wordsworth wrote his 'Prospectus to the Recluse' – the epic poem for which *The Prelude* was to be the preparation – he deliberately called on Milton for guidance, while also making clear that his own region was 'the soul of man' (Wu, 481–2). Wordsworth had no need to portray 'Jehovah with his thunder, and the choir of shouting angels', because he had learned to find 'paradise and groves Elysian', in 'the growth of common day' (21–2, 35–40; Wu, 481). In other words, the world was charged with divine power, if only people knew where and how to look. It would have been difficult for Wordsworth to make his point about the marvellous potential of the everyday so effectively, however, without the contrasting example of Milton's monumental poem.

Whether Wordsworth's allusions to Milton are as easily grasped by a twenty-first as by a nineteenth-century audience, however, is another matter. A modern reader, unfamiliar with *Paradise Lost*, might initially feel disadvantaged by editorial notes pointing out Miltonic parallels, and may even be deterred from carrying on with *The Prelude* as a result. Since Wordsworth's literary recollections are generally so well blended with his personal experience, however, *The Prelude* can be read and enjoyed quite independently of *Paradise Lost*. As evident in the two passages discussed above, epic momentousness is invested in encounters with a breeze or a full moon, while the quality of Wordsworth's writing is such that the experience is conveyed with vivid immediacy. In a sense, *The Prelude* rewrites *Paradise Lost* for a modern audience, who may respond more easily to a description of the recognizable physical world than to an imagined prelapsarian ideal.

For those who have read Milton, however, the allusions add extra dimensions to *The Prelude*, and identifying them can help shed light on the subtle complexity of Wordsworth's descriptions. Once aware of the additional layers of possibility, those unfamiliar with Milton's epic may also feel eager to read it. The growth of a poet's mind, after all, includes his own reading, even if only one book of *The Prelude* is explicitly devoted to 'Books' (Book V). By drawing on his own reading so naturally and unostentatiously, Wordsworth demonstrates the 'invisible workmanship' that blends so many diverse elements into a single, creative mind. Encounters with great poets are just as much part of an individual's experience as the landscape of childhood, family, friends and formative events. *The Prelude* gives no obvious indication that reading *Paradise Lost* was as intense an activity as *King Lear* was for Keats, but it still reveals at every turn the far-reaching effect of Milton on Wordsworth's growth as a poet.

Native Traditions

Milton's great epic had demonstrated, beyond any doubt, that the English language was equal to the highest forms of poetry and therefore did much to establish a sense of national pride in the literary tradition. While his elevation of British culture to classical heights had strong appeal for many readers of the eighteenth century, however, its unavoidable erudition was not always inviting to those conscious that their education had had its limitations. Keats, for example, who did not have the opportunity to go to University (unlike Wordsworth, Coleridge, Byron and Shelley) felt his inability to read ancient Greek keenly, and hence his profound gratitude to Chapman's English translation of Homer. During the Romantic period, no universities were open to women, so unless they learned from governesses, schoolteachers or the men in their family, classical literature remained a closed book.

Like Blake, Clare, Burns, Bloomfield and most women poets of the period, Keats's knowledge of Ancient Greece came through English literature, through translations, through classical handbooks, through mythological paintings, vases and sculptures, and not directly from Greek texts. When he imagined the sacrificial heifer in 'Ode on a Grecian Urn', for example, he seems to have been thinking of the Elgin marbles, which he had visited when they were opened for public view in 1816. Often poets of the period drew on the classical references in English texts, relying more on contemporary Hellenism than on Homer. Though few were deterred from attempting classical forms, from pastoral to epic, ode to lyric, many poets in the period were also drawn to other literary kinds. Ancient Greece maintained a powerful hold over Romantic imaginations, but the eighteenth century had seen a steady rise in the publication of home-grown culture – ballads, songs, lyrics and legends that belonged to the ordinary people of Britain.

Joseph Addison had surprised readers of *The Spectator* in 1711 when he wrote of his admiration for the old ballad of 'Chevy Chase', but by the 1790s ballads were the height of literary fashion. Thomas Percy had done much to raise interest in the native tradition by publishing *Reliques of Ancient English Poetry* in 1765, but in the last decade of the century, the popularity of German Gothic ballads by Gottfried Bürger gave new impetus to the trend for folk poetry. Walter Scott's first ventures into poetry were translations from German ballads, but he rapidly saw the potential for a collection of popular Scottish poems, and produced three volumes of *Minstrelsy of the Scottish Border* in 1802–3. When he turned his hand to longer narrative poems, such as *The Lay of the Last Minstrel* and *The Lady of the Lake*, Scottish legends and scenes supplied him with materials perfectly suited to the taste of contemporary readers. His novels, too, drew on Scottish traditions and history, and woven into the central adventures were snatches of popular song, original lyrics and quotations from other poets. Poetry was part of national culture and Scott's voluminous publications reflected a new, widespread awareness of regional and national identity.

Like Scott, Coleridge was a great admirer of Percy's *Reliques*, and 'Dejection', though 'An Ode', begins with explicit reference to 'the grand old ballad of Sir Patrick Spens', which had appeared in Percy's collection (O'Neill and Mahoney, 235). When Coleridge and Wordsworth published their anonymous volume of *Lyrical Ballads* in 1798, they gave 'The Rime of the Ancyent Marinere' prime position, puffing it in the Advertisement as a poem 'written in imitation of the style as well as of the spirit of the elder poets' (O'Neill and Mahoney, 187). The archaic language, mysterious characters, use of dialogue, simple imagery, repetition, and long tale about an extraordinary voyage, were all carefully chosen to suggest authentic folk tradition, even though the concerns of the ballad were so much those of its modern creator. It was a shrewd choice for the opening poem, given the popularity of Bürger's 'Lenore' – a tale of a wild horse ride, in which a young woman is lured to the grave by her demon lover. In fact 'The Ancient Mariner', with its powerful religious imagery and focus on the protracted suffering of the principle narrator, had more in common with spiritual autobiography than with Bürger's sensational Gothic tale; the very form of Coleridge's poem would nevertheless have whetted the appetites of readers with a taste for supernatural thrills or traditional adventures. What's more, the choice of the ballad genre signaled sympathy with the common people and suggested that these were poems to be enjoyed by all, irrespective of their educational and social backgrounds.

Ballads had the authority of antiquity, without the potential obstacles of classicism. Romantic poets who adopted the form were indicating their awareness of literary tradition just as much as when they alluded to Greek or Roman authors, but their choice had the additional attractions of seeming patriotic and egalitarian. During the eighteenth century, the notion that the arts flourished in a free society had become firmly established, as evident in Gray's 'The Progress of Poetry'. During the Romantic period, however, as much of Europe fell under Napoleon's conquering army and the wartime Government clamped down on free speech, the precariousness of Britain's proud liberty was felt acutely. When Wordsworth visited France in 1802, during the short-lived peace, the sonnet 'Composed in the Valley near Dover', which he wrote on his return expressed a powerful sense of Europe's subjugation and the preciousness of Britain's contrasting freedom. Felicia Hemans's 'The Homes of England' was not published until 1827, twelve years after Waterloo, but the experience of prolonged war and threatened invasion still gave a powerful charge to the hope that 'the free, fair Homes of England' might remain safe for ever (33; O'Neill and Mahoney, 406–7).

In such a context, the appeal of poetic kinds that were not only quintessentially British, but whose long history might provide hope for the future continuity of native values, is understandable. Almost all the major poets of the Romantic period, whether classically educated or not, tried their hands at ballads, and in the process a form traditionally used for simple, orally transmitted, narrative was transformed into something highly sophisticated, literary and surprisingly capacious. Whether readers embark on 'The Ancient

Mariner', 'Simon Lee', 'La Belle Dame Sans Merci', 'The Mental Traveller' or 'The Mask of Anarchy', the immediate pleasure of the strong rhymes and rhythms are quickly complicated by the interpretative challenges. Romantic ballads may have signaled sympathy with the common people, but the form was often used as a vehicle for ideas that were anything but commonplace.

In one of the most popular literary ballads of the nineteenth century, Hemans's 'Casabianca', what appears to be a straightforward celebration of youthful courage in the face of dire odds becomes more complicated as soon as readers recognize that the boy on the burning deck is French, his death the result of British naval power. Given the public enthusiasm for Nelson, a poem that focused on a ten-year-old French victim of his famous victory at the Battle of the Nile was an unlikely bestseller, but its success shows the powerful appeal of a successful ballad:

> The boy stood on the burning deck
>   Whence all but he had fled;
> The flame that lit the battle's wreck,
>   Shone round him o'er the dead.
>
> Yet beautiful and bright he stood,
>   As born to rule the storm;
> A creature of heroic blood,
>   A proud though childlike form.
>   (1–8; O'Neill and Mahoney, 428)

The simple language and alliteration, pounding iambic meter, easily memorized monosyllables and, above all, the striking image of the boy standing at his post on a burning warship, makes it easy to see why Victorian school boys were encouraged to learn the ballad by heart. At the same time, the poem could as easily be regarded as a protest song, directing public outrage towards the plight of a child combatant, with the flags streaming 'above the gallant child' an ironic image of appalling exploitation. The pared down character of the verses, in keeping with ballad tradition, means that readers are given the narrative, but not the interpretation. Ballads in the old, oral tradition often dealt with violence, warfare, feuds, local tragedies, but their anonymity meant that the response generally depended on the audience. The literary ballads of the Romantic period were similarly given to presenting short narratives packed with striking images, memorable phrases and simple dialogue, which nevertheless combined to invite very varied and often antithetical readings.

Interest in native culture tends to thrive during periods of warfare, but during the late eighteenth-century conflict with France, patriotic enthusiasm was complicated by the relative novelty of the idea of 'Britain'. Although the war did much to consolidate a sense of internal unity between England, Wales and Scotland, the rising of the United Irishmen in 1798 underlined differences that the British Government were keen to suppress. The ensuing Union with Ireland in 1800, together with ongoing wartime rhetoric of Britishness contributed to the deeper awareness of what it meant to be English, Irish, Scottish, Welsh and/or British, which in turn fed the interest in national culture. The Welsh poetry of Iolo Morganwy and the Irish collections of Sydney Owenson and Thomas Moore were all published to popular acclaim in the Romantic period and reveal a widespread desire to trace and maintain distinct national traditions within the larger idea of 'British' literature.

Burns, especially, did much to re-establish older native traditions, though his poems were not always widely recognized as part of a sophisticated cultural heritage. Many of his verse forms derived from the distinct literary traditions of Scotland, including the so called 'Burns stanza' or 'Standard Habbie' – whose name derived from Robert Sempill of Beltrees's 'Lament for Habbie Simpson'. The combination of long and short lines and numerous rhymes is by no means an easy stanza to master, so Burns's pose of the 'simple bard' throwing off 'rhymin-ware' was every bit as artful as Gray's adoption of the Pindaric Ode:

> Gie me ae spark o' nature's fire,
> That's all the learning I desire;
> Then, though I drudge through dub an' mire
>   At pleugh or cart,
> My Muse, though hamely in attire,
>   May touch the heart.
>   ('Epistle to Lapraik', 67–72; Wu, 264)

So skilful was he that many readers hardly noticed his technical ability, enthusing instead over the astonishing 'spark o' nature's fire'. The direct, colloquial language of his 'Epistle to Davie', too, means that it is easy to overlook the complexity of the fourteen line stanzas, adapted from the seventeenth-century Court poetry of Alexander Montgomery, while the riotous scenes of 'Holy Fair' are described in elaborate eight-line stanzas in the tradition of the old Scottish poem, 'Christis Kirk on the Green'. Burns's reading was quietly evident in his forms and subtle allusions.

Indeed, the wish for 'ae spark o' nature's fire' was in itself a reference to *Tristram Shandy*, though he was more inclined to point to the influence of Scottish poets than to a Yorkshire based novelist. *Poems, Chiefly in the Scottish Dialect* included a pastoral in the same stanza that Byron would adopt for *Childe Harold* and Keats would choose for 'The Eve of St Agnes', but the Spenserian 'The Cotter's Saturday Night' idealises Scottish rural life and draws on eighteenth-century Scottish poets such as James Thomson and James Beattie as much as on *The Faerie Queene*. In his fusing of different traditions, Burns was at once distinctive and representative. His enthusiastic reading meant that his poems reflected many of the literary trends of his age, including the confident adaptation of any material that might serve a creative purpose, while still emphasising the distinct character of Scottish traditions. For Burns, adoption of an older form was also a statement of independence.

Although Gray's 'The Progress of Poetry' had followed the flight from classical Greece to Renaissance England, it had also acknowledged the independent existence of poetic inspiration in Northern Europe. Gray himself had serious antiquarian interests in Old Norse, Welsh and Celtic literatures and was aware that the decline of the early cultures of Britain could not be regarded unequivocally in terms of a peaceful 'progress'. In another poem of the 1750s, 'The Bard', Gray had imagined the last Welsh Bard, plunging to death in the Conway rather than submit to the invading army of Edward II and chose a Pindaric Ode for recreating the wild energy of the early Celtic poet. Memories of the violent suppression of Welsh culture and dramatic suicide of the last Bard were not easily reconciled with the ideal of artistic freedom in Britain that informed 'The Progress of Poetry', however. Images of the native past might be stirring to later generations, but were often resistant to any grand, unifying idea of national progress. At the same time, the discovery of ancient Celtic languages and a native heroic culture had strong appeal to those seeking new kinds of literature in the newly United Kingdom.

As an alternative to the classical and Christian idea of antiquity inherited from English Renaissance poets, the Celtic world offered an exciting source of inspiration. The image of the Celtic Bard, memorably depicted in a painting by John Martin, on a precipice high above the white water, became an important figure for the entire Romantic movement. The ancient Welsh poet was both a Romantic solitary, standing heroically against the forces of oppression, and yet the representative of an entire community. According to Gray's poem, the Welsh Bards were the spiritual ancestors of the great British poets who flourished under the Tudors and so, by turning directly to them, Romantic poets seemed to have recovered a native spring of inspiration as ancient and invigorating as the Hippocrene. Felicia Hemans, for example, who spent her early years in North Wales, drew on local legends for her collection of *Welsh Melodies*, which appeared in 1822 as a Welsh answer to Moore's highly successful *Irish Melodies*. In 'The Rock of Cader Idris', she revived the old bardic tradition relating to the mountain summit of Cader Idris, by which anyone spending the night there 'would be found in the morning either dead, in a state of frenzy, or endowed with the highest poetical inspiration' (Wu, 1247). Her poem accordingly relates the experience of lying on the mountain-top and waking 'to inherit / A flame all immortal, a voice, and a power!' (27–8; Wu, 1248).

While Shelley was offering himself as heir to a great European poetic lineage in the beautiful forests of Italy, Hemans was reclaiming the ancient British tradition in Wales. During the Romantic period, the remote mountainous areas of England, Ireland, Scotland and Wales offered the possibility of encountering the sublime – and therefore of producing a kind of poetry capable of aspiring to Miltonic heights. In 1800, Madame de Stael identified the 'literature of the North' as a powerful alternative to the long-revered literature of the Mediterranean, seeing in the cold landscapes of Northern Europe a spirit fiercely independent and an environment perfectly suited to nurturing originality. When Wordsworth concluded his own exploration of the epic impulse with a momentous ascent of Snowdon, he was therefore drawing not just on personal experience of walking in the Welsh mountains, but also on the new recognition of the power inherent in the ancient landscape and culture of Britain.

The translation of oral poetry into modern print culture is addressed more fully in the next chapter, but it seems appropriate to bring this one to a close with reflection on the variousness of the poetic traditions inherited by Romantic writers. Though admiration for Renaissance poetry continued to dominate Romantic literature, it was only one of many influences. Poets of the period read voraciously and seized on forms, images, lines and themes wherever they found them. Adaptation and allusion were as much part of Romantic poetry as originality and individual experience – and it was often the fusion of reading and living that propelled the most exciting writing.

Further Reading

Excellent discussions of Romantic adaptations of genre include Stuart Curran, *Poetic Form and British Romanticism* (Oxford: Clarendon Press, 1986) and David Duff, *Romanticism and the Uses of Genre* (Oxford: Oxford University press, 2009). More general studies include David Duff (ed.) *Modern Genre Theory* (Harlow: Longman, 2000); Alastair Fowler, *Kinds of Literature* (Oxford: Clarendon Press, 1982); Angela Leighton, *On Form* (Oxford: Oxford University Press, 2007). For a useful reference guide to all aspects of poetry, with analysis of numerous Romantic poems, see John Lennard, *The Poetry Handbook*, 2nd edn. (Oxford: Oxford University Press, 2005).

Influential theories of belatedness include Harold Bloom, *The Anxiety of Influence* (New York: Oxford University Press, 1973) and W. J. Bate, *The Burden of the Past and the English Poet* (Cambridge, Mass.: Harvard University Press, 1970).

For Shakespeare's pre-eminence in the period, see Jonathan Bate, *Shakespeare and the Romantic Imagination* (Oxford: Clarendon Press, 1986); (ed.) *Romantics on Shakespeare* (Harmondsworth: Pen guin, 1992); for interest in Dante, see Ralph Pite, *The Circle of our Vision: Dante's presence in English Romantic Poetry* (Oxford: Clarendon Press, 1994); for Spenser, see Greg Kucich, *Keats, Shelley and Romantic* Spenserianism (University Park, Pa: Pennsylvania State University Press,1991); David Hill Radcliffe, *Edmund Spenser: A Reception History* (London: Camden House, 1996).

The sonnet revival has been examined by Curran in *Poetic Form* (1986) and in his edition of *The Poems of Charlotte Smith* (Oxford: Clarendon Press, 1993); see also Stephen Behrendt, *British Women Writers and the Romantic Writing Community* (Baltimore: Johns Hopkins University Press, 2010); Paula Feldman and Daniel Robinson (eds.) *A Century of Sonnets: The Romantic Era Revival* (New York and Oxford: Oxford University Press, 1999).

The influence of *Paradise Lost* has been analyzed in detail by Lucy Newlyn in *Paradise Lost and the Romantic Reader* (Oxford: Clarendon Press, 1994); see also M.H. Abrams, *Natural Supernaturalism* (New York and

London: Oxford University Press, 1970); Leslie Brisman, *Milton's Poetry of Choice and its Romantic* Heirs (Ithaca: Cornell University Press, 1973); Robin Jarvis, *Wordsworth, Milton and the Theory of Poetic Relations* (Basingstoke: Macmillan, 1991); Beth Lau, *Keats's Paradise Lost* (Gainesville: University of Florida Press, 1998); Joseph Wittreich (ed.) *Romantics on Milton* (Cleveland: Cape Western Reserve University Press, 1970); Lisa Low and Anthony John Harding (eds.), *Milton, the Metaphysicals and Romanticism* (Cambridge: Cambridge University Press, 1994).

Details of what the Romantic poets read are often included in scholarly editions of their works, for example James Kinsley (ed.), *The Poems and Songs of Robert Burns*, 3 vols (Oxford: Clarendon Press, 1968); Jerome McGann (ed.) *The Complete Poetical Works of Lord Byron*, 7 vols (Oxford: Clarendon Press, 1980–1993); J.C.C. Mays, *The Poetical Works of Samuel Taylor Coleridge. Volume 16 of The Collected Works*, 6 vols (Princeton: Princeton University Press, 2001); John Keats, *The Complete Poems*, ed. Miriam Allott (Harlow: Longman, 1970); Kelvin Everest et al. (ed.) *The Complete Poems of Percy Bysshe Shelley*, 3 vols (Harlow: Pearson, 1989–2011); *The Cornell Edition of the Poems of William Wordsworth*, general editor Stephen Parrish, 22 vols (1975–2005).

Critical studies are also helpful, including Douglas Dunn, '"A Very Scottish Kind of Dash": Burns's Native Metric', in Robert Crawford (ed.), *Robert Burns and Cultural* Authority (Edinburgh: Edinburgh University Press, 1997), 58–85; Mina Gorji, *John Clare and the Place of Poetry* (Manchester: Manchester University Press, 2009); Robert Griffin, *Wordsworth's Pope* (Cambridge: Cambridge University Press, 1995); Moyra Haslett, *Byron and the Don Juan Legend* (Oxford: Oxford University Press, 1998); John Spencer Hill, *Imagination in* Coleridge (Basingstoke: Macmillan, 1978); Beth Lau, *Keats's Reading of the Romantic Poets* (Ann Arbor: University of Michigan Press, 1991); David Sergeant and Fiona Stafford (eds.) *Burns and Other Poets* (Edinburgh: Edinburgh University Press, 2011); Timothy Webb, *The Violet in the Crucible* (Oxford: Clarendon Press, 1976); *Shelley: A Voice Not Understood* (Manchester: Manchester University Press, 1977); Kathleen Wheeler, *Sources, Processes and Methods in Coleridge's Biographia Literaria* (Cambridge: Cambridge University Press, 1980); R. S. White, *Keats as a Reader of Shakespeare* (Norman: University of Oklahoma Press, 1987); Duncan Wu, *Wordsworth's*

Reading, 2 vols (Oxford: Oxford University Press, 1993–5). Major Biographies also shed important light on the reading and education of Romantic poets – see Further Reading section for Chapter 2 for details.

On the revival of native traditions in the period and the importance of regional and national identity, see Gerard Carruthers and Alan Rawes (eds.), *England and the Celtic World* (Cambridge: Cambridge University Press, 2003); Robert Crawford, *Devolving English Literature* (Oxford: Clarendon Press, 1992); Leith Davis, Ian Duncan, Janet Sorenson (eds.) *Scotland and the Borders of Romanticism* (Cambridge: Cambridge University Press, 2004); David Duff and Catherine Jones (eds.) *Scotland, Ireland and the Romantic Aesthetic* (Lewisburg: Bucknell University Press, 2005); Richard Gravil, *Wordsworth's Bardic Vocation* (Basingstoke: Palgrave Macmillan, 2003); Murray Pittock, *Scottish and Irish Romanticism* (Oxford: Oxford University Press, 2007); Nicholas Roe (ed.) *English Writers and the West Country* (Basingstoke: Palgrave Macmillan, 2010); Katie Trumpener, *Bardic Nationalism* (Princeton: Princeton University Press, 1997); Damian Walford-Davies and Lynda Pratt (eds.), *Wales and the Romantic Imagination* (Cardiff: University of Wales Press, 2007).

For the ballad revival, see Nick Groom, *The Making of Percy's Reliques* (Oxford: Clarendon Press, 1998); Mary Jacobus, *Tradition and Experiment in Wordsworth's* Lyrical Ballads *1798* (Oxford: Clarendon Press, 1976); Maureen Maclane, *Balladeering, Minstrelsy, and the Making of Romantic Poetry* (Cambridge: Cambridge University Press, 2008).

5

Reading or Listening? Romantic Voices

The Solitary Reaper appears suddenly before the eyes of Wordsworth's readers:

> Behold her, single in the field,
> Yon solitary Highland Lass!
> (1–2; O'Neill and Mahoney, 169)

Before we know anything of the landscape, we are directed to focus on the figure at the centre of the scene who, oblivious to her audience, remains utterly involved with her own private thoughts as she carries out her task. Although 'Behold', with its powerful, Biblical resonances, seems more of a command than an invitation, we never actually discover what it is we are meant to see, for the reaper is described only through her actions. We do not know her age, her height, her hair color or her choice of dress, for, having paused to look, we are being asked rather to 'listen!' It is her singing that is so arresting, the verb hidden within the initial adjective, 'single', which provokes admiration. And yet, being encouraged to 'behold' someone, who remains withheld from view, is a suitable introduction to a poem evoking songs that cannot be enjoyed. This is in some ways a lyric celebrating what Keats would later describe in his 'Ode on a Grecian Urn' as 'unheard melodies' – sweeter than those we can hear. It can also be read, however, as a more wistful reflection on the transience of the visionary moment, with the speaker left to wonder, in a mood similar to that of 'Kubla Khan', 'Could I revive within me / Her symphony and song?' (42–3; O'Neill and Mahoney, 187).

Reading Romantic Poetry, First Edition. Fiona Stafford.
© 2014 Fiona Stafford. Published 2014 by John Wiley & Sons, Ltd.

A poem that initially seemed a simple record of a passing encounter lives on as a perplexing memorial, stimulating further thought and inviting comparison with other poems. As with many Romantic lyrics, 'The Solitary Reaper' is both silent and overflowing with sound, entirely self-sufficient and yet suggesting thoughts of other poems and places. Both the fascinations and frustrations associated with representing the human voice on the blank page are caught in Wordsworth's haunting lyric, which makes it the perfect starting point for a chapter concerned with orality and writing.

Although the reader of Wordsworth's poem cannot hear the Reaper's voice, an *idea* of perfect pitch is conveyed through the analogy with birdsong:

> No Nightingale did ever chaunt
> So sweetly to reposing bands
> Of Travellers in some shady haunt,
> Among Arabian Sands:
> No sweeter voice was ever heard
> In spring-time from the Cuckoo-bird,
> Breaking the silence of the seas
> Among the farthest Hebrides.
> (9–16)

The very comparisons, however, emphasize remoteness and mystery. How many readers can identify with unknown travellers who hear the nightingale's song on their journey across the desert? Or imagine a cuckoo's annual arrival in the Western Isles? We may gain some sense of the marvellousness of these unexpected delights, but it is difficult to formulate any specific voice or call. These are parallels that baffle as much as they illuminate.

Even when the speaker attempts to give an indication of the kind of song being sung, what he offers is a series of questions rather than any clear definition:

> Perhaps the plaintive numbers flow
> For old, unhappy, far-off things,
> And battles long ago:
> Or is it some more humble lay,
> Familiar matter of today?
> Some natural sorrow, loss or pain,
> That has been, and may be again!
> (17–24)

The unanswerable questions only generate further conjecture, leaving readers with a strong sense of general significance, but little idea as to what might be signified. Does the speculation really relate to the subject of the reaper's song, or to some mysterious aspect of the singer herself, or the listener's experience?

As the speaker ponders over the possible themes, he is also considering kinds. Is this an old war-song or ballad about a battle? Or is it a modern folk-song, dealing with love and loss? A 'Highland Lass' might well be singing a traditional Gaelic air, or one of Burns's popular songs – in either case, the lyrics could present problems for a visitor. A strong accent and Scots vocabulary often cause English listeners to struggle with precise meanings, while Scottish Gaelic is a completely different Celtic language largely unknown to people outside the Highlands and Islands. Whatever the song's language, if unintelligible to the English speaker, its effects must be entirely non-verbal. In other words, the poem is about the power of sound and the ability to move a listener independently of clearly defined linguistic meanings.

Rather than address the singer in words, the speaker responds to her with his 'heart'. That he 'bore' the music, however, suggests both continuing experience and growing distance – since the verb might mean enduring intensity or carrying something away. The concluding emphasis on the lasting effect of the song, preserved in the heart 'long after it was heard no more' sustains both interpretations. The sudden shift to the past tense testifies to the power of the song, even as it affirms its elegiac nature, emphasizing presence and absence simultaneously. Awareness of the passage of time also shows that the impulse to write the poem has come much later than the original experience. The difference between the poem's direct opening and retrospective close suggests a primary imaginative experience that was intensely physical and private, in contrast to words that have come later, in an attempt at recapture and preservation. The baffling nature of the Highland song is not only a historical detail relating to linguistic and cultural translation, but also a metaphor for the frustrated desire of a poet longing for the proper language to embody what he feels most deeply.

Throughout, the speaker appeals to the reader of the poem, issuing direct commands – 'Behold', 'O listen!', or posing questions, 'Will no one tell me?… Perhaps… Or is it?' And yet, these are communications that require no reply, for the speaker seems engaged in private internal communion, just as the Highland Lass is reaping and singing by herself.

Readers may similarly become involved with the images and ideas embodied in the poem, but their own response is also likely to be silent. The poem celebrates the capacity of the mind to conjure up beautiful sounds from within, to entertain itself with internal harmonies and lyrics, but as it worries over the meaning of the reaper's song, it underlines the unreliability and illusory nature of imaginary music. Readers are asked simultaneously to listen and to accept that nothing very definite can be heard.

The entire poem is playing on the nature of hearing – and whether we hear with our minds or with our ears. The speaker is conveying a moment of delight arising from the experience of unexpected sound, but the medium is that of the printed word, with the distance between the words on the page and the living voice being acknowledged throughout. Thoughts of the solitary young woman, reaping and singing by herself, underline the silence of reading and the separation between different minds. At the same time, she seems to represent the self-sufficiency of the inner world and the capacity to participate in the collective tradition of song even when physically isolated. The four eight-line stanzas, in a predominantly eight-syllable tetrameter, are perfectly poised to present alternatives without reaching any firm conclusion, while the final stanza accordingly demonstrates the lyric's resistance to closure. The young woman sings, 'As if her song could have no ending' and so the speaker replies with a confirmation of the music's impact, 'Long after it was heard no more' (31–2). Whether the words of the poem will ensure the longevity of the song remains uncertain, however, since the lyric itself depends on future readers for survival.

'The Solitary Reaper' was first published in 1807, in *Poems, in Two Volumes*, which included many of the poems inspired by Wordsworth's tour of Scotland, as well as the Sonnets to Liberty, 'Resolution and Independence' and the 'Ode: Intimations of Immortality'. When read alongside 'Rob Roy's Grave', 'Glen Almain', 'Address to the Sons of Burns', 'To a Highland Girl' or 'Stepping Westward', early readers might have assumed that 'The Solitary Reaper' was another record of the poet's experience on his tour. Wordsworth, however, disturbed the simple equation between his life and his lyric by including a note that attributed his central image to Thomas Wilkinson, who had recorded the following sentence in his own *Tours to the British Mountains*, 'Passed a female who was reaping alone: she sung in Erse as she bended over her sickle; the sweetest human voice I ever heard: her strains were tender melancholy, and felt delicious, long after they were heard no more' (O'Neill and Mahoney, 169).

As soon as the haunting last line of Wordsworth's poem has been glossed as a virtual quotation, 'The Solitary Reaper' becomes even more perplexing. For what had appeared to be a dramatic recreation of a profoundly personal moment is now revealed to be a response to the experience of reading. The Highland Lass, whom readers of Wordsworth's poem were invited to behold, had not after all been seen by the author of the poem, and nor had he heard her haunting song – which does turn out to have been in 'Erse' – Gaelic. Far from negating the pleasure of the poem, however, the revelation merely accentuates its elusiveness, as fresh questions erupt. Is the Solitary Reaper an individual, seen by Thomas Wilkinson and vividly imagined by Wordsworth as a reader of his friend's manuscript? Or is she an emblematic figure, representative of all the reapers seen by William and Dorothy Wordsworth when they visited the Highlands in 1803? Or perhaps she is both of these things, and a great deal more. Like her own song, she is resistant to definition and as such, endlessly fascinating.

As Wordsworth presented the arresting lyric and its perplexing note, he was confronting readers with a searching question. Where do poems come from? From what is heard, or what is read? For while the lyric offers an image of aural inspiration, the note points to the imaginative resources of the printed page. If Keats was right about 'unheard melodies', then an image of singing might be more pleasing than the actual sound of a human voice; but equally, it might not. Even if a reader succeeded in conjuring up beautiful music within, the intensely private nature of such experience might still be less satisfying than the shared pleasure of a live performance. Such questions may seem strange to modern readers, who are able to listen to recorded music whenever they choose, but in an era in which popular culture was gradually shifting from oral to printed media, these were issues that mattered very much – especially to poets.

For although improved literacy and cheaper printing methods had done much to transform eighteenth-century British society, by putting books, pamphlets, chapbooks and newspapers into the hands of those who had largely been denied educational opportunities in the past, the advent of modern print culture was not without its cost. Popular songs, stories and ballads, passed on by word of mouth, had entertained people for many generations, but were now in danger of being superseded by the new kinds of literature, which were easily available in libraries and bookshops. Mass production increased not only choice but also uniformity, however, and so in place of hearing the unique tones of an individual performer, readers experienced texts quietly, through identical, printed copies. Something of the older, oral habits survived in the practice of reading aloud but, in general, books were the companions of silent readers. Since reading was a much less sociable activity than attending a live performance, print was a potentially isolating force, even as it offered virtual connections between strangers. Poets might reach out metaphorically through their verse, using images of binding together society through shared emotions and awakening fellow-feeling among strangers, but such links were very different from those formed within living communities where people chatted to each other, exchanging personal stories and opinions on a daily basis.

The new connections between contemporaries that were being forged by print technology might even threaten the older ties of inherited culture that had always connected individuals to their collective past. In a self-consciously modern age, the disappearance of older traditions was often perceived in terms of profound loss, which in turn prompted nostalgia for the culture of earlier generations. As new publishing houses boomed, so did enthusiasm for antiquarianism, ballad-collecting and the recovery of old songs. The speaker of Wordsworth's poem may be musing over the song of a single Highland girl, but in doing so he is also reflecting contemporary concerns over whether popular poems and songs were now largely 'old, unhappy, far-off things', or whether they might still constitute 'familiar matter of today.' Should the traditions of the ordinary people simply be allowed to disappear as they went out of fashion, or did they somehow embody the spirit of the past – vital, precious and, once destroyed, impossible to recreate?

As discussed in Chapter 4, Joseph Addison had alerted his early eighteenth-century audience of predominantly urban *Spectator* readers to the naturalness and passion of the old popular rhymes. When he compared the old ballad of 'Chevy Chase' to Virgil's *Aeneid*, Addison was stirring up both sentimental memories of childhood and patriotic pride in the heroic deeds of earlier ages. He was also reminding the reading public of the rich resources of the oral tradition. The simple ballad style might not measure up to modern standards of literary and linguistic sophistication, but there was an energy in the older poems that matched their stirring subjects. They were also prized for their increasing rarity: part of Percy's appeal was the idea of the 'relique' – these poems might be the cultural inheritance of the common man, but they were by no means common.

Realization of the special qualities of oral forms went hand in hand with recognition of their vulnerability in the modern world. When Macpherson introduced his old Highland tales of to the modern reading public, he emphasised the retreat of the oral tradition in the face of irreversible social change: Ossian's mournful poems seemed poised on the brink of destruction even at the moment of publication. The oral tradition depended on materials being handed down through generations and so any major social change threatened its survival. Macpherson was therefore as much creator as translator, in his attempt to recover wholeness from the fragmentary remains of his native culture, while his ancient poet, Ossian, as the last of his race, was doomed to ultimate silence by the death of his entire community. With no audience, nor heir to pass on the tradition, the oral poet could speak only words that were destined to die with him. The urge to record and collect oral tales and folksongs was therefore often prompted by an awareness of traditions under threat. And though few areas were subject to changes as devastating as those afflicting the Scottish Highlands in the eighteenth century, factors as diverse as increasing social mobility, rising literacy rates, the gravitation of labour towards expanding cities and the boom in publishing, meant that the old forms of storytelling were beginning to disappear.

When Wordsworth's Solitary Reaper is described as singing 'As if her song could have no ending', interpretation of the line depends very much on which end arrests the reader's attention. Given the traditional associations of the figure of the 'Reaper' and the continuous action of cutting the cornfield, ideas of permanent ending are never far way. On the one hand, Wordsworth's poem might be joining a contemporary lament for the steady diminution of songs that had long sustained ordinary people into 'old ... far-off things'. On the other hand, it seems to treat native tradition as a vital resource for modern poets, exploring the crucial transformation of the human voice to the fully embodied poem on the page. The Highland Lass binds as well as cutting the corn, so her work may be read as a metaphor not for the death of the living tradition, but rather for the capacity of song to gather people together or bind a community of isolated individuals through shared culture. For it is when corn is harvested – cut and bound – that it begins to sustain new life. As in Burns's song, 'John Barleycorn', it is only after the barley has been cut, tied, submerged, roasted and crushed that its reviving strength can be shared by all, in glasses of whisky. The transformation from inspiration to song to print could thus be regarded as a kind of distillation of original experience, in which extraneous elements are purged away and all that is left is pure and lasting.

Many writers of the Romantic period attempted to capture something of the living voice through the medium of print, whether through a lyric moment such as this, or in the more practical shape of song-books and ballad-collections. The urge to record speech and song often gave rise to elegiac acknowledgements of vanishing folk traditions, but it also introduced exciting new dimensions to Romantic poetry. Some of the most striking poetic innovations of the period arose from the new awareness of the relationship between orality and literacy, whether through the revival of the ballad as a sophisticated literary form, or through the development of new kinds. The same poets who saw the creative potential of the ballad also recognised the benefits of using direct speech in their verse, whether through developing 'Conversation Poems' or in revitalizing the epic with witty digressions. Forms such as the verse epistle frequently adopted a more colloquial style, mimicking spontaneous verbal exchanges even as they stressed their status as letters. Once 'real' speech became a more acceptable element in poetry, literary language began to expand and allow non-standard forms and dialect into print. Many Romantic poems share Wordsworth's fascination with hearing a human voice and with the related task of conveying sounds through the visual medium of the printed word. The acoustic qualities of Romantic poetry form the subject of the next chapter, but the focus here is on one of the major concerns of the period: the relationship between the spoken and written word.

The Language of Conversation: *Lyrical Ballads*

Wordsworth's concern with the living voice was not something he discovered on his Scottish journey, nor in his reading of Thomas Wilkinson's *Tour*. The first edition of *Lyrical Ballads* had introduced the collection as 'experiments' on the grounds that the poems had been 'written chiefly with a view to ascertain how far the language of conversation in the middle and lower classes of society is adapted to the purposes of poetic pleasure' ('Advertisement', Wu, 331). In other words, these were poems that were using what Wordsworth would subsequently term 'the real language of men', rather than the poetic diction learned from reading books ('Preface to *Lyrical Ballads*', Wu, 495). Some of the poems begin accordingly, with idiomatic phrases, as in 'Goody Blake and Harry Gill', 'Oh what's the matter? what's the matter?', or plunge straight into direct speech, as in the dramatized debates over books and nature in 'Expostulation and Reply' and 'The Tables Turned'. The reader is immediately engaged through the direct address, even if the poem subsequently reveals an implied interlocutor within.

Coleridge's 'The Nightingale' takes up similar arguments to 'Expostulation and Reply', in rebuking those who attempt to understand the natural world from their reading, rather than from first-hand physical experience. The choice of blank verse rather than reported dialogue makes this seem more like extended personal meditation than Wordsworth's concise lyric, but 'The Nightingale' is nevertheless presented as 'A Conversational Poem' and includes direct, almost dramatic, addresses – 'Come, we will rest on this old mossy bridge!' (4; O'Neill and Mahoney, 229). The speaker's companions, later revealed as 'My Friend, and thou, our Sister!' (40), stand in for readers in the poem, apparently hearing both the nightingale's song and the speaker's reflections. Since Coleridge's poem quotes directly from Milton (13), as well as echoing numerous other sources, its advocacy of the primacy of hearing over reading is no more straightforward than the claim that its elaborate language resembles ordinary speech. But what Coleridge does provoke is an active response from the reader, who seems required to engage with the argument just as much as being invited to surrender his senses. We are at once placed in the position of the baby, holding up his hand in wonder at the joy of the nightingale's song, and also reminded of literary tradition and the tendency of striking lines to harden into commonplace and misconception. The 'conversation' is with other poets and readers, just as much as with nature or the 'Friends' inside the poem. Indeed, in some of the other 'Conversation poems' written at this time, Coleridge presented himself entirely alone – as in 'This Lime-Tree Bower My Prison' and 'Fears in Solitude' – or accompanied only by a sleeping child - as in 'Frost at Midnight'.

Coleridge's 'Conversation Poems' adopted a kind of flowing blank verse reminiscent of Cowper's technique in 'The Task', but *Lyrical Ballads* included a number of other poems that recalled traditional ballads in their form and in their use of direct speech and dialogue. Wordsworth's 'The Thorn' for example, relies on an idea of conversation, but is very different in style from Coleridge's 'The Nightingale'. The main voice in the poem is that of an elderly narrator, drawing on his local knowledge to arouse the curiosity of an unnamed visitor, who interrupts the narrative at various points with increasingly urgent questions:

> 'But what's the thorn? and what's the pond?
> 'And what's the hill of moss to her?
> 'And what's the creeping breeze that comes
> 'The little pond to stir?'
> (210–13; O'Neill and Mahoney, 87)

Unlike the direct speech employed elsewhere in *Lyrical Ballads*, the gossipy tone of the principal speaker reveals a man who enjoys his power and uses language to insinuate rather than clarify:

> I cannot tell; but some will say
> She hanged her baby on the tree,
> Some say she drowned it in the pond,
> Which is a little step beyond,
> But all and each agree,
> The little babe was buried there,
> Beneath that hill of moss so fair.
> (214–20)

Though very different in tone from the later 'Solitary Reaper', Wordsworth's fascination with the openness of orality is abundantly evident in 'The Thorn'. For here is another list of questions with answers that resolve nothing, though this time working on the listener through lurid suggestion. These sensational possibilities are no sooner offered than undermined, however, by the obvious unreliability of the speaker. Conversation may be but another name for hearsay, which unsettles the emphasis in the Preface to *Lyrical Ballads* on the truthfulness of the language really used by men. The oral source, by definition unrecorded, is open to endless interpretation, alteration and retelling. To convey its fluid character through the fixed, permanent medium of the written word therefore required careful narrative strategies. While 'conversation poems' tended to rely on unrhymed verse to reflect the natural movement of speech or private thought, rhyming stanzas could achieve a sense of openness through the use of questions and alternative points of view. 'The Thorn's 'Some will say … some say … all and each agree' are versions of the more sophisticated, 'Will no one tell me … Perhaps … Or is it…?' of 'The Solitary Reaper'. In both poems, the uncertainty of the speaker is crucial to their baffling nature and refusal of absolute meaning.

When Wordsworth included 'The Thorn' in the enlarged edition of *Lyrical Ballads* in 1800, he added a substantial note, distinguishing himself from the carefully constructed narrator of the poem, who is described as a retired sea Captain, 'prone to superstition' ('Note to The Thorn', Wu, 508). He was also at pains to explain that the numerous repetitions in the verse were not accidental, but deliberately chosen to convey both the character of the narrator and the urge to communicate powerful emotion to an audience. Wordsworth pointed out the difficulty of representing deep feelings 'without something of an accompanying consciousness of the inadequateness of our own powers, or the deficiencies of language', arguing that it was the mind's 'craving' for adequate expression that made a speaker 'cling to the same words, or words of the same character' (Wu, 508). Far from being a straightforward record of conversation, Wordsworth's note makes clear that the words of 'The Thorn' are crafted with a particular artistic purpose, making the poem as much dramatic monologue as simple ballad.

Even though he advocated the use of a 'plainer and more emphatic language' (Wu, 497) for poetry in the Preface to his collection, Wordsworth still felt the need to reveal his own sophistication – hence the addition of the substantial Preface and the 'Note to The Thorn' to the newly enlarged edition of *Lyrical Ballads* in 1800. With the 'real language of men' came the forms popular with real audiences that survived through oral transmission, but Wordsworth's profound thoughts on the repetitions of 'The Thorn' are not concerned with the mere practicalities of memorizing verse. Instead, his note dwelled on the very nature of language with all the seriousness of an experimental artist addressing highly literate readers. And though he distinguished so carefully between the poet and the narrator of 'The Thorn', his note is in itself a kind of craving, because it asks readers to imagine a language that remains unarticulated – as elusive as the words of the Solitary Reaper's song.

Whether or not 'The Thorn' is enhanced by the prose note is open to question, since the explicatory tone might strike some as destructive of imaginative illusion – an editorial unweaving of the rainbow. Once aware of it, readers may nevertheless respond more positively to the poem, for the repetition of words and phrases ('what's the thorn? and what's the pond?') can now be understood in relation to the essential inadequacy of language, pointing not just to the limitations of the speaker, but also to the enormity of what is being suggested. If the note seems to divert readers from the story to the narrative method, however, it is really concentrating attention on Martha Ray, whose only words are 'Oh misery! Oh misery! / Oh woe is me! Oh misery!' (65–6; 76–7; 252–3). Martha clings to the same words, just as she clings to the same spot, 'The heap that's like an infant's grave, / The pond – and thorn, so old and grey' (93–4), as if her entire being is distilled into the one emotion. The narrator of the poem may be pointing an accusatory finger, but his rather limited story-telling is transformed by the intensity of feeling embodied in her refrain. What matters in the poem – what continues to haunt readers – is the image of the woman beside the old thorn and her obsessive repetition of 'Oh misery!'

In 1798, Wordsworth had allowed 'The Thorn' to stand without commentary, though the Advertisement to the volume had described it as a poem 'spoken' not by the author, but by a 'loquacious narrator', whose character would rapidly reveal itself (Wu, 331). Two years and a few hostile critical responses later, however, he evidently felt the need to offer an interpretation of the direct speech that constituted his poem. Robert Southey, for example, had singled out 'The Thorn' in his review of *Lyrical Ballads* with the caustic observation that 'he who personates tiresome loquacity, become tiresome himself' (*William Wordsworth: Critical Heritage*, 66). The openness of the oral method might, after all, have its disadvantages, if it led to serious misinterpretations of his poems.

Wordsworth recognized the value of simple language as both the original Advertisement and the later Preface to *Lyrical Ballads* made plain, but he was discomforted by the possibility of a simple response of the wrong kind. The addition of the extended Preface was, in itself, a sign that neither Wordsworth nor Coleridge remained confident that their 'experiments' could safely speak for themselves – and the more urgent the need to persuade the public of the virtues of plain language, the more elaborate their prose commentaries became. Apparently spontaneous utterances gradually acquired a framework of deeply considered literary thought, prompted by the consciousness of a readership.

Reconsideration of the oral ideal is most obvious, however, in Coleridge's main contribution to *Lyrical Ballads*: 'The Rime of the Ancyent Marinere.' As discussed in Chapter 3, the ballad first appeared, unadorned by glosses, in the anonymous collection of 1798, but when Coleridge republished it under his own name in *Sibylline Leaves*, it appeared with a modernised title – 'The Rime of the Ancient Mariner', extensive marginal annotations and a substantial epigraph from the works of Thomas Burnet. By 1817, the very attractions of orality had come to require some means of containment. Even the original 1798 version, 'The Rime of the Ancyent Marinere', had shown an acute awareness of the more dangerous aspects of oral delivery, however. In prime position at the start of the volume, the ballad startled readers with the Wedding-guest's dramatic re-enactment of his first impression of the principle narrator:

> It is an ancyent marinere
>   And he stoppeth one of three:
> 'By thy long grey beard and thy glittering eye
>   Now wherefore stoppest me?
>   (1–4; Wu, 332)

This is not a tale that the listener in the poem, whose own sense of purpose (as a wedding guest) is clear, wishes to hear. His very reluctance proves irresistible to readers, however, who are not only given the Mariner's reported speech, but also evidence of its power:

> He holds him with his glittering eye –
>   The wedding-guest stood still
> And listens like a three years' child;
>   The Marinere hath his will.
>   (17–20)

Even without the marginal glosses, Coleridge's use of the frame narrative enabled him to reveal the power of the direct word over listeners. Unlike the speaker in 'The Solitary Reaper', whose injunction to 'listen' is an invitation to share something of intense beauty, the Ancient Mariner's repeated insistence on being heard seems designed to overpower the wedding-guest. The reader stands witness to the subjugation of an unwilling stranger, making the tale that follows seem dangerous and unbidden, before it has even begun. This is a very different atmosphere from the elegiac 'Solitary Reaper', even though the Highland song was just as compelling. The oral tale, in Coleridge's hands, seems to possess an uncanny power, moving unpredictably to target particular listeners.

Readers watch the effect of the Mariner's words on another human being, as well as seeing exactly what he says, so Coleridge's 'Listen, Stranger!' (45, 49) works very differently from Wordsworth's 'O listen!' in 'The Solitary Reaper'. What is immediately apparent to readers of the 'Rime' is the way in which the Mariner's words are enforced by his physical presence – he holds the wedding guest not with his eloquence alone, but with his 'skinny hand' and the even more arresting 'glittering eye'. If the detail seems drawn from folk-lore to emphasise the traditional nature of the seaman's tale, however, it also reflects contemporary philosophical interest in the effects of non-verbal communication. Scottish Enlightenment thinkers had devoted considerable attention to the development of different kinds of communication in the history of human society (from dance and oratory to discursive prose), often commenting on the retreat of passion and imagination in the face of improved accuracy and abstraction. Among the topics most under debate was body language.

Hugh Blair, for example, whose *Sermons* and *Lectures* were best-sellers, wrote passionately about the importance of the body in the delivery of any speech, arguing that the 'voice of the living Speaker, makes an impression on the mind, much stronger than can be made by the perusal of any Writing' (*Lectures*, I, 160–1). For Blair, speech was more powerful than the most accurate writing, because 'tones, looks, and gestures are the natural interpreters of the sentiments of the mind' (*Lectures*, I, 161). The physical presence of the speaker would always be more persuasive than the inanimate printed page, because 'sympathy is always awakened more by hearing the Speaker than by reading his works in our closet' (*Lectures*, I, 161). Given the importance of 'sympathy' for poets in the period, as discussed in the opening chapter of this book, the idea that writing might somehow be a less effective medium than speech was a matter for deep concern. It was easy enough to assert that poetry was derived from powerful emotion and might be instrumental in communicating feeling, but the real challenge for poets was to capture the force of speech in their published works.

With these ideas in mind, the image of the Ancient Mariner seizing the wedding-guest at the start of his recital can be read as a metaphor for the arresting quality of speech and its capacity to dominate listeners. Coleridge was effectively demonstrating the truth of Blair's theory, by dramatizing the reaction of the listener to the presence of the Mariner. For the modern poet, the image of the spellbound audience also had particular appeal, since it suggested that poetry was capable of stopping even the most purposeful in their tracks. Modern book-buyers, unlike the traditional audiences attending a recitation, could dip into their purchases at will, abandoning stories if they were not to their taste or skipping to the end of the tale. The Wedding-guest, however, represents a much more manageable audience, utterly under the spell of the teller.

Despite the appeal that such an image might hold for some poets, fearful perhaps of public neglect, it was also indicative of enforced passivity and so ultimately not very satisfactory. Since Coleridge shared Wordsworth's poetic ideal of rousing dormant faculties and awakening people to a better society, it was difficult to reconcile this with an image of the poet as mesmerist. In the light of this, the image of a speaker so powerful that his listener's critical faculties are completely nullified was alarming rather than reassuring – this was an image of powerful speaking that might inspire a dictator just as readily as a prophet. The Mariner's hold on the wedding guest shows that the power of spoken eloquence could be dangerous as well as dazzling, so the urge to contain the oral might not, after all, be a repressive reaction. Coleridge's later glosses can be seen, in this light, not as readings that restrict the freedom of the speaker, but rather as cues for interpretation, whose divergences from the poem work to stimulate the active participation of the reader in the pursuit of meaning.

If 'The Rime of the Ancyent Marinere', with its dramatic opening and different voices, originally seemed to be a kind of performance poem, it also drew attention to its own condition as a written text. The first published version adopted numerous archaisms more likely to catch the reader's eye rather than the listener's ear – 'Ancyent Marinere', 'Minstralsy', 'Emerauld', 'withouten', 'gossameres', 'Pheere', 'clombe', 'Countrée'. For readers in 1798, such words looked strange because of their antiquated spelling. The poem's situation on the printed page was emphasized, too, by the brief prose 'Argument', summarizing the voyage and the Mariner's return, which offset the dramatic opening. Despite the immediacy of the Wedding-guest's present tense – 'It is an ancyent marinere' – the reader is placed at a distance from the speaker's perspective because of the advanced knowledge of the conclusion. In other words, it is and it isn't an ancyent marinere.

The original Advertisement to *Lyrical Ballads* made clear that the poem was 'written in imitation of the *style*, as well as the spirit of the elder poets' (Wu, 331), so there was no intention to pass it off as a genuine old ballad, in the way that Lady Wardlaw's 'Hardiknute' had hoodwinked eighteenth-century readers. Instead, Coleridge was conducting an 'experiment' and his self-conscious modernity, quite distinct from the Mariner's quasi-medieval expressions, is evident throughout. The 'Rime' reveals and conceals its literariness by combining simple language with hidden allusion. As John Livingstone Lowes revealed in astonishing detail many years ago, the poem is overflowing with echoes of Coleridge's voluminous reading, even the albatross deriving, via Wordsworth, from the pages of George Shelvocke's *Voyage Round the World*. As a modern, printed ballad, it is evoking the power of orality, while exploiting the rich possibilities of print.

The skill with which Coleridge plays on the relationship between the oral and the written is often greatest when least apparent. The verbs in line 105, for example, 'And we did speak only to break', look like a full rhyme, but sound like a half-rhyme – unless we imagine the Mariner with an accent that pronounces 'speak' and 'break' in similar style. The rest of the stanza, however, with words such as 'breeze' and 'sea', works towards a standard pronunciation of 'speak', so that 'break' stands out appropriately enough, as a rupture to the regular rhyme pattern of preceding stanzas – 'weft/left', 'day/play', averred/bird', 'they/slay', 'first/burst' (84, 87, 91, 95, 97, 101). Once disrupted, the regular rhymes within the third line of these stanzas give way to unrhymed lines of irregular awkwardness and increasing desperation – 'Right up above the mast did stand', 'As idle as a painted ship', 'Water, water, everywhere', 'Yea, slimy things did crawl with legs' (109, 113, 117, 121). Speech itself breaks down in this sequence, as the sailors' tongues wither, until 'We could not speak, no more than if / We had been choked with soot' (133–4). The double negative emphasises the difficulty of finding words, its clumsiness an ironic echo of the line that started the collapse of language – 'And we did speak only to break'. In retrospect, the crew's need 'to break the silence of the sea' seems an ominous act of corroboration for the motiveless destruction of the albatross.

In 'The Solitary Reaper', the image of the cuckoo, 'breaking the silence of the seas' implicitly brings a confirmation of spring to the wind-swept, winter-bitten coast of the northernmost reaches of Scotland. The sound of a human voice, for Wordsworth's isolated speaker, is a thrilling experience, descending like a blessing when it is least expected. 'The Rime of the Ancient Mariner', however, is much more wary of the power of the voice, provoking fear as well as fascination in its presentation of the Mariner's words. Far from treating oral forms as part of a vanishing heritage, Coleridge's poem stresses the need to circumscribe the potentially uncontrollable power of direct speech, encouraging different perspectives to combat his mesmerizing rhyme. This very emphasis on the power of the spoken word is also an affirmation of his own creation, which has continued to possess an extraordinary hold over readers ever since its first appearance, as evident in the numerous illustrated editions that have been published since. Unlike 'The Solitary Reaper', Coleridge's play on listening to the silent page avoids any elegiac tone and dwells instead on the haunting nature of what has been heard.

Oral and Rural

Coleridge's increasing uneasiness over oral forms is evident not only in the glosses he added to 'The Ancient Mariner' in 1817, but also in the repudiation of the Preface to *Lyrical Ballads* which he published the year before in *Biographia Literaria*. Coleridge's literary memoir includes an extended analysis of the Preface, dwelling especially on Wordsworth's claim that the natural speech of 'low and rustic life' was the poet's language of choice. In his sustained demolition of Wordsworth's ideas about language, Coleridge argued that very little of Wordsworth's poetry bore much resemblance to words 'taken from the mouths of men in real life', because of the poet's unusual sensitivity, imagination, wide reading, powers of reflection and the special 'music of his own thoughts' (*Biographia Literaria*, II, 42; I, 37). The 'uneducated rustic', in contrast, 'would furnish a very scanty vocabulary' (*Biographia Literaria*, II, 53). Despite the warm tributes to the beauties of Wordsworth's poetry and of his imaginative powers, which came 'nearest of all modern writers to Shakespeare and Milton' (*Biographia Literaria*, II, 151), Coleridge was damning his old friend's critical theory and idealistic attitude to ordinary speech. In rhetoric reminiscent of Thomson's distinction between the 'sage-instructed eye' of the philosopher and the ignorant 'swain', Coleridge was effectively abandoning responsibility for the ideas presented in the preface to their joint volume. Ironically, the brilliant dissection of Wordsworth's strongly-worded sentiments carried authority because of Coleridge's unique relationship with the volume under discussion. His own commitment to the common man seemed long forgotten, the more recent breach with Wordsworth only too fresh in mind. According to Coleridge, 'low and rustic life' provided the language of poetry only when the main influences on rural speech came from the Bible or Prayer Book. The great ideal of 'conversational' poetry, which he had once promoted with such enthusiasm, was therefore being rejected, very publicly, in favour of the superiority of the written text.

Coleridge's lack of sympathy for those living and working in the countryside becomes especially apparent when he refers to the 'provincialism and grossness' of 'a rustic's language' – charges that played directly to the commonplace prejudices of an urban readership. That the idea of poetry being compatible with 'provincialism' should seem quite so unthinkable was not, however, a view shared by everyone in the Romantic period. The powerful appeal of traditional rural communities during the Romantic period is evident from the enormous success of poems such as Bloomfield's *The Farmer's Boy* or Cowper's *The Task*, as well as from the continuing popularity of Thomson's *The Seasons* and Goldsmith's *The Deserted Village*. These were not poems that necessarily mirrored the experience of their readers, but represented images of worlds no longer immediately available to urban readers – rather like the paintings of British landscapes that were now so much in demand.

During the later eighteenth century, towns and cities gradually expanded, common land was enclosed and traditional cottage crafts became increasingly mechanized, but the long war with France accelerated the transformation by demanding more efficient agricultural production and a constant supply of soldiers and sailors. As the face of Britain changed, fascination with traditional rural life intensified. Wordsworth's 'Michael', for example, is presented as a tale learned by the narrator when he was 'yet a boy / Careless of books' ('Michael', 27–8; O'Neill and Mahoney, 130). The poet's source is part of the shared oral inheritance of Grasmere, whose vulnerability is only too evident as the tale of Michael's broken inheritance and vanished way of life unfolds. At the same time, Wordsworth emphasizes the exemplary nature of a story that has survived through telling and retelling, until his own version gave it new life through publication. The elegiac aspect of 'Michael' is abundantly apparent, but there is no sense in the poem that the shepherd's life and what he represents is no longer important. On the contrary, Michael matters very much to Wordsworth and to generations of readers, as almost five hundred lines of blank verse and continuous republication of the poem demonstrate.

Wordsworth's reverence for tales recalled from his youth was part of his wider pursuit of essential truths and faith in the imaginative powers of childhood. The recreation of Michael's story in blank verse nevertheless reveals a new willingness among Romantic poets to seek material from oral sources and a taste among readers for traditional tales. In the 1820s, James Hogg offered readers of the sophisticated, new *Blackwood's Edinburgh Magazine* images of life in the Scottish countryside, styling himself as the Ettrick Shepherd. His collections of short stories such as *Winter Evening Tales* or *The Shepherd's Calendar* were presented similarly: not as the inventions of a desk-tied author, but as versions of material collected from the people of the Scottish Borders. When Hogg included his own poems, they seemed as much part of the local tradition as the anecdotes, pen portraits and old stories. For the Ettrick Shepherd's urban readers, the rural and the oral were natural companions.

When John Clare published his first volume of *Poems, descriptive of Rural Life and Scenery* in 1820, he was described on the title-page as a 'Northamptonshire peasant'. His publisher, John Taylor, was well aware of the appeal of rural life to the London book market and did much to promote Clare's success. Clare's own *The Shepherd's Calendar* appeared in 1827, two years before Hogg's collection, but adopted descriptive poetry rather than short stories to conjure up the countryside. The importance of orality to rural communities is just as obvious in Clare's volume nevertheless, which follows the life of a rural community from January to December. Even though the Preface made clear that Clare was the sole author, the opening book of the poem pays special tribute to the old stories known from childhood:

> When listning on the corner seat
> The winter evenings length to cheat
> I heard my mothers memory tell
> Tales superstition loves so well
> Things said or sung a thousand times
> In simple prose or simpler rhymes
> Ah where is the page of poesy
> So sweet as theirs was wont to be
> The majic wonders that decievd
> When fictions were as truths believd
> The fairy feats that once prevaild
> Told to delight and never faild
> ('January', 238–48; Wu, 1225)

The power of orality was quite unlike that of modern print culture, since it is the familiarity of the tales that makes them, rather than any suspense or surprise. 'Things said or sung a thousand times' had a very different appeal from experimental poetry or a new novel; and yet their perennial pleasure offered a quiet challenge to the prevailing emphasis on originality or novelty. Clare is recalling old favourites as affectionately as he talks of his own mother – and no 'page of poesy' could ever measure up to such longstanding intimacy.

Even as he affirms the superiority of storytelling over reading, however, Clare emphasizes the power of print through his persistent *ubi sunt* – 'Where are they fled wi their delights' (236), 'Where are they now their fears and sighs' (249). Tales that had so long maintained 'the life of other years' had now been 'nipt' and withered away (262–6). 'Reason', which is associated directly with adulthood and books, eventually triumphs over the 'majic wonders' of cultural tradition, making the characteristic Romantic recollection of childhood a metaphor for social transformation. Clare's account of winter story-telling offers a quiet critique of the dominance of reason in its emphasis on 'fictions' so compelling that they were 'as truths believd'. Like Wordsworth's 'The Rainbow', *The Shepherd's Calendar* suggests that the child is father of the man, but it also registers deep anxieties about the growing amnesia of modern society and attendant loss of essential truths.

By 'June', the old country way of life, which the oral tradition had helped to sustain, was explicitly upheld as the model for a better society than the present:

> And ale and songs and healths and merry ways
> Keeps up a shadow of old farmers days
> But the old beachen bowl that once supplyd
> Its feast of frumity is thrown aside
> And the old freedom that was living then
> When masters made them merry wi their men
> Whose coat was like his neighbours russet brown
> And whose rude speech was vulgar as his clown
> Who in the same hour drank the rest among
> And joined the chorus while a labourer sung
> All this is past – and soon may pass away
> The time torn remnant of the holiday
> As proud distinction makes a wider space
> Between the genteel and the vulgar race
> Then must they fade as pride oer custom showers
> Its blighting mildew on her feebler flowers
> ('June', 153–68; Wu, 1227)

The widening gulf between masters and men was a herald of the Victorian 'Two Nations' – the rich and the poor. For Clare, memories of the good 'old farmers days' were not merely sentimental recollections of a picturesque past, but a means of expressing serious social comment on the erosion of ancient human rights and the growing disempowerment of those without land and capital. 'Ale and songs' were vital to the 'healths and merry ways' of the British people, not merely because they offered a moment of respite in a hard working week, but because they kept alive the memories of greater social cohesion. In the past, the spoken word had united the classes because the master's 'rude speech was vulgar as his clown' (160). In contemporary Britain, however, the distinction between 'the genteel and the vulgar race' was only too marked and, as the wealthier members of society were educated into Standard pronunciation, spelling and grammar, their distance from those who lived on their estates became ever greater.

Clare's own perspective on the language divide is obvious to modern readers encountering *The Shepherd's Calendar* in Duncan Wu's anthology because of his use of dialect, colloquial contraction and lack of punctuation. For those who bought the poem in 1827, however, Clare's personal alignment with the men rather than the 'genteel' masters would have been less apparent, because of the editorial amendments made by Clare's publisher. The first published edition of *The Shepherd's Calendar* is now easily available in a helpful parallel text edited by Tim Chilcott, which shows at a glance how Clare's lines were carefully punctuated and rendered into Standard English for the reading public. A couplet such as 'And turning as he claims the custom kiss / Wi stifld smiles half ankering after bliss' ('June', 141–2) became, after Taylor's editing, 'He rises, to obtain the custom'd kiss – / With stifled smiles, half hankering after bliss' (Chilcott, 119). Throughout, Clare's individual spelling and often ambiguous punctuation was tidied up in order to make his text easier for readers. In many instances, however, ease of reading also meant ease of mind, as Clare's more recalcitrant lines vanished under the editorial smoothing iron. In the published version of 'June', for example, the line reading 'Keeps up a shadow of old farmers days' (154) in the manuscript turned into 'Keep up a shadow still of former days', which effectively removed the poem's admiration for 'old farmers' (Chilcott, 118). Soon afterwards, the lines about the masters drinking and singing with the men were cut entirely, along with the passage about 'proud distinction' and the destruction of custom by 'pride'. Clare might have been making a strong case for the value of older social attitudes and traditions, but the very medium in which he embodied his ideal was subject to the tastes of 'the genteel'. Oral traditions, song culture, dialect and idiomatic speech might still help to redeem British society, but not if their distinct forms were neutralized by publishing practice. The genteel readers who enjoyed Clare's poetry were to be spared the more uncomfortable expressions of 'the vulgar race'. If the elegiac tone became ascendant in the transformation of manuscript to print, however, the original versions of Clare's texts now visible to modern readers enable a recovery of their more resistant qualities.

Dialect words and punctuation, especially, often attracted editorial attention, often with very significant implications for the meaning of a stanza. The opening to Clare's manuscript of *The Shepherd's Calendar*, for example, reads 'Dithering & keen the winter comes / While comfort flyes to close shut rooms', a passage that continues without comma, semi-colon or full stop for 220 lines. The poem published by John Taylor, on the other hand, begins 'Withering and keen the Winter comes, / While Comfort flies to close-shut rooms,' with the first sentence ending at line six, the next at line 18. Taylor retained the sense of a scene built from many co-existent details, but introduced standard punctuation to help his readers follow the parallel clauses. What he removed, however, were the additional meanings springing from the use of dialect words or fluid syntax. The substitution of 'Withering', for example, makes Winter seem a more destructive and decisive agent than if it were 'Dithering', which not only suggests uncertainty but also, for those familiar with East Midlands dialect, 'shivering with cold'. Withering might work better alliteratively and conjure up a more literary tradition, but 'Dithering' animates the season in such a way as to make it seem more afflicted than 'comfort' in its cosy corner by the fireplace. The introduction of standard punctuation similarly strips Clare's verse of some of its originality, because the compound 'close-shut', precluding the possibility of 'close' being a verb, forces the life out of the personified 'comfort'. Taylor's decisions, though designed to clarify Clare's meanings, often inadvertently closed them shut.

Standard English and the Freedom of Speech

Although the changes to Clare's texts were especially marked, many writers of the period were affected by the growing emphasis on Standard English and correct pronunciation, exhibiting either a Coleridgean disdain for regional usage or awkwardness over their own accents and dialects. Those living in Scotland, especially, worked hard to eradicate 'Scotticisms' from their work, with even the leading intellectuals of the Enlightenment getting their prose checked for northern peculiarities before venturing into print. Burns, however, celebrated the old language of his country, just as he drew inspiration from local traditions. 'Tam O'Shanter', for example, was composed for his friend, the antiquarian, Francis Grose, but instead of presenting the tale as a specimen of quaint superstition to amuse a more sophisticated readership, Burns plunged readers into Tam's world adopting the present tense and inviting participation through his use of the first person plural:

> When chapman billies leave the street
> And drouthy neebors, neebors meet,

> As market-days are wearing late,
> And folk begin to tak the gate;
> While we sit bowsing in the nappy,
> And getting fou, and unco happy,
> We think na on the lang Scots miles,
> The waters, mosses, slaps and styles,
> That lie between us and our hame,
> Where sits our sulky sullen dame,
> Gathering her brows like gathering storm,
> Nursing her wrath to keep it warm.
> (1–12; Wu, 270)

If some of the words were unfamiliar to those outside Scotland, the situation evoked was one that anyone could understand. As a narrative opening, it brilliantly sets up the different perspectives on the man in the pub and the homeward journey he is leaving rather later than is sensible, creating the blend of sympathy and tongue-in-cheek observation that continues throughout. Even when the tense shifts to describing Tam's ride in the past, the narrator still breaks in with direct addresses to both the hapless protagonist and to the reader, so that the sense of being told something that is at once remarkable and yet oddly perennial is maintained.

The narrator is a skilful mediator between different kinds of speech, for when he addresses Tam, he uses Scots, 'Oh Tam, hadst thou but been sae wise / As taen thy ain wife Kate's advice!' (17–18), while his general reflections, like 'the snow-falls in the river / A moment white, then melts for ever' (61–2), tend to adopt Standard English. The narrator adopts a much wider range of vocabulary and tone than either Standard English or Scots could have furnished alone, and it is largely the colloquial flexibility of his narrative that allows for this linguistic richness. The ease with which he uses language that would be familiar to Tam means that even when the drunken hero is seen to least advantage there is little sense of condescension from the narrator. As Murray Pittock has pointed out, the narrator's offer of his only pair of breeks from off his 'hurdies' for 'ae blink o'the bonie burdies!' (161–2) brings him close to Tam in both sentiment and language (Pittock, 162). At the same time, key moments in the poem are offered in words that those familiar only with English could understand instantly:

> Tam lost his reason a'thegither
> And roars out 'Weel done, Cutty Sark!'
> And in an instant all was dark
> (191–4)

The dramatic moment when Tam cries out in excitement over what the lively dance and short shift have revealed would be much diminished if readers were unable to share the immediacy of the consequences.

Burns's unapologetic use of Scots may have unsettled some of his first readers, but his almost instantaneous fame showed that it was possible to compose highly acclaimed poetry irrespective of the prevailing linguistic standard. For aspiring poets whose own way of speaking did not conform to the received pronunciation of the educated, Burns was therefore welcomed as the great liberator. James Hogg, for example, who began his working life as a shepherd in the Scottish Borders, recalled the staggering effect of discovering Burns's poetry, when he heard a 'half-daft' man reciting 'Tam o'Shanter': 'I was delighted! I was more than delighted – I was ravished! I cannot describe my feelings!' (Hogg, *Memoir*, 18). Without any knowledge of the poet behind the poem, Hogg was able to respond directly to Burns's narrative, which told a local tale in Scots, brilliantly and unapologetically. Instead of the classical heroes, nymphs and dryads of so much eighteenth-century poetry, here was a very unheroic tale, rooted in Scottish folklore, but wonderfully presented in tetrameter lines that matched the beat of Maggie's hooves. For Hogg, as for numerous men and women of the time, Burns offered a thrilling example of possibilities hitherto unimaginable. He understood the multi-faceted nature of the oral tradition and instead of consigning it to the antiquarian specimen-tray, unleashed its energy on a startled reading public. 'Tam O'Shanter' included landmarks distinguished by oral rather than architectural, geographical or historical significance:

> By this time he was cross the ford,
> Where in the snaw the chapman smoored;
> And past the birks and meikle stane,
> Where drunken Charlie brak's neck-bane;
> And through the whins and by the cairn
> Where hunters fand the murdered bairn
> (89–94; Wu, 272)

Drunken Charlie provides a cautionary memory for Tam's unsteady homeward journey, while setting the distinctive tone of a comic-Gothic narrative as innovative as it was traditional.

Awareness of the languages and forms that remained distinct from the mainstream of British culture increased during the later eighteenth century, being felt most strongly in regions furthest from London. When Burns published his *Poems, Chiefly in the Scottish Dialect*, in 1786, reviewers in Edinburgh were delighted to discover such an accomplished poet writing in his own native Scots. One of Burns's major contributions to Romanticism was his willingness to write poetry in language that resembled ordinary speech, rather than feeling the need to adopt what Wordsworth would later scorn as 'poetic diction' – the elevated classical or sub-Miltonic phrases that became the staple of so much eighteenth-century poetry. Burns's invitation to John Lapraik, suggesting 'a swap o' rhyming-ware / Wi' ane anither' (106–7; Wu, 265) over a drink is hardly in the tone of a man stepping forward to awaken the great 'Lyre' that Milton had passed down from his classical forefathers. And yet, in its down-to-earth language and lively rhythm, Burns was introducing a vital new dimension to the literature of his day. For those like Hogg, who earned a living from hard physical work, the revelation of 'Tam O'Shanter' cannot be understated. Here was a poet who dared to use Scottish dialect and tradition and still succeeded in impressing critics and ordinary readers alike.

Burns's unreserved confidence in the kinds of life and language that flourished far from the metropolis gave his work a political dimension even when his subject was ostensibly personal. From the standpoint of Ayrshire or Dumfries, debates in the Houses of Parliament seemed rather remote from lived experience, while the social structures of the Britain offered little security to those uncushioned by land and wealth. Burns's poems frequently included wry observations on the attitudes and behaviour of those who considered themselves his superiors, including Scottish landowners or Ministers of the Kirk, while 'The Dream' employed Scots to offer explicit satire on the Royal Family. Often, when addressing a farmyard subject, Burns was making very human observations, using his local vocabulary to express sympathy with the poor. In 'To a Mouse', for example, a trivial, everyday incident is magnified to create an image of overwhelming disaster, as the farmer who has ploughed through the mouse's nest imagines the horror of domestic demolition. Crucial to his treatment of the subject is Burns's use of language that suggests intimate understanding of the mouse and her world, while revealing the wider implications of her misfortune:

> That wee-bit heap o' leaves an' stibble
> Hast cost thee monie a weary nibble!
> Now thou's turned out, for a' thy trouble,
>   But house or hald,

> To thole the winter's sleety dribble,
> An cranreuch cauld!
> ('To a Mouse', 31–36; Wu, 269)

The poem shows deep imaginative sympathy with a mouse-eye view of the world, but in doing so, it also brings thoughts of sudden homelessness vividly before the reader. The same crass casualty that left the mouse with nothing could just as easily strike human beings – especially those with no resources to rebuild their lives. In a period of economic hardship and rural dispossession, the fate of the mouse was shared by numerous agricultural workers and Burns himself was only saved from having to emigrate to Jamaica by the success of his first volume of poetry. Many of his poems reveal the fear of sudden homelessness afflicting those whose livelihoods were insecure, even though such anxieties were often combated by the spirited camaraderie that could turn beggars into kings.

Dialect poetry offered a way of expressing sympathy with – rather than pity for – those who were not very high on the social ladder. Burns's example helped people such as the Cumberland poet, Robert Anderson, to find ways of developing their local modes of speech into comments on the consequences of decisions made by the distant policy-makers. In his *Ballads in the Cumbrian Dialect*, published in Carlisle in the year of Trafalgar, 1805, Anderson created the comic figure of 'Nichol the Newsmonger', to offer an alternative perspective on current affairs:

> The clogger has bowt a new wig;
> Dalston singers come here agean Sunday;
> Lord Nelson's ta'en three Spanish fleets,
> And the Dancing schuil opens on Monday.
> (Anderson, *Ballads*, 7)

If such verses appeared to be poking fun at the ignorance of the Cumbrian newsmonger, however, they were also giving vent to anger over contemporary foreign policy. When Nichol brings news of the Peace of Amiens in 1802, for example, dutiful celebration of the nation's leaders turns rapidly into a catalogue of local suffering, focusing on figures such as 'the peer sarvent man', Peter:

> They said a captain he sud be,
> Alang wi' t' Duke o'York:
> Wi' powder'd head away he march'd,
> And gat a wooden leg:

> But monie time he's rued sin syne,
> For now he's fworced to beg.
> (Anderson, *Ballads*, 37)

Physical distance from the centres of power had not saved the people of Cumbria from the pains of prolonged warfare and so Anderson used his traditional oral forms and language to register a protest against the remote figures at whose hands his neighbours' lives could be devastated. The Duke of York's disastrous campaign in Flanders, which ended with his defeat at the Battle of Tourcoing in 1794 was already old news, but the long-term consequences were still visible in the maimed veterans who had survived. Comments hidden in collections of local dialect poems published in provincial towns were not likely to attract the attention of Government officials. As Seamus Heaney pointed out in an essay on 'John Clare's Prog', regional dialects have often been used by poets who felt the need 'to body-swerve past the censor' – whether the restrictions were grammatical or political (Heaney, 291). Burns may have posed as a simple bard writing to please himself and his friends, but his poems simmered with indignation over social injustice and the abuse of power. His admirers similarly conveyed their humanitarian concerns in poetry that stood for the ordinary people of Britain, resistant to attitudes imposed from elsewhere. The more limited the audience, the bolder the sentiment could afford to be.

Not all dialect poetry was composed in opposition to the Government, of course, for the military songs that emerged during the Napoleonic war often drew on regional expression to drum up native loyalties. Burns's own song, 'The Dumfries Volunteers', for example, rallies the local volunteers gathering to defend their country against the likelihood of a French invasion from the Solway Firth. One early collection of regional poetry published during the Napoleonic War under the title, *The Yorkshire Dialect*, includes a poetic dialogue between two Yorkshiremen called Willy and Roger. 'The Invasion' is presented as an 'eclogue', but far from portraying peaceful otium, it is a declaration of local – and therefore national strength:

> But let the Franch be turn'd to what they will,
> They'll find 'at Inglishmen are Inglish still.
> (Yorkshire Dialect, 8)

The anonymous dialogue was hardly immortal verse, but it shows very clearly the varied uses of poetry and the continuing power of orality in the

Romantic period. Local pride could easily be roused through dialect songs, which incited the men of Cumbria, Dumfriesshire or any other county to rally and defeat the French. War songs were very much part of the oral tradition and war was very much part of human experience during the Romantic period. Rather than body-swerving past the censor, the lyricists who wrote or revived songs in the regional languages of the United Kingdom were just as likely to be rousing their communities in support of the national crisis.

The eighteenth-century retreat of orality in the face of an expanding print culture, then, was by no means steady or straightforward. In many ways, books stimulated fresh interest in old, half-forgotten stories as well as in the variousness of living language. Translation of the traditional ballads, songs and speech of different communities into the permanent and portable medium of print often meant widening the audiences rather than restricting the sources of culture. And although the relationship between the written and spoken prompted elegiac reflection in some writers, for others the potential for transformation offered a means of preservation, distillation and renewal. Many Romantic poems are poised between loss and recovery, at once elegiac and forward-looking – just like 'The Solitary Reaper'.

Further Reading

For insightful readings of 'The Solitary Reaper', see Geoffrey Hartman, *Wordsworth's Poetry, 1787–1814* (New Haven and London: Yale University Press, 1964); Susan Wolfson, 'Wordsworth's Craft', in Stephen Gill (ed.), *The Cambridge Companion to Wordsworth* (Cambridge: Cambridge University Press, 2003), 105–24; Peter Manning, *Reading Romantics: Text and Context* (New York and Oxford: Oxford University Press, 1990).

On 'Conversation' Poems and *Lyrical Ballads*, see C. Barfoot, *A Natural Delineation of the* Passions (Amsterdam: Rodopi, 2001); Patrick Campbell, *Wordsworth and Coleridge: Lyrical Ballads* (Basingstoke: Macmillan, 1990); Heather Glen, *Vision and Disenchantment: Blake's Songs and Wordsworth's Lyrcal Ballads* (Cambridge: Cambridge University Press, 1983); Mary Jacobus, *Tradition and experiment in Wordsworth's Lyrical Ballads 1798* (Oxford: Clarendon Press, 1975); Stephen Parrish, *The Art of Lyrical Ballads* (Cambridge, Ma.: Harvard University Press, 1973); Seamus Perry and Nicola Trott, (eds.) *1800: New Lyrical Ballads* (Basingstoke: Palgrave Macmillan, 2000); Susan Wolfson, *The Questioning Presence: Wordsworth, Keats and the Interrogative Mode in Romantic Poetry* (Ithaca and London: Cornell University Press, 1986).

On orality and literacy, see Walter Ong, *Orality and Literacy* (London: Routledge, 1982); Penny Fielding, *Writing and Orality* (Oxford: Oxford University Press, 1996); and for 'reading aloud', Lucy Newlyn, *Reading Writing and Romanticism: The Anxiety of Reception* (Oxford: Oxford University Press, 2000). For the ballad revival, see the further reading for Chapter 4 above.

For depictions of rural life in the period, see Jonathan Bate, *The Song of the Earth* (London: Picador, 2000); John Barrell, *The Dark Side of the Landscape* (Cambridge: Cambridge University Press, 1980); John Goodridge, *Rural Life in Eighteenth-Century English Poetry* (Cambridge: Cambridge University Press, 1995); John Goodridge (gen. ed.) *Eighteenth-Century Labouring-Class Poets*, 3 vols (London: Pickering and Chatto, 2003); John Goodridge and John Lucas (eds.) *Robert Bloomfield: Selected Poems*, rev. edn. (Nottingham: Trent editions, 2007); Bridget Keegan, *British Labouring-Class Nature Poetry* (Basingstoke: Palgrave, 2008); Raymond Williams, *The Country and the City* (London: Chatto, 1971).

For an accessible parallel text of Clare's poem, see John Clare, *The Shepherd's Calendar*, ed. Tim Chilcott (Manchester: Carcanet, 2008); see also, Simon Kovesi, 'Beyond the Language Wars: Towards a Green Edition of John Clare', *John Clare Society Journal*, 27 (2007), 61–75. For further discussion of editing see Chapter 7 below. The rise of Standard English has been analyzed by Lynda Mugglestone, *Talking Proper: The Rise of Accent as Social Symbol* (Oxford: Oxford University Press, 1995). See also, Michael Baron, *Language and Relationship in Wordsworth's Writing* (London and New York: Routledge, 1995); Fiona Stafford, *Starting Lines in Scottish, English and Irish Poetry: From Burns to Heaney* (Oxford: Oxford University Press, 2000). On dialect poetry in the period and associated political questions, see Liam McIlvanney, *Burns the Radical* (East Linton: Tuckwell, 2002); Seamus Heaney, 'John Clare's Prog', *Finders Keepers* (London: Faber, 2000); Fiona Stafford, 'Scottish Poetry and

Regional Literary Expression', in John Richetti (ed.), *The Cambridge History of English Literature 1660–1780* (Cambridge: Cambridge University Press, 2005), 340–62.

For the poetry of war, see Simon Bainbridge, *British Poetry and the Revolutionary and Napoleonic Wars* (Oxford: Oxford University Press, 2003); Betty T. Bennett, *British Poetry in the Age of Romanticism: 1793–1815* (New York: Garland, 1976).

6

Sweet Sounds

For poets of the Romantic period, the world was full of noises, sounds and sweet airs that gave delight. Looking back on his earliest experiences, Wordsworth paid tribute to the River Derwent for making 'ceaseless music through the night and day' (*Prelude*, I, 279; *William Wordsworth*, 309), while for Coleridge, memories of his birthplace were accompanied by the sound of church bells, ringing 'so sweetly, that they stirred and haunted' him with 'wild pleasure' ('Frost at Midnight', 28–32; O'Neill and Mahoney, 223). Sounds spoke to poets, long before they recognized their own calling, and many of the poems written in maturity reflect a life-long delight in the music of the everyday. The unfailing quality of aural enjoyment meant that familiar sounds often provided a reassuring sense of continuity in a world where so much pleasure seemed transient. The natural music of streams, breezes and birds or the regular ringing of church bells not only awakened immediate delight, but also recollections of pleasures past and therefore hope for similar experience in the future. Recognition of the familiar in unexpected circumstances was often the prompt for a Romantic lyric, and when the inspiration was aural, the poet had to make special efforts to measure up acoustically. As Wordsworth reflected, the ideal poet 'murmurs near the running brooks / A music sweeter than their own' ('A Poet's Epitaph', 39–40; *William Wordsworth*, 126).

Whether poets could necessarily achieve a music sweeter than that of the natural world was, however, not always subject to such confident claims. Many poets of the period sought resemblances between their art and the music of the natural world, but often seemed more conscious of the differences. Nor were all poets as ready as Wordsworth to express

Reading Romantic Poetry, First Edition. Fiona Stafford.
© 2014 Fiona Stafford. Published 2014 by John Wiley & Sons, Ltd.

gratitude for the reassuring memories embodied in familiar sounds – Byron, for example, rhymed 'sound' with 'wound' in *Childe Harold*, listing 'a sound – / A tone of music – summer's breath' as among the things that 'bring / Back on the heart the weight which it would fling aside for ever' (*Childe Harold*, IV, 23, 202–206). Byron's melancholic reflection on the power of sound provided an epigraph for Felicia Hemans, whose 'The Spirit's Mysteries' begins by musing on 'The power that dwelleth in sweet sounds to waken / Vague yearnings, like the sailor's for the shore' (O'Neill and Mahoney, 407). Hemans was as alert to the memory-waking qualities of sound as Wordsworth or Coleridge, but in her poem the past is vanished and the harp, broken with 'deserted strings' (7–9). 'Sweet sounds' were as likely to provoke unfulfilled longings as grateful celebrations, though many Romantic lyrics encompassed both.

When Shelley, for example, leapt to defend poetry from the satirical jibes of his friend, Thomas Love Peacock, sound was a crucial part of his rhetorical strategy. The 'uniform and harmonious recurrence of sound', which poets in all ages had preferred was, in Shelley's view, 'scarcely less indispensable' to the reception of their work 'than the words themselves' (*Defence*, Wu, 1188). For Shelley, the language of great prose writers such as Francis Bacon also possessed a 'sweet and majestic rhythm', which satisfies 'the sense no less' than its wisdom satisfied the intellect (Wu, 1188). The distinction between prose and verse was one that concerned many writers of the period, but for his *Defence of Poetry*, Shelley was eager to enlist as many powerful writers to his cause as possible, and hence his inclusion of Plato, Bacon and a host of other creative spirits. Rather than emphasize any essential difference between prose and poetry, Shelley drew attention to the elements shared by the greatest practitioners of each – their imaginative powers, progressive ideas, capacity for expressing truths and, crucially, the technical skills that rendered these qualities so persuasive to others. Plato's prose had a 'melody' just as distinctive as that of Milton's majestic poetry, and both demonstrated the poet's ability to convey newly acquired knowledge in rhythmic, orderly language.

Since concepts are inseparable from the 'melody' of a text, they cannot to be abstracted: 'Sounds as well as thoughts have relation both between each other and towards that which they represent' (Wu, 1188). This is why it is also impossible to paraphrase a poem or reduce it to a mere message, and why the translation of poetry is so often unsatisfactory: 'it were as wise to cast a violet into a crucible that you might discover the formal principle of its colour and odour, as seek to transfuse from one language into another the creations of a poet' (Wu, 1188). Poems have a special life of their own, springing from the intricate patterns of sound within the individual form, and good prose, similarly, should have its own distinctive acoustic qualities.

According to Shelley, the best prose, like the best poetry, expands and then 'bursts the circumference of the reader's mind' (Wu, 1188) and so his own *Defence* seeks to render the doubts of the unsympathetic irrelevant – readers will either be carried away with its beauty or left, baffled and stranded. His own excitement shimmers in every sentence, awakening in readers a desire to share in the intense pleasure of poetry by presenting lyrical phrases that sound as lovely as the images they create: 'its secret alchemy turns to potable gold the poisonous waters which flow from death through life' (Wu,1196); 'Veil after veil may be undrawn and the inmost naked beauty of the meaning never exposed' (Wu,1192); 'the mind in creation is as a fading coal which some invisible influence, like an inconstant wind, awakens to transitory brightness' (Wu, 1195). Sentences such as these, filled with alliteration and assonance, even resembling hexameters in their rhythmic balance, are not easily paraphrased or refuted. Ideas, emotions, images and acoustics all contribute to the full *Defence of Poetry*.

When Shelley comes to describe the poet, his chosen metaphor accordingly makes sounds rather than concepts primary:

> A poet is a nightingale who sits in darkness to cheer his own solitude with sweet sounds; his auditors are as men entranced by the melody of the unseen musician, who feel that they are moved and softened, yet know not whence or why.
>
> (Wu, 1189)

The image suggests that 'sweet sounds' are cheering to both artist and audience irrespective of any precise ideas being communicated, a point reinforced by the alliterative sequence of 's's and 'm's, culminating in the passive 'moved and softened'. A nightingale's song, like any beautiful piece of music, has its own physical and emotional power and is capable of moving listeners without words. Poetry, too, should delight the reader at once, through its distinctive acoustic quality, whatever sentiment or argument might also be conveyed. The nightingale, singing in the dark, could be heard very clearly, but not seen – and hence its suitability for an image of pure sound. The attention commanded by a nightingale is focused entirely on the astonishingly varied song rather than the invisible bird and so, as an image for the poet it is self-effacing and sound-enhancing.

Poems of the period overflowed with natural music, from melodious rivers and murmuring springs to whispering breezes and roaring winds, one of the most resonant images being that of the eolian harp, whose strings made music in response to gusts of wind. Of all the natural sources of music in the world, however, it was song birds that probably attracted most frequent admiration from poets. Birds, alighting unannounced and disappearing at will, were figures of freedom, especially appealing to an age obsessed with human liberty. They were also images of 'unseen companionship', capable of banishing solitude in a moment, as evident in Wordsworth's tribute to his sister, Dorothy:

> Where'er my footsteps turned,
> Her voice was like a hidden Bird that sang;
> The thought of her was like a flash of light
> Or an unseen companionship.
> ('Home at Grasmere', 109–112;
> *William Wordsworth*, 191')

The 'hidden bird' is an unexpected blessing, a sudden delightful presence that appears when least expected. The poet, too, as a 'nightingale', might hope to provide similar company, despite remaining personally unknown to his readers as long as his song happened to please them. Birdsong, though wordless, seemed capable of expressing many of the literary concerns of the day, not least those relating to the relationship between the poem and the reader.

Song birds flit through the pages of Romantic poetry collections, both as images of artistic perfection and as elusive ideals that leave the writer lamenting the inescapable limitations of mortal beings. The medium of the poet is language and so the ideal of moving readers through 'sweet sounds' alone is always compromised by the meaning of the words that constitute the sounds; hence, very often, the fascination with the 'unheard melodies' or 'the damsel with a dulcimer' half-recalled from a vanished vision, but never realized on the page for readers. At moments such as this, the poet seems more like the reader than the creator, catching at notes that can no longer be fully heard. Though Shelley imagined the poet as the nightingale, it was also possible to see him in the position of the auditor, entranced by the song and left in a state of bewildered wonder.

For the Romantic poet, the creation of natural, spontaneous music in words was at once an ideal for which to strive and yet one that often seemed maddeningly unattainable. A sense of loss was nevertheless part of the creative experience, as Shelley acknowledged in *A Defence of Poetry*: 'when composition begins, inspiration is already on the decline, and the most glorious poetry that has ever been communicated to the world is probably a feeble shadow of the original conception of the poet' (Wu, 1195). The flight of a bird, after pouring out a glorious and unexpected song, was a perfect image for the deflation that followed the exhilaration of the visionary moment.

Despite the despondency that so often accompanied attempts to capture the inexpressible, writers of the Romantic period continued to pour out their own poems in astonishing numbers. Their acute awareness of the difficulty of their task generally contributed great subtlety to many Romantic lyrics, which are often as much about writing poems as they are about the ostensible subject. Poets of the period may have been racked with doubts about their ability to create a 'music sweeter' than what was audible to everyone on a daily basis, but they still achieved an extraordinary beauty in their verse, creating poems that work primarily through rhythm, melody and harmony to leave readers moved and softened, though often unable to analyze quite why this should be so. This chapter explores the attempt to create 'a music' as sweet or even sweeter than that of the natural world, by poets for whom sound was at once an idea and an instrument.

Romantic Nightingales

When Shelley observed in 1821 that 'a poet is a nightingale', he was drawing on a well-established motif. Numerous poets of the period had felt compelled to address poems to nightingales, including Ann Radcliffe, William Cowper, Mary Hays, Mary Robinson, William Wordsworth, Samuel Taylor Coleridge, George Dyer, Cornelius Webbe, Francis Hoyland, Josiah Conder and, of course, John Keats. In many such poems, explicit parallels were drawn between the woodland songster and the would-be poet, though the natural virtuosity of the reticent bird often seemed an image of the unattainable. Charlotte Smith's address to the nightingale as 'Sweet poet of the woods' in her *Elegiac Sonnets*, for example, had been inspired by the bird's departure, making what appeared to be a greeting, in fact 'a long adieu!' ('Sonnet VII', Wu, 87). The full title of William Cowper's 'To a Nightingale which the Author Heard Sing on New year's Day, 1792' appears to indicate a spontaneous response to the natural world, but since nightingales are summer migrants, Cowper was probably using the image of a retiring bird to express feelings about his own art. For though the poet gives thanks for the privilege of hearing 'the melody of May' in freezing January, he also identifies with the difficulty of putting 'forth ...song / Beneath a wintry sky'. Cowper was well aware, too, of the difference between his own hard-won craft and the nightingale's effortless harmonies:

> Sing'st thou, sweet Philomel, to me
>   For that I also long
> Have practis'd in the groves like thee,
>   Though not alike in song?
>   ('To the Nightingale', 9–12,
>   Cowper, III, 180).

The nightingale seemed to demand poetic tributes, but these often vacillated between a thrilling sense of kinship and self-punishing recognition of inadequacy.

As nightingales became established figures for the poet in successive lyrics, further anxieties intruded, for it became difficult to make spontaneous responses to the sound of a bird singing without feeling the presence of a host of earlier poems on the same subject. When Coleridge took fellow poets to task in 'The Nightingale' for adopting ideas from books rather than directly from the woods, he was himself contributing another voice to the contemporary chorus of bird poems. Coleridge's desire to represent nightingales more accurately, 'With skirmish and capricious passagings, / And murmurs musical and swift jug jug' ('The Nightingale, 59–60; O'Neill and Mahoney, 230), is indicative of a culture in which virtual nightingales abounded, but real birds were very hard to find. Many of those who tuned their lyres to the nightingale's note would never actually have heard the bird sing and so drew inspiration solely from earlier poems.

Despite the much admired lightness, variety and spontaneity of their song, literary nightingales came weighted with associations that stretched back to the classical world. Ovid had recounted the painful myth of Philomel in the *Metamorphoses*, describing how she turned into a nightingale after being violated and mutilated by her brother-in-law, Tereus. Philomel was prevented from calling out for help because her tongue was cut out, and so the ancient image of the nightingale was associated with horrific recollections and the agonizing failure of words. The bird who finally flies away from her bloody experiences was unable to tell her own story, but it continued to inspire generations of later poets and would give women writers such as Charlotte Smith special scope for expressing affinity with the nightingale. Smith's third sonnet, 'To a Nightingale', for example, acknowledges a debt to Petrarch, but behind Petrarch's nightingale hovers the old myth of Philomela, one of 'Pale Sorrow's victims' (Wu, 85). With the nightingale's song came ideas of passionate experience too intense to be allowed utterance in words, too traumatic to be forgotten.

The violence of Ovid's tale often softened into a more gentle mood of sadness in the English tradition, however, and, as Coleridge was only too aware, the association of nightingales with melancholy was established most firmly by Milton's 'Il Penseroso'. In Milton's poem, Melancholy is invoked as a 'pensive Nun', moving in silence, unless 'Philomel will deign a song, / In her sweetest, saddest plight' ('Il Penseroso', 56–57). There is little emphasis on ancient atrocities in this evocation of the 'Sweet bird, that shunn'st the noise of folly, / Most musical, most melancholy!' ('Il Penseroso', 61–2), although the myth makes Milton's use of the superlative seem anything but hyperbolic. The unspecific sadness of the bird-song in 'Il Penseroso', which fascinates and eludes the solitary poet in the woods at night added a new cluster of ideas to post-Miltonic nightingales and fed the fashionable melancholy of much later eighteenth-century poetry. Milton's nightingales were not reserved exclusively for the pensive solitary, however, as his first sonnet, which figures the nightingale as the herald of 'success in love' (7) demonstrates. Nightingales, as the only British birds to sing at night, were obvious candidates for accompanying love scenes and in *Paradise Lost*, Adam and Eve are accordingly, 'lulled by nightingales' in their nocturnal embraces (*Paradise Lost*, IV, 771). If the myth of Philomel carried memories of violence and discord, the nightingales of Milton's prelapsarian Eden offered tenderness and harmony, albeit beyond the reach of mere mortal ears.

Perhaps the most influential evocation of the nightingale for Romantic writers, however, was to be found in the third book of *Paradise Lost*, which opens with a long meditation on the hard task of the poet. In spite of his blindness, which now precluded him from independent reading and writing, Milton described his undiminished 'love of sacred song' and compared his own practice to that of a nightingale, feeding

> On thoughts that voluntary move
> Harmonious numbers, as the wakeful bird
> Sings darkling, and in the shadiest covert hid
> Tunes her nocturnal note.
> (*Paradise Lost*, III, 37–40)

To find such a learned and verbally ambitious poet aligning his work to that of a song bird, emphasizing not his hard-won knowledge of ancient languages and theology so much as his 'harmonious numbers' and perfectly tuned 'note' was striking to say the least. Milton's blindness, made apparent to all readers of his great poem, meant that he was unable to gain inspiration from the source so gratefully acknowledged by eighteenth-century writers – the natural world, as perceived by the eye. Whereas Addison would identify sight as the chief source of the imagination, Milton had included in *Paradise Lost* a confession of his own physical limitation:

> ever-during dark
> Surrounds me, from the cheerful ways of men
> Cut off, and for the book of knowledge fair
> Presented with a universal blank
> Of Nature's works to me expunged and razed,
> And wisdom at one entrance quite shut out.
> (III, 45–49)

In spite of his inability to see God's creation, Milton had nevertheless succeeded in composing the great English epic.

As discussed in Chapter 4, *Paradise Lost* still dominated the literary landscape of the Romantic period and, among its many influential aspects, was a heightened awareness of the significance of sound rather than sight for poetry. If Milton cast himself as a nightingale, then anyone with poetic aspirations was likely to be attracted by an image of the poet, hidden from sight but singing with notes as near-heavenly as was possible in the darkness of the earth. Such a figure had powerful appeal for rural poets like John Clare, for example, who was acutely conscious of his own social obscurity, but still able to express himself and celebrate natural plenitude through local details. In his sonnet, 'The Nightingale', the bird is heard by the speaker, 'from the little blackthorn spinney', while 'the ploughman feels / The thrilling music as he goes along' (8, 10–11; *Poems*, II, 443) at dusk. Even the most unassuming corners and unlikely listeners could be transformed by 'thrilling music', as Clare's own verse demonstrated.

Milton's suggestion that darkness was not necessarily uncongenial to the creation of poetry also found a sympathetic supporter in Keats, who created his own enduring 'Ode to a Nightingale' in 1819. Although the darkness of the ode is less permanent than Milton's blindness, insofar as it derives from the ordinary experience of nightfall, there are still moments in Keats's poem where the simple statement, 'But here there is no light'

(38; O'Neill and Mahoney, 445) seems an ominous summary of the human condition. The ode's gloomier tendencies are nevertheless held in check by the emphasis on the deep pleasure that may be gained from visual deprivation:

> I cannot see what flowers are at my feet
>   Nor what soft incense hangs upon the boughs,
> But, in embalmed darkness, guess each sweet
>   Wherewith the seasonable month endows
> The grass, the thicket, and the fruit-tree wild
>   (40–45)

Images of death linger in the embalmed darkness, but the absence of light intensifies the other senses, making the air almost palpable, the evening fragrances overpowering. Above all, the poem dwells on the effect of sound on the speaker, which is abundantly evident from the opening line: 'My heart aches, and a drowsy numbness pains / My sense'. What seems initially to be a physical condition, with symptoms as dramatic as that of a drug-induced lapse from consciousness, turns out to be a reaction to the nightingale's song, heard unexpectedly on a summer evening. Pleasure so intense is figured as pain, just as sound is conveyed through each of the other senses.

Keats's poem takes Milton's image of the nightingale, echoing key words, 'numbers', 'sings', 'darkling', and exploring the parallels between the poet and the bird. Far more physical than Milton's invocation, Keats's ode creates links between the 'full-throated' bird-song and his own thirst for a draught from the 'blushful Hippocrene' – the classical spring of inspiration, envisaged as red wine, bubbling from Mediterranean soil. As the nightingale pours forth its soul, the speaker longs to drink and free himself from the troubles of suffering man. The bird's song has the power to move, console and free listeners, just as it has for centuries, as the evocations of the ancient emperor and clown, or the Biblical Ruth, in tears amid the alien corn, affirm.

The sound of singing, intensified by darkness, transports the speaker into an imaginative world, unfretted by the pains and problems of life. It is not Milton's divine light that shines inwardly in Keats's poem, but a secular vision, nourished by the senses and by memories of poetry. Keats's ode recreates the movement from an earthbound consciousness to visionary flight, as the 'viewless wings of Poesy' begin to approach the unseen nightingale:

> Away! Away! For I will fly to thee,
>   Not charioted by Bacchus and his pards,

> But on the viewless wings of Poesy,
>   Though the dull brain perplexes and retards:
> Already with thee! Tender is the night,
>   And haply the Queen-Moon is on her throne,
>   Cluster'd around by all her starry Fays;
>   But here there is no light,
> Save what from heaven is with the breezes blown
>   Through verdurous glooms and winding mossy ways.
>   (31–40)

Unlike Coleridge, who attempted to recreate a sense of the nightingale's song, Keats shows that human beings have a music of their own. His 'Poesy' is described as moving on 'viewless wings', which readers can hear for themselves in the beauty of his rhythms and language. This stanza, for example, opens with a regular iambic pentameter line, a rhythm repeated in the third line, but then varied in all the rest to create not just an ordered harmony, but also gentle surprises and a sense of powerful internal tension. Indeed, the second and fourth lines of this stanza seem to counter their immediate predecessors not just in sense, but by opening with a stressed syllable ('Not', 'Though'). The varied stresses are also interlaced with internal rhymes and assonance, which similarly work to balance the regularity of the end-rhymes. The full rhyme of 'Away' and 'away', followed by that of 'I' and 'fly', for example, pre-empt the attention that is inevitably demanded by the end word, 'thee', and its pair, 'Poesy', while 'pards' and 'retards' are recalled from their commanding position by 'starry'. The internal struggle conveyed by the literal meaning of the words is thus matched by the rhythmic tensions of the verse.

Heavy alliteration also contributes to the internal bracing, as the line-ends are linked aurally to numerous words within – 'thee' (31) recurs in line 35, for example, but also resembles 'Though', 'there' and 'Through'. 'Bacchus' similarly, shares vowel sounds with 'charioted', 'viewless' and 'verdurous', and consonants with 'But', 'brain', 'breezes blown', 'Queen' and 'Clustered'. The train of v's that link 'viewless' with 'verdurous' help to emphasize 'Save' and 'heaven', which in turn create a subliminal sense that the viewless wings of poesy may be a way to reach salvation and eternity; the alliteration reveals the possibility of the pun in 'save', transforming it from conjunction to verb, exception to promise. It is not that the aural dimensions of Keats's words make them operate independently of their normal definitions, but rather that the careful arrangements of sounds and stresses greatly enrich the overall meaning of his poetry. Keats's ode has a very distinctive acoustic quality, making it worthy to accompany the nightingale, whose ecstatic notes are constantly evoked without ever being fully realized. Readers may only imagine the singing of the 'light-winged Dryad', but they can enjoy the sounds of Keats's virtuoso performance again and again, finding deeper satisfaction with every new reading.

Keats's attention to the sound of his poetry means that even his gloomiest sentiments offer a strange satisfaction to readers. The opening stanza speaks of heart-ache, pain and numbness, but the melody of the verse, with its rich alliteration and aural satisfaction turns the pain into pleasure, even before the speaker explains that his feelings result from excessive happiness. From the very beginning of the poem the internal vowel sounds are perfectly chosen, with the long a's of 'aches', 'pains', 'opiate', 'drains' playing against both the repeated 'My', 'my', which leads to 'I', 'thy' and 'light' 'Dryad', and the assonance of 'sense', 'hemlock' and 'empty', later picked up in 'envy' (1–5). In line 4, 'Lethe' sets up another dominant sound pattern, which recurs in 'being', 'trees', 'beechen green' before culminating in the last word of the stanza, 'ease' (9–10). Almost every word is linked acoustically to another word in the stanza, creating a sense of numerous invisible connections for the solitary speaker.

Since the opening stanza is a single sentence, the emphasis provided by the network of different sounds offers a quiet challenge to conventional syntax, which means that readers are more likely to be struck first by the sounds, feelings and images conveyed than by any very clear idea of action or thought. Initially, at least, the 'sense' of the ode is primarily physical. As the reader follows these complicated lines, the pain of the first line turns out to have been an expression of excessive pleasure, the slump towards death a result of great joy, corresponding to the sudden perception of happiness in another being. What appears to be an opposition between the speaker and the bird in line 5, 'Tis not through envy of thy happy lot', rapidly collapses with the repetition of 'happy', to encompass both the bird ('too happy in thine happiness') and the speaker, 'being too happy in thine happiness', 6). The emphasis on 'happiness' also invites recognition of the play on 'hap', implicit in 'happy lot' and recalled in stanzas four ('haply the Queen-Moon') and seven ('perhaps the self-same song'). The opening stanza abounds with words that similarly carry more than one meaning, such as 'numberless', which means both 'numerous' and 'without songs', or 'light-winged', which encompasses both weightlessness and brightness, and anticipates later angelic imagery of pouring forth the soul in ecstacy (57–8). As an introduction to a poem that perpetually vacillates between a sense of similarity and difference, closeness and distance, the opening stanza with its unexpected twists, puns and acoustic harmonies is pretty much perfect.

Each stanza has its own distinctive character, its rhymes, rhythms and alliteration creating a mood that follows naturally from the preceding verse while maintaining its own completeness. The ode reads almost like a condensed sonnet sequence, its ten-line stanzas suggesting a fusion of the English and Petrarchan sonnet forms – ababcdecde. In the third stanza, as the ode begins to dwell on a world 'where youth grows pale, and spectre-thin, and dies' (26), the technical brilliance of the verse still carries its own consolation. Readers are being at once reminded that they habitually 'hear each other groan' and offered a very different set of sounds, beautiful, rhythmic, haunting. The word 'Here' at the start of the line may be a straightforward indication of the speaker's situation, but for anyone listening to the ode, it also sounds like an injunction to listen – 'Hear', thus connecting the reader's experience with the speaker's comment on the human condition. In a poem where being 'full of sorrow / And leaden-eyed despairs' is so pleasurable to the ear, the profound melancholy of the world seems almost contained by the beauty of its presentation. Like the nightingale's song, Keats's poetry emerges startlingly from the darkness to delight readers in perpetuity.

If sound has the capacity to triumph over the most adverse circumstances, however, it can also destroy the visionary moment, as the sudden recollection that brings the poem to a conclusion demonstrates. The very word 'Forlorn' is enough to recall the speaker to his condition, the ecstatic 'soul' returned once more to the 'sole self' (71–2). Keats uses the sound of his own words to take his poem back to earth, rhyming 'sole' with 'toll' to emphasize the association with mortality. If words can evoke the song of a nightingale, they can also generate meanings through their own syllabic sounds, to accentuate the familiar linguistic connotations. 'Forlorn' is like a bell, not just because it recalls the sadness from which the speaker had momentarily escaped, but also because its vowel sounds resemble the tolling from the bell-tower. It is orderly, repetitive, and as unlike the varied cadences of the nightingale's song as it could be. 'Forlorn' repeats the last word of the preceding stanza to usher in a series of dull, monosyllabic words ('like a bell / To toll me back from thee to my sole self', 71–2), which contrast starkly with the earlier fluidity of the verse,

> The same that oft times hath
> Charm'd magic casements, opening on the foam
> Of perilous seas, in faery lands forlorn.
> (68–70)

In stanza seven, 'forlorn' follows alliteratively from 'faery', 'foam' and 'oft', its twin 'o' sounds flowing gently from 'oft', 'opening on', 'foam' and 'of'. When it recurs at the start of the eighth stanza, however, 'Forlorn' seems isolated from its immediate surroundings, a counterpart of the sole self who has been temporarily cheated into consolation. As the 'plaintive anthem fades', the speaker is left, bereft of the ravishing music and uncertain of everything that it seemed to represent (75). 'Was it a vision or a waking dream? / Fled is that music: – Do I wake or sleep?' (79–80). It is a very different point from that reached by Milton after his soul-searching into the nocturnal inspiration of the poet / nightingale. And yet the unresolved question leaves open more hopeful possibilities. The flight within the ode has revealed the way in which music can illuminate the darkest situations, even carrying listeners into a spiritual existence that transcends the ordinary, everyday world. 'Harmonious numbers' reveal a transcendent realm that is real and eternal, rendering ordinary existence, with all its limitations, the unreal. The speaker's question, 'Do I wake or sleep?' does not necessarily arise from a condition of solitary half-consciousness in the dark, but may represent a return from a truly awakened state into more customary experience. After all, the elegiac note of 'Fled is that Music' is countered by the poem on the page: the nightingale may have flown away, but Keats's poem remains.

Hidden Birds that Sing

Although the Romantic admiration for the hidden bird tended to find most frequent expression in poems addressed to nightingales, the period was also a nesting ground for numerous literary cuckoos, linnets, robins, wrens, lapwings, yellow-hammers, doves, thrushes, and sky-larks. John Clare wrote an entire series of poems celebrating birds less frequently featured in literature such as the blackcap ('A nightingale in melody') or the wren, who 'raised / One's heart to ecstacy and mirth' as well as the 'madly praised' nightingale ('The Black Cap', 2, 'The Wren', 5, 2; *Poems*, 225, 245). Clare understood the different kinds of birds native to his local area and although he used such standard terms as 'melody' or 'minstrelsy', his poems also included onomatopaeic words, in an attempt to represent the distinctive calls of different birds. He was, in a sense, taking up Coleridge's challenge to represent nature as she really was, rather than as the poets had painted her, though his poems suggest a genuine fascination with the life of the birds themselves, irrespective of philosophical anxieties about the workings of the associative faculty. Clare's chiffchaff makes a 'chippichap' sound, for example, quite unlike the 'churring noise' of the fern-owl, the 'tweet-tut' of the redstart or the 'eejip' of the spotted fly-catcher, and all feature in his sequence of poems about birds. Nor were their cries always the same, as evident in 'The Firetail's Nest', with its images of birds under threat:

> 'Tweet' pipes the robin as the cat creeps by
> Her nestling young that in the elderns lie,
> And then the bluecap tootles in its glee,
> Picking the flies from orchard apple tree,
> And 'pink' the chaffinch cries its well-known strain,
> Urging its kind to utter 'pink' again
> ('The Firetail's Nest', 1–6; *Poems*, 246.)

Clare also understood that birds were often 'hidden' because of the dangers posed by human beings, and so their cries might be warning-signals rather than jubilations or gestures of companionship. Fear could provoke a 'tweet' from the normally tuneful robin or a distinctly unmelodious 'pink' from the chaffinch, while the fire-tail, alarmed by the hedge-cutter close to her nest, 'pipes her 'tweet-tut' fears the whole day long' (14; *Poems*, 246). His poems nevertheless celebrated the wonders of what lay hidden from sight, recreating on the page what might not otherwise be seen by readers. Clare knew only too well that one of the functions of a bird's call was the defence of its territory, and his own sense of beleaguered isolation gave him special affinity with the local birds. If Shelley enlisted the nightingale for his *Defence of Poetry*, Clare brought forward an entire morning chorus to help perform the music of the unassuming.

Although birds were subject to many dangers, they also enjoyed a freedom prized by Clare, especially after his experience of being confined in an asylum. Birds were images of liberty, free to fly where they would, independent of any authority figures. They also offered songs that everyone could enjoy, irrespective of income. The 'fern-owl's cry', for example, intrigues the woodman on his way home from work just as the hidden nightingale's song in Keats's ode had perennially fascinated both emperor and clown. Indeed, the 'thrilling music' of Clare's nightingale was as delightful to the ploughman as to the poet and represented a kind of aesthetic and emotional pleasure open to everyone. Birdsong might appeal to men and women, rich and poor, young and old, and required no special training to appreciate, nor large fortune to enjoy. Indeed, part of its appeal for poets lay in its freedom from the materialism of modern society. Even the greediest getters and spenders could not possess the songs of the wild birds of the British countryside.

Clare's 'The Wren' is both a response to hearing the 'minstrelsy' of wrens and robins, and an expression of praise for the tiny birds 'Whose song hath crowds of happy memories brought' (4, 8). Bird-song was often linked to the reassurance of the long familiar: the wren that brings back memories to Clare was also prompting literary recollections, which are evident in the sonnet's Wordsworthian sentiments, despite its opening repudiation of 'poet's rhymes'. For Wordsworth, part of the wonder of bird-song lay in its consistency over many years – like the rainbow, it was one of the things that had made his heart leap as a boy and would continue to do so until old age deprived him of sensory pleasures. The sound of the cuckoo that delighted the adult poet, for example, was not from the same bird he had chased after as a schoolboy, but the call was identical nevertheless. As Keats acknowledged in 'Ode to a Nightingale', the individual singer was as mortal as those listening, but the song continued through generations.

When Wordsworth gave thanks for the 'hidden bird that sings', he was writing of his sister, but the metaphor chosen reflects a delight in birdsong that inspired him to write numerous lyrics. 'To the Cuckoo', published along with a number of other bird lyrics in *Poems, in Two Volumes*, in 1807, displayed a similar impulse to respond thankfully to the unexpected sound of an invisible bird. Like Keats (who was, of course, responding to Wordsworth as well as to the nightingale in his garden when he wrote his ode), Wordsworth emphasized the strange elusiveness of a creature so evidently present and yet always out of reach – 'Still longed for, never seen!' ('To the Cuckoo', 24). For the speaker, the cuckoo is 'No bird, but an invisible thing, / A voice, a mystery' (15–16). The difficulty of finding words to describe an object heard, but not seen, is manifest in the unspecificity of Wordsworth's 'invisible thing'. Even the generic 'Bird' doesn't seem quite right, as admitted in the first stanza – 'O Cuckoo! Shall I call the Bird, / Or but a wandering voice?' (3–4). Wordsworth later explained that his question reflected 'the memory that the cuckoo is almost perpetually heard throughout the season of spring, but seldom becomes an object of sight' (Preface to *Poems*, 1815). Since all that is known of the cuckoo is its distinctive call, it has acquired a name indicative of its most striking feature – not only in English but also German (kuckkuck), French (coucou), Italian (cucolo), Spanish (cuco), Dutch (koekoe), Hungarian (kukuk), Polish (kukulka) or Finnish (kaki). For writers exercised by the complex relationships between words, sounds and objects, the cuckoo held out a promise of union – only to slip away again as 'an invisible thing'. Wordsworth's poem therefore mimics the sound of the cuckoo, rather than attempting visualization. Its palindromic phrases ('O Cuckoo!' 'Shall I call', 'hill to hill') not only imitate the falling rhythm of the familiar birdsong, but also suggest the poet's desire to find a corresponding language. The rhythm and repetition within the lines at once evokes the cuckoo's presence and emphasises its absence – the hidden bird is everywhere and yet nowhere.

Throughout the poem, the cuckoo represents a paradoxical familiarity and unattainability, as the perennially futile search for the source of that most recognizable song is recalled with affection. For Wordsworth, failure to spot the cuckoo was no reason to be downcast, since its very elusiveness sustained its promise:

> To seek thee did I often rove
> Through woods and on the green;
> And thou wert still a hope, a love;
> Still longed for, never seen.
> (21–24)

Like Keats's nightingale, the Cuckoo has a transformative capacity, but rather than offer imaginative escape from a world of pain, it reveals the hidden wonders all around:

> O blessed Bird! The earth we pace
> Again appears to be
> An insubstantial, faery place;
> That is fit home for Thee!
> (29–32)

It is not that the earth we pace is unreal in comparison to the realm inhabited by the mysterious voice, but rather the cuckoo's presence means that this world is more remarkable than it might otherwise have seemed.

By re-examining the familiar experience of hearing a relatively common bird, Wordsworth shows that nothing should be taken for granted, that blessings may be received in the most unlikely forms. If the eye was dominant in conventional understandings of the world, sound had the capacity to startle new perceptions and challenge poets to find a language adequate to its mysterious power. When Coleridge tried to summarize Wordsworth's literary aims, he highlighted the capacity of his friend's poetry to alert people 'to the loveliness and the wonders of the world before us; an inexhaustible treasure, but for which in consequence of the film of familiarity and selfish solicitude we have eyes that see not, ears that hear not, and hearts that neither feel nor understand' (*Biographia Literaria*, II, 7). Coleridge was well aware that the revitalizing power of Wordsworth's poetry operated through the ear just as much as through the eye or emotions.

'To the Cuckoo' was published in the same volume as Wordsworth's 'To a Skylark', which was even more obviously concerned with representing bird-song on the page. The simple, repetitive language and innovative stanzaic form offer an acoustic image of the lark ascending, which is very different from the shorter, 'twofold', line patterns of 'To The Cuckoo':

> Up with me! Up with me into the clouds!
>   For thy song, Lark, is strong;
> Up with me, up with me into the clouds!
>   Singing, singing,
> With all the heav'ns about thee ringing,
>   Lift me, guide me, till I find
> That spot which seems so to thy mind!
>   ('To a Sky-Lark', 1–7;
>   *William Wordsworth*, 228)

The heavily rhymed, irregular verses are highly innovative and show Wordsworth's desire to experiment with the acoustic possibilities of poetic language. Although the opening line is a pentameter, the dactyls create a very different rhythm from a routine iambic, encouraging an unexpected stress on the first syllable of 'into' which continues the line's succession of liftings, like the movement of a lark. The mood continues with the short, trochaic 'Singing, singing', before slowing in the fourth line to suggest a momentary pause, as if to relish the echoing sky. Although the verse tries to keep pace with the lark's song, however, the speaker's earthbound condition gradually overcomes the sense of release, and the poem ends with rather less rapturous lines:

> I on the earth will go plodding on,
> By myself, chearfully, till the day is done.
> (28–9)

Despite the speaker's resolute cheerfulness, the image of the poet as plodder shows that not all the reflections inspired by Romantic song-birds were wholly reassuring.

The lark was the morning equivalent of the nightingale, an invisible spring of strikingly beautiful sounds. Although Shelley chose the traditional Miltonic nightingale as his figure for the poet in *A Defence of Poetry*, his own most famous bird lyric was addressed to the more Wordsworthian sky lark. It also drew on Wordsworth's 'The Green Linnet' and 'To the Cuckoo' for its opening apostrophe – 'Hail to thee, blithe spirit!' ('To a Skylark', 1, Wu, 1181). Shelley was inspired by both his reading and by his own first-hand experience of listening to birds, however, just as Keats had been when composing his ode in the previous year. For 'To a Skylark' was informed not just by reading Wordsworth, but also by the Italian larks Shelley had witnessed, flying higher and higher until 'their soft and still receding forms had at length vanished' (Wu, 1182). The brightness of the Italian summer sky gave rise to a glittering succession of images, though Shelley was as concerned as Wordsworth or Keats with the condition of hearing something imperceptible to the eye:

> Like a star of heaven
>   In the broad daylight
> Thou art unseen – but yet I hear thy shrill delight
> (18–20)

The sky lark, like the nightingale or the cuckoo, is heard but not seen. In Keats's Ode, the word 'unseen' may refer to the poet (flying from 'the world unseen', or unnoticed) or to the world ('unseen' in that it cannot be seen at night), as well as to the hidden bird that inspired the poem. For Shelley, the separation between the poet and the bird remains much more clearly marked, even though the poem keeps moving towards a fully realized identification. It is a poem that both claims and denies likeness, poised between exhilarating pursuit and doubtful pauses, full of desire and yearning. The very analogy between the bird and the morning star sets it high above the speaker, who can only hear and feel its presence:

> Keen as are the arrows
> Of that silver sphere,
> Whose intense lamp narrows
> In the white dawn clear,
> Until we hardly see – we feel that it is there.
> ('To a Skylark', 21–5; Wu, 1182)

The poem seems to fuse the senses by comparing the bird-song to a star, normally a visual image; but then it turns, as swiftly as the lark, to reveal that it is an image of the morning star, rendered invisible by daybreak. If the traditional nightingale was hidden in darkness, Shelley's Skylark is lost in the light.

It is also lost in words, however, for the comparison with the morning star is only one of many analogies drawn by the poet in response to the song. Like Wordsworth addressing the Cuckoo, Shelley begins by dismissing any conventional designation for the lark – 'Bird thou never wert', but this leaves open the question of how to define the 'blithe spirit'. It is 'Like a cloud of fire', 'Like an unbodied joy', 'Like a star of heaven', 'Like a poet', 'Like a high-born maiden', 'Like a glow-worm', 'Like a rose', like so many different things, in fact, that it gradually becomes plain that it resembles none of them very closely. As Shelley reaches for language sufficient to match the natural music of the bird, he seems engaged in the pursuit of something endlessly deferred, for ever eluding the perfect union of word, sound and thought. No wonder critical readings of Shelley in the 1980s, influenced by post-structuralism, focused so intensively on his language and linguistic theory. Self-consciousness over the difficulty of describing sound is an essential part of addressing a song-bird and, as the similes mount, the lark seems to ascend further and further from reach, just as it had in Wordsworth's poem. 'What thou art we know not; / What is most like thee?' (31–2) asks Shelley's speaker, effectively negating all the beautiful analogies drawn in the poem. How can words capture the astonishing sound of the bird? Whether this is a question tending towards despair or exhilaration depends a great deal on the individual reading, but it is certainly one that exercised the technical skills of the poet.

Wordsworth had attempted to render something of the lark's song through his unusual choice of verse and Shelley, too, experiments accordingly in his lyric. His build-up of short, trimeter lines to a strikingly extended hexameter mimics the sense of a song that is at once rising and vanishing. The reader's sense of the sky lark, after all, depends on the perspective chosen – are we nearer the singing bird or the listening poet? In the first four stanzas, the reader seems to be ascending with the lark, as the meter accentuates the syllables in 'high', 'spring', 'fire', 'wing', 'sing' and 'soar':

> Higher still and higher
>   From the earth thou springest
> Like a cloud of fire;
>   The blue deep thou wingest,
> And singest still dost soar, and soaring ever singest.
>   (6–10)

It is only when the 'I' of the speaker appears in line 20 that the perspective shifts back to the earth, while the lark seems to disappear in the shower of similes scattered by the poet as he attempts to find words true to what he hears.

'To a Skylark' is as much about the failure of language as it is about a bird:

> Better than all treasures
>   That in books are found –
> Thy skill to poet were, thou scorner of the ground!
>   (98–100)

If only the poet could create something of the skylark's song, his words would overwhelm an audience – just like the ideal poet / nightingale imagined in *A Defence of Poetry*:

> Teach me half the gladness
>   That thy brain must know,
> Such harmonious madness
>   From my lips would flow
> The world should listen then, as I am listening now.
>   (101–105)

If the lark's 'unpremeditated art' excels all the treasures to be found in books, however, there seems little hope that any poet will ever match its easy accomplishment. The closing stanza of 'To a Skylark' recalls Wordsworth's lines on the fate of poets in 'Resolution and Independence', 'We poets in our youth begin in gladness / But there of comes in the end despondency and madness' (48–49, O'Neill and Mahoney, 158). Although 'To a Skylark' seeks to transmute 'madness' into harmony, the ominous recollection of the likely future for young, idealistic poets makes Shelley's dream of entrancing the world seem far from certain.

The year before he wrote 'To a Skylark', Shelley had been provoked into a furious denunciation of the British Government by the bloody suppression of a peaceful demonstration at Peterloo Fields in Manchester in August 1819. His poem, 'The Mask of Anarchy', composed within weeks of the massacre, had appealed directly to the people of England to 'Rise like lions after slumber / In unvanquishable number' ('Mask of Anarchy', 368–9, Wu, 1175), in the cause of Liberty. The very power of the poem, and its explicit political message, meant that no one would dare publish it, however, not even Shelley's close friend, the radical publisher, Leigh Hunt. The difficulty of achieving a world in which people 'should listen' was not to be underestimated: the 'should' of Shelley's 'Skylark' is as wistful as it is commanding. Failure to find a public voice for overtly political poetry created another dimension for Shelley's struggle with the difficulty of linguistic expression. Although his emphasis on the sound of poetry was partly aesthetic and philosophical, it also reflected a frustration with reaching the British public through direct arguments. The image of the poet as a nightingale or unseen musician probably derived as much from feelings of unjust neglect by contemporary society as from Shelley's admiration for the great poets of the past.

Despite disappointments over publication and sales, Shelley nevertheless maintained an optimistic note in his poetry that tended to be accentuated rather than silenced by the doubts. Unlike Milton, who consoled himself in the midst of physical and political darkness with an unshakable religious faith, Shelley rejected the consolations of Christianity and sought a better world through secular enlightenment. Where Milton had adopted the image of birdsong to celebrate the redemptive power of inner, divine light, Shelley exalted the sky lark as a poet transfigured by brilliance from an unspecified source:

> Like a poet hidden
> In the light of thought,
> Singing hymns unbidden,
> Till the world is wrought
> To sympathy with hopes and fears it heeded not.
>   (36–40)

'The light of thought' may issue from the individual poet, or from the collective wisdom of generations, all contributing to the improvement of human society. When read in conjunction with *A Defence of Poetry*, it becomes clear that both meanings are probably present in 'To a Skylark', since Shelley was developing ideas about the mutual enlightenment of writers and their age, and though he saw Milton standing 'alone illuminating an age unworthy of him', he attributed the 'electric life' burning in the words of his own great contemporaries to 'the spirit of the age' (Defence, *Poems and Prose*, 160, 278). Poets were at once heralds and participants, generators and receivers of the light of thought.

Italian light offered Shelley an image for secular enlightenment, but his praise of the skylark still drew upon the Miltonic ideal of the poet hidden from sight and moved to 'unpremeditated' devotional song. The lyric overflows with religious language – of the heavenly spirit, of hymn-singing, of divine rapture – as if Shelley could only find words approximating to the ravishing sounds of the song-bird by delving into remembered literary and religious traditions. Though celebrating a song encountered first-hand in a foreign country, his own language is suffused with Milton, Wordsworth, Shakespeare and even Keats – and indeed, assumes much of its resonance from such echoes. To see Shelley as merely repeating the achievements of other poets would, however, be to misunderstand his work. The purpose of his *Defence of Poetry* is to demonstrate the centrality of art to society in all ages, and so the great writers of the past are enlisted as allies and models, not as opponents for the newcomer. Dante, for example, is presented as 'the first awakener of entranced Europe', each of his words being 'a spark, a burning atom of inextinguishable thought', many still 'pregnant with a lightning which has yet found no conductor' (*Defence*, Wu, 1192).

In Shelley's account, great poetry had the capacity for infinite regeneration, not just because the full meaning of a poem changed through successive ages, but also because it created the universe 'anew', after it had been obliterated 'by the recurrence of impressions blunted by reiteration' (Wu, 1197). In other words, poetry renewed the entire world by stripping 'away the veil of familiarity' (Wu, 1197) – a view very similar to those expressed elsewhere by Coleridge and Blake. As long as a poem could startle audiences into seeing the world as if for the first time, it did not matter if the materials were as old as chaos. Shelley's attempt to find a proper analogy for the skylark need not, therefore, be read as an exercise in increasing desperation, but rather as a way of awakening the reader to the 'wonder of our being'. Familiar images, of the rose, the star or the maiden in her tower, are rendered unfamiliar by the unexpected parallels being drawn until, cumulatively, they bewilder the reader into a state of delight. By the end of the poem, we are still not clear how a song can resemble any of the images that have been conjured up and abandoned, but an overall sense of 'All that ever was / Joyous, and clear and fresh' (59–60) remains, even though the bird's voice is still unknown.

When Shelley imagined the world listening, just as he listened to the lark, his analogy did not suggest the experience of receiving a carefully argued, rational argument, nor indeed, a clear political view. What the conclusion of 'To a Skylark' suggests is something closer to the idea of poetry in the *Defence*: of a mysterious, quasi-divine 'instrument of moral good', that encourages 'a going out of our own nature and an identification of ourselves with the beautiful which exists in thought, action, or person, not our own' (Wu, 1190). It was not that Shelley, in celebrating the non-verbal outpourings of the skylark, was despairing of poetry, but rather that he saw an unexpected relation between the beauty of the bird's music and his own chosen art. His lyric poem is just as much an unbidden hymn as Milton's more explicitly devotional invocation to the third book of *Paradise Lost* and its power was equally unquantifiable.

Sound and Sense

When Wordsworth and Shelley addressed song birds, they were also addressing the forms and meters of lyric poetry. In their poems to the sky lark and the cuckoo, the representation of sound on the page is explored as an idea and as a method. Aural experimentation was made easier by their choice of verse, because the lyric allows for greater variety in line lengths, rhyme-schemes and stanzaic form than many other poetic genres. As we saw in Chapter 4, revitalization of inherited genres was a defining feature of the Romantic period and so the various transformations of the lyric were part of a far-reaching reconsideration of what could be done with particular kinds. In the preface to his *Poems* of 1815, Wordsworth defined 'The Lyrical' (which includes the Hymn, Ode, Elegy, Song and Ballad), as a kind of poem for which 'an accompaniment of music is indispensable', though he rapidly explained that his own lyrics' required nothing more than an animated or impassioned recitation, adapted to the subject.' Since 'Poems cannot read themselves', Wordsworth was deeply aware of the role of the reader in modulating 'the music of the poem', making clear in his discussion that a poem's meter should not be so strong and inflexible that any individual interpretation was precluded. The poem's 'music', must be enjoyed in concord with its 'sense'. The individual reader's modulation was, indeed, part of the complexity of poetry, which Wordsworth had already discussed in his preface to *Lyrical Ballads*, when explaining his preference for writing poetry rather than prose. In the earlier essay, he had pondered at some length on the 'continual and regular impulses of pleasurable surprise' arising from 'metrical language' and the way in which the movement of meter imparted 'passion to the words' (Preface to *Lyrical Ballads*, Wu, 503). Far from being incidental to the poem's meaning, meter was a vital part of it, at once intensifying and complicating the feelings denoted by the words.

For Wordsworth, true poetic language spoke to the reader's emotions, understanding and senses. As he explored the workings of the imagination in his preface to *Poems*, 1815, he devoted considerable attention to the effects of sound, analysing a line from 'Resolution and Independence' to illustrate his point: 'Over his own sweet voice the Stock-dove broods' (5). Wordsworth glosses the line by defending his choice of the verb 'brood' for the dove's action, in place of the more conventional 'coo', explaining that it helps to suggest 'the manner in which the bird reiterates and prolongs her soft note, as if delighting herself to listen to it, and participating of a still and quiet satisfaction, like that which may be inseparable from the continuous process of incubation' (Preface to *Poems*, 1815). Wordsworth's choice embraces not only the simpler, onomatopeic 'oo' sound of the dove, but also a host of subtler observations arising from the imaginative sympathy of one who has brooded on the nature of the bird. Though he does not mention the Miltonic suggestion of the Holy Spirit, which 'dove-like sat'st brooding' over the opening of *Paradise Lost*, ideas of the great original creation and the accompanying sacred song are also implicit in his choice. Wordsworth's anthropomorphic reading of the dove also has parallels with his definition of poetry as 'emotion recollected in tranquillity' (Preface to *Lyrical Ballads*, Wu, 504), in the combination of immediate delight and the quieter satisfactions gained through the passage of time. The self-delighting stock-dove is a perfect objective correlative for the poet at the opening of 'Resolution and Independence'.

A poem's sound, as Pope had advised a century before, was indeed, an echo of the sense. But it was far more than an echo for Wordsworth, because the vivid perceptions of the senses deepened as the imagination gathered related thoughts, ideas, and feelings, fusing them into rhythmic forms that could offer readers a pleasure much more profound. And hence the hope expressed in 'A Poet's Epitaph' that, unlike 'the mere Proseman', the poet

> murmurs near the running brooks,
> A music sweeter than their own.
> (39–40; *William Wordsworth*, 126)

Wordsworth's preoccupation with the distinctions between prose and poetry helped to draw attention to the importance of sound in literary works, and those who read his extensive prose prefaces were led to explore the questions he had identified so authoritatively. The publication of *Biographia Literaria* in 1817 made Wordsworth's views on meter seem even more significant, because Coleridge spent so much time and energy on refuting the arguments of the preface to *Lyrical Ballads*. Entire chapters were devoted to comparing 'Metrical Composition and Prose' or the 'neutral style, common to Prose and Poetry', as Coleridge demolished Wordsworth's metrical theories while praising 'the music of his own thoughts' (*Biographia Literaria*, II, 69). As discussed in Chapter 5, Coleridge was distancing himself from the preface to *Lyrical Ballads*, but in devoting his critical energies to the same questions, he brought them firmly back into the literary debates of the second decade of the nineteenth century.

For the younger poets emerging in the wake of Wordsworth and Coleridge, such technical literary questions increasingly became part of their own poetry. Poems about writing poems were as characteristic of the Romantic movement as of the Modernist. Far from limiting themselves to the purposes of poetry or its social and philosophical justification, Romantic poets frequently considered technical questions, including acoustics. In *Don Juan*, for example, the demands of the rhyme scheme are emphasized from the start, as the narrator, distinguishing his epic method from that of classical predecessors, announces that his opening cost 'half an hour in spinning' (*Don Juan*, I, 7). Instead of coming as naturally as Keatsian leaves to a tree, Byron's lines had been carefully spun by a poet keen to remind readers of his presence. The stanza that had taken him half an hour certainly lives up to its expectations, with its challenging triple rhymes – 'city', 'pity', 'pretty' – and memorable concluding couplet:

> Don Juan's parents lived beside a river,
> A noble stream, and call'd the Quadalquivir.
> (*Don Juan*, I, 8, O'Neill and Mahoney, 265)

Not every poet would wish to be confronted with 'Quadalquivir' at the end of a rhyming stanza. Spectacular rhymes of this kind nevertheless provide one of the principal pleasures of Byron's poem and once the reader becomes accustomed to the ottava rima, anticipation of the rhymes becomes a major impetus through the long, digressive narrative. The surprise of finding a line ending with 'homily', for example, invites a rapid mental search for any possible rhyme, which can only to be answered by Byron's own choices of 'Romilly' and 'anomaly' (I, 15). For the poet who had the audacity to rhyme 'Plato' with 'potato', 'Aristotle' with 'bottle', 'goddesses' with 'bodices' or 'intellectual' with 'hen-pecked you all', anything seems possible.

Though much of Byron's brilliant rhyming has comic or satiric purpose, *Don Juan* also raises serious literary questions about the relationship between sound and sense. In Canto IX, for example, Byron describes rhyme as the 'good old steamboat which keep verses moving /'Gainst reason' (IX, 74), thus reminding readers that the progress of his poem depended as much on the rhyme-scheme as on the narrative, themes or intellectual comment. Indeed, many stanzas seem created especially for satisfactions offered by their elaborate rhymes, as if the poet has taken a word and challenged himself to fit the ottava rima around it. 'Quadalquivir' is a good example of the unlikely rhyme words in Byron's poem, but we might also consider the difficulties of 'Cadiz', 'problem', 'O'Reilly', 'juventa', 'Quarterly', 'pyramid', 'Cazzani' or 'Corydon', all of which find an acoustic twin or even triplets over the course of *Don Juan*. Throughout the poem, the adventures of the protagonist are frequently subordinated to the cleverness of his creator, whose efforts often seem every bit as engaging.

At times, however, the joke is on the poet, who is presented as the servant rather than master of his form:

> And then he swore, and sighing, on he slipped
>   A pair of trousers of flesh-coloured silk;
> Next with a virgin zone he was equipped,
>   Which girt a slight chemise as white as milk.
> But tugging on his petticoat he tripped,
>   Which, as we say, or as the Scotch say, whilk
> (The rhyme obliges me to this; sometimes
> Monarchs are less imperative than rhymes)
>
>   (*Don Juan*, V, 77)

Manuscript evidence indicates that this stanza caused considerable difficulty, since the trousers were initially 'fine crimson satin', which means the joke on the final choice of 'whilk' (as dictated by silk) probably results from some genuine frustration. The poetic difficulties emphasized in the couplet are nevertheless a perfect match for Juan's discomfort over being forced into ill-fitting clothes, and as the sentence continues over the stanza break, it becomes applicable to both narrator and protagonist:

> Whilk, which (or what you please) was owing to
>   His garment's novelty, and his being awkward.
>   (V, 78)

Forcing men into awkward garments inevitably resulted in the occasional trip-up. Since Byron's purpose was to convey a sense of resistance being overpowered by external pressures, the apparent faltering of his verse is thus a perfect echo of the sense of the passage, even if initially it suggests loss of control.

Don Juan is a brilliant poetic performance, whose colloquial tone suggests easy spontaneity even though the complexity of the stanza tells a different story. In the ninth Canto, when Byron rebukes himself for digressing into philosophical speculation, his tone approaches that of a dramatic soliloquy:

> But I am apt to grow too metaphysical:
>   'The time is out of joint,' – and so am I;
> I quite forget this poem's merely quizzical,
>   And deviate into matters rather dry.
> I ne'er decide what I shall say, and this I call
>   Much too poetical. Men should know why
> They write, and for what end; but, note or text,
> I never know the word which will come next.
>
> So on I ramble, now and then narrating,
>   Now pondering:
>   (IX, 41, 42)

Although he claims to be uncertain about his poem's progress, the style is remarkably controlled for a ramble. Often comments such as this are as much jokes on contemporary aesthetics as on his own practice, for this stanza is strongly reminiscent of Shelley's rather more serious account of the unpredictability of poetic composition ('Poetry is not like reasoning, a power to be exerted according to the determination of the will. A man cannot say "I will compose poetry"' (*Defence*, Wu, 1195). Byron was at

In the light of these lines, 'The Tyger' may suggest that once people have dared to seize the fire, they will cease to be the willing prisoners of conventional thought.

Blake's 'Tyger', however, might also be presenting creative power as something overwhelming and terrifying, as opposed to the cosy, reassuring pastoral imagery of a piper, singing about a Lamb. If Blake's vision of the divine encompasses the 'dread grasp' that might 'dare its deadly terrors grasp', it seems to look forward to Gerard Manley Hopkins at his most intense. The poet who celebrated 'Energy', 'Desire', 'Pride', 'Lust' and 'Wrath' as divine in *The Marriage of Heaven and Hell*, might express his idea of God more fully in 'The Tyger' than in *Songs of Innocence*. At the same time, Blake's questions point as readily to the creator of the poem as to the Creator of the world, for he who made 'The Tyger' had already made 'The Lamb' (O'Neill and Mahoney, 24). Whether the poem suggests pride in his creation or horror is unclear, since none of the questions are answered by the poet. The mesmeric beauty of the lyric might make the idea of the creator dreading his own creation seem absurd, and yet such a fear surfaces frequently in the Romantic period, most obviously in *Frankenstein*. 'What the hand dare seize the fire?' may refer to God's great original act of creation, or to the artist's inspiration, or to the craftsman working in the printing press, or to Prometheus, stealing the fire of heaven. It is usually assumed, on the basis of Blake's other works, that any Promethean rebel must be a positive figure, but in a poem made almost entirely of questions, it is dangerous to feel too certain of anything.

Given the apparent discrepancy between the image and the poem, a sense of unease about the plate might not be inappropriate. This is not to suggest necessarily that Blake was disappointed by his illuminated poem, but it might reflect some of the artist's frustration about representing a creature known largely through reading. Modern readers are generally familiar with tigers from childhood, whether from zoos and safari parks, computers, picture books, nature documentaries, films or advertisements. For Blake and his contemporaries, however, the tiger was known largely from stories, Biblical texts, travel books or natural histories – in other words, more distantly and much less visually. There were tigers in the zoo at the Tower of London, but the conditions in which they were kept meant that they hardly seemed the terrifying beasts of legend. Whether Blake was reflecting ironically on the poor creatures imprisoned in the Tower, or on his own difficulty in finding a satisfactory visual image for something that lived so magnificently in the mind, remains unanswerable – like so many aspects of this poem. The images e poem, the chanting rhythm of the verse, seem to create something quite independent of any tiger existing in the natural world, so even considering the practical business of the artist's reference seems somewhat wide of the mark. It is possible nevertheless to see the smiling or melancholic cat (depending on the copy viewed) as an ironic comment on the energy so forcefully conveyed through the words above. In the more dejected versions, the tiger might even seem defeated by the ubiquitous 'mind-forged manacles', a dark comment on what man had made of God's astonishing creation. But the image may, after all, have been a Blakean joke.

From Vision to Volume

Blake's determination to present his poems with such individuality was part of his resistance to any kind of imposed system. *The Marriage of Heaven and Hell* contains a 'Memorable Fancy' describing 'a printing-house in Hell', where the wonderful process of creation involves 'an Eagle with wings and feathers of air', 'Eagle-like men' and 'Lions of flaming fire' (Wu, 212). After all the 'clearing', 'adorning', 'raging' and 'melting metal into living fluids', however, the final chamber is occupied by Men, who 'took the books and were arranged in libraries.' Once published, it seems, the creative process is over, and what remains is only a lifeless shell. While Blake is often seen to be representing his own printing methods here, it is also possible to read the 'Fancy' as an allegory for modern publication, which takes the living thoughts of artists and poets and turns them into standardized blocks of printed paper, tightly bound and identical to each other. With its imagery of caves and heat, it could also be an extended metaphor for the creation of a poem, taking fire in the mind, but cooling as it goes through the processes of composition and eventually reaches readers. The introduction to *Innocence*, for example, can be read similarly, as the laughing child in the cloud of inspiration vanishes once the poet begins to write, staining the clear waters with his ink. As discussed in Chapter 1, Shelley described the mind in creation 'as a fading cold' awakened to 'transitory brightness' and saw poetry as an attempt to arrest the moment of translucence (*'Defence'*, Wu, 1195). The very act of composition, however, meant that the inspiration was 'already on the decline', so even the greatest poetry was 'probably a feeble shadow of the original conception of the poet' (Wu, 1195). The artist might be compelled to record the visionary moment, but the urge to find words and communicate the experience was as destructive as creative.

Blake found his own way to combat the sense of collapsing into words and standard typography by making each of his books unique and glowing with color. For those who had to be content with more normal methods of preserving and sharing their private inspiration, the sense of producing only feeble shadows seems to have descended with dismaying frequency. Indeed, the gap between inspiration and printed page became a recurrent theme in Romantic poetry, enabling what was often an intensely private anxiety to become representative of the larger cultural shift towards a modern print culture. As internal experience was externalised on the printed page and sold to anonymous readers, the marvellous, original moment seemed irredeemably distant. And yet, many poets still sought to recreate the visionary moment in words that might enable others to share the sudden, intoxicating, lightness of being.

Often the intensity of vision was conveyed most powerfully through the expression of loss, as readers were made to sympathize with feelings of emptiness and aftermath, and so imagine just what might have caused such a reaction. The very conventions of modern publication were easily adapted to such strategies, because a printed page offered such obvious contrasts between prose and verse. In an oral recitation, it is impossible to listen to the words of a poem and the editorial annotation at the same time, but on the page, the words of the speaker and an editor can be seen simultaneously. When awareness of the gap between inspiration and composition is important to a poem, the visual reminder of the poem as an object to be interpreted contributes quietly to the overall reading experience. It is surely no coincidence that in a period when new ideas about the creative process became such an important preoccupation for writers, the conventions for printing poetry increasingly included notes, prefaces and epigraphs. Such details were there to help readers understand the poem, but they also reflected a later stage of the poet's relationship with the work – reflective, interpretative and even directive. The printed page could offer an illusion of spontaneous emotion, while also emphasizing the poet's capacity for recollection. As discussed in Chapter 5, details dependent on print might be read elegiacally, as nails in the coffin of an older oral tradition, but they are also signs of a new kind of literature, in which the complicated, multiplicity of ideas made possible by technology transformed the relationship between the poet, text and reader.

Even within the constraints of the printed book, there were ways of suggesting that the poem on the page was only 'a feeble shadow' of whatever might have illuminated the poet's mind. Such a suggestion was, of course, rhetorically effective, since it both encouraged sympathy for the bereft poet and contributed to the sense of his astonishing powers. When Coleridge published 'Kubla Khan', for example, he was able to convey a dual image of himself as both a quasi-prophetic figure, astonished, and therefore astonishing, *and* as a heroic failure, appealing in his confused abandonment. The poem captures this duality in its final section, as the speaker recalls 'A damsel with a dulcimer / In a vision once I saw', before uttering a longing to 'revive within… / Her symphony and song' ('Kubla Khan', 37–8; 42–3; O'Neill and Mahoney, 187). The sense of loss in turn promotes a desire to create, but this brings with it an awareness of audience – and isolation:

> I would build that dome in air,
> That sunny dome! those caves of ice!
> And all who heard should see them there,
> And all should cry, Beware! Beware!
> His flashing eyes, his floating hair!
> Weave a circle round him thrice,
> And close your eyes with holy dread,
> For he on honey-dew hath fed,
> And drunk the milk of Paradise.
>
> (46–54)

Inspiration seems at once something to be desired and dreaded, the poet a figure commanding admiration and fear. In his isolation and uncertainty (conveyed through the use of conditionals – 'could I', 'I would', 'all should'), he also comes across as one crippled with self-doubt, conscious that his thoughts of future glory are as insubstantial as the memory of his lost vision.

Since the words of 'Kubla Khan' are so mysterious, its imagery of sunny domes, honey-dew and Abyssinian maids quite remote from early nineteenth-century Britain, the suggestion that the speaker might represent the modern poet might not be immediately persuasive. However, when the poem was published in 1816, Coleridge prefaced it with an account of its composition in the summer of 1797. He describes 'The Author, then in ill health', recuperating in a Devon farmhouse, where one afternoon he took a strong painkiller and fell fast asleep over the book he was reading: *Purchas's Pilgrimage*. Coleridge even includes the sentence he read before dropping off ('Here the Khan Kubla commanded a palace to be built, and a stately garden thereunto. And thus ten miles of fertile ground were inclosed with a wall' (O'Neill and Mahoney, 185)). As he slept, he recalls images rose up before him as *things*, with a parallel production of the correspondent expressions, without any sensation or consciousness of effort. On awaking he appeared to have a distinct recollection of the whole, and taking his pen, ink, and paper, instantly and eagerly wrote down the lines that are here preserved.

(185)

With the ill-timed arrival of 'a person on business from Porlock', however, all spontaneous composition ceased, leaving the poet with only scattered recollections of his dream and the most famous example of poeticus interruptus in English literary history. Apart from the lines already caught and transcribed, 'all the rest had passed away like the images on the surface of a stream into which a stone has been cast, but, alas! without the after restoration of the latter!' (185). What Coleridge was now allowing into print was apparently a fragment of some much larger visionary narrative – the precious record, snatched before oblivion descended. As a way of whetting the appetite of readers, the account could hardly have been better.

While the details about Coleridge's reading, the precise location of the farmhouse, the matter-of-fact reference to the businessman's home town combine to make this seem an authentic memory and help to explain the strangeness of the opening lines, the passage is also creating a sense of something beyond comprehension. The beginning of 'Kubla Khan' is so arresting that the idea of something even more magnificent is almost too much to conceive. And yet, the prose passage works with the poetry to conjure up some unrealized imaginative experience that can never again be seen or told. The preface ends with a quotation from one of Coleridge's own poems, 'The Picture', as if to underline the limitations of prose and thus prepare readers for a rare glimpse of the enchanting 'phantom-world' offered in 'Kubla Khan' (185).

Christabel, and Other Poems, 1816

The full title given to the poem published in 1816 was 'Kubla Khan: Or, A Vision in a Dream. A Fragment' – so readers understood at once that what they were about to encounter was only the surviving record of something insubstantial. The slim volume in which 'Kubla Khan' first appeared also included 'The Pains of Sleep' – introduced by Coleridge as 'a fragment of a very different character' – and the unfinished narrative, 'Christabel.' It was an unassuming volume for such a remarkable group of poems, but oddly suited to the sense of fragmentation and haphazard survival that was emphasized in the poet's commentary. As modern readers, it is helpful to consider the original presentation of the poems, to see whether Coleridge's prefatory remarks are as much part of the text as Blake's illuminations for his *Songs*, and whether the choice of companion poems might affect the interpretation of each one.

Coleridge described 'Kubla Khan' as a 'fragment', published at the request of a fellow poet, rather than as a complete work, written for readers. That he did not identify the other poet as Byron only added to the mystery. Throughout the preface, Coleridge seemed to be evading responsibility for the text, dismissing it first as a 'psychological curiosity', and then, in the more elaborate account, as automatic writing following a dream. Since 'Kubla Khan' – and the other two poems – could easily be associated with opium or with repressed sexual feelings, some unease about publication may have resulted from understandable, personal reasons. The prefatory emphasis on fragmentation is as much rhetorical as autobiographical, however. Ideas of the poem's incompleteness and mysterious origins contribute brilliantly to its hold over the reader, for at every turn, things seem not fully explained – and all the more compelling as a result:

> In Xanadu did Kubla Khan
> A stately pleasure-dome decree:
> Where Alph, the sacred river, ran
> Through caverns measureless to man
>   Down to a sunless sea.
> So twice five miles of fertile ground
> With walls and towers were girdled round
> And there were gardens bright with sinuous rills,
> Where blossomed many an incense-bearing tree;
> And here were forests ancient as the hills,
> Enfolding sunny spots of greenery.
>   (1–11)

The Khan's decree appears to be carried out instantaneously, but instead of describing the pleasure dome, the poem dwells on the perimeter walls, the gardens, hills and forests. The dome never appears directly, but always at a remove, in a decree, as a shadow, floating midway on the waves, or as 'a miracle of rare device, / A sunny pleasure-dome with caves of ice!' The combination of sun and ice is as disconcerting as 'A savage place! As holy and enchanted / As e'er beneath a waning moon was haunted / By woman wailing for her demon-lover!' How the deep, romantic chasm can be 'holy and enchanted' remains baffling, while the spectacular force with which the 'sacred river' is flung from such a place makes its origins seem as diabolical as divine. The powerful sexual imagery of the woman wailing, the seething turmoil, the earth's panting breath and the bursting fountain, all combine to suggest some vast orgasmic intensity, which is somewhat at odds with conventional ideas of the sacred.

Though the opening specifies a circumference of 'twice five miles', the poem conjures up ideas of uncontainable vastness in its 'caverns measureless to man', 'mighty fountain' and 'huge fragments'. The irregular rhymes and line lengths suggest a struggle to bring order to forces far greater than man, while the sudden disappearance of the dome makes the effort seem both heroic and futile. 'That sunny dome! Those caves of ice!' We never discover what they are, what they look like, how they might feel to the touch, and are left, with the speaker, haunted by a vision that we have never quite been able to visualise. How to express the inexpressible? 'Kubla Khan' succeeds better than most Romantic attempts, but it does so by emphasizing its own failure and incompletion. The prefatory account of its composition is at once a rhetorical trope of false modesty and a careful guide to reading a poem that might otherwise seem too strange to be anything more than a dazzling fantasy. By dismissing it as a 'psychological curiosity', Coleridge was artfully prompting ways of reading the poem which anticipated Freud by almost a century.

Coleridge's prefatory emphasis on psychology and personal history mean that a poem that might otherwise seem quite remote from the experience of readers, with its evocation of Medieval Mongolia and inexplicable shifts from image to image, can be interpreted as a dream vision. Not only does this possibility offer traditional interpretative approaches to those familiar with the dream visions of Chaucer and his contemporaries, but it also opens the way to more individual responses for any reader who has ever had a dream. Jennifer Ford has shown in her study of *Coleridge and Dreaming* that the eighteenth century saw intense speculation over the nature of dreams, as traditional ideas about their prophetic or supernatural origins persisted, alongside theories of natural causes, relating to diet or waking experience. As Enlightenment philosophers probed the workings of the mind, energetic debate continued over whether dreams were generated from the individual's experience, whether they represented a different kind of thought from that of the conscious mind, or whether they were sent from some external power, divine or malignant. For Coleridge, who was not only extremely well read in ancient and modern literature, but also prone to vivid day dreams and disturbing nightmares, the issue was of pressing personal concern. Inclusion of the recollection of drifting off into a semi-drugged stupor meant that the nature of dreaming was already in the mind of his readers, before they were transported to Xanadu.

If read in the company of 'Christabel' and 'The Pains of Sleep', 'Kubla Khan' may seem an artistic exploration of the workings of the unconscious mind, especially given the prefatory description of it as a 'psychological curiosity'. Since 'The Pains of Sleep' is explicitly describing nightmares, readers of the 1816 volume were encouraged to read 'Kubla Khan', the 'Vision in a Dream', as part of the same poet's tempestuous unconscious experience. The night-terrors of 'The Pains of Sleep' are not conveyed through the kind of images represented in 'Kubla Khan', but remain largely abstract:

> the fiendish crowd
> Of shapes and thoughts that tortured me:
> A lurid light, a trampling throng,
> Sense of intolerable wrong,
> And whom I scorned, those only strong!
> (16–20; O'Neill and Mahoney, 233)

However, the idea of things not fully realized, or at least withheld from the reader ('Sense of intolerable wrong', 'Deeds to be hid which were not hid') is strongly reminiscent of the rhetorical strategies of 'Kubla Khan'. The confusion of the afflicted speaker in 'The Pains of Sleep' also serves as an oblique commentary on the companion poem. For although the preface to 'Kubla Khan' points to the dream's origins in the poet's waking experience, the poem itself, with its inexplicable creation, supernatural imagery, prophetic voices and vision of the damsel, suggests more mysterious sources – a possibility strengthened by the other poems in the volume.

The preface to 'Kubla Khan' describes 'The Pains of Sleep' as a 'fragment of a very different character, describing with equal fidelity the dream of pain and disease', but again, the poem itself is more ambiguous. The cause of the speaker's nightmares remains bewildering, because of the immediacy of the horrifying experience – 'all confused I could not know / Whether I suffered, or I did' (28–9). The repetition of the word 'fiendish', however, and the desperate cry, 'But wherefore, wherefore, fall on me?' (50)

nevertheless suggests some external, malevolent force, against which the speaker is powerless. This might well be interpreted by many modern readers as a way of representing drug addiction or psychological illness, but for a deeply religious poet living in an age where the nature of dreaming was open to numerous theories, the possibility of dreams being 'punishments' (43) or even diabolical visitations was only too real. The sense of guilt in the poem is palpable, but the mental anguish is so vividly conveyed that the relationship between the speaker's daylight actions and his dreams remain inexplicit.

Although 'Christabel', the title poem in the 1816 collection, is not presented as a dream, the detail of its original composition in 1797 – the year of 'Kubla Khan' – and its dramatic midnight opening help to suggest connections with the other poems in the volume. Coleridge offered no clues about the inspiration of 'Christabel' in his 1816 preface to the poem, being more concerned to combat charges of imitation, since his meter had been put to very popular use by Scott in 1805 in *The Lay of the Last Minstrel*. The companion poems in the 1816 volume, however, enhanced the dreaminess of the strange Gothic narrative, and thus invited psychological rather than sceptical interpretations. By 1816, the craze for Gothic had abated, as Jane Austen realized when considering whether or not to revise the manuscript of *Northanger Abbey* for publication at this time. Coleridge may well have feared that 'Christabel' had missed its moment, but by publishing it with the 'psychological curiosity', 'Kubla Khan', and 'The Pains of Sleep', he was able to play to the new taste for intense psychological drama, which Byron would exploit a year later in *Manfred*, as well as suggesting dimensions to the poem that may not have been so visible in the 1790s. The unsettling tone of 'Christabel' and its arresting present tense are certainly easier to accept once readers suspend any expectations of a realistic poem. As it continues, its weirdness becomes more and more apparent, but thoughts of dreams only add to the sense that anything is possible in this unfamiliar, moonlit scene.

In keeping with the other poems in the volume, 'Christabel' is filled with half-articulated suggestions to readers. We notice that the mastiff bitch is 'toothless' (7), that 'naught was green upon the oak / But moss and rarest mistletoe' (33–4; O'Neill and Mahoney, 207), though we are not given any real clues as to what these details mean. That the narrator knows more than the reader is allowed to hear is clear very early on, with the offhand comment on the dog's 'sixteen short howls' – 'Some say, she sees my lady's shroud' (13). Which Lady is this, we may well wonder? The sounds in the eerie, moonlit wood are conjured up in quick succession, but because we cannot see what is there, we are left to guess. If the mastiff is howling, the owls hooting, the cock crowing drowsily, Christabel sighing, what is it that is moaning 'as near as near can be' (39)? Christabel 'cannot tell', and nor can the reader, because the narrator chooses to delay any explanation and thereby build suspense.

The pun on 'telling' becomes clearer later in the poem, when Geraldine is giving Christabel the account of how she has come to be beneath the oak, after her abduction, 'Whither they went I cannot tell' (99). At this point, the reader cannot be sure whether Geraldine means that she does not know where the warriors went, or that she is unable, or unwilling, to say any more to Christabel. It is not until the horrifying climax of the first part of the tale, however, that the full force of the connection between knowing and speaking becomes plain, as Geraldine undresses:

> Beneath the lamp the lady bowed,
> And slowly rolled her eyes around;
> Then drawing in her breath aloud,
> Like one that shuddered, she unbound
> The cincture from beneath her breast:
> Her silken robe, and inner vest,
> Dropped to her feet, and full in view,
> Behold! her bosom and half her side –
> A sight to dream of, not to tell!
> O shield her! shield sweet Christabel!
>   (245–54)

The refusal to describe what the loosened robe has revealed not only brings home the narrator's persistent evasiveness, but also sends the reader's imagination racing. We cannot tell what Geraldine's body might be like, and so the idea of its being something 'to dream of' depends on the imaginative experience of the individual reader. The bedroom scene might titillate or terrify, conjuring up a beautiful, inviting, woman or that of a grotesque monster. In the manuscript, Coleridge had been much more graphic, writing 'Behold! Her bosom and half her side / Are lean and old and foul of hue', but the reticence of the published version, leaving everything to the imagination, offers far more varied possibilities. Once the scene shifts to the following morning in Part II, Christabel's own inability to speak about what has happened intensifies the reader's speculation and, with it, the contradictory impulses to know and not to know. We are placed in the strange situation of knowing more than Sir Leoline and yet, not really understanding anything.

Christabel's silence raises further doubts about the narrator's power, since it now seems that the uncertainties and gaps in the story may follow from the narrator's own glimpse of forbidden secrets – and consequent inability to tell. The protagonist's difficulty in relating her experience can be interpreted in numerous ways – from the silence of the rape victim or traumatised witness, to the fairytale motif of the enchanted tongue:

> For what she knew she could not tell,
> O'er-mastered by the mighty spell.
> (619–20)

When the poem is read along with 'Kubla Khan' and 'The Pains of Sleep', it may seem another study of the workings of the unconscious mind, as Christabel is haunted by nightmarish images, though unable to recapture quite what she has seen. The details in lines 457–8, 'Again she saw that bosom old / Again she felt that bosom cold' seem to recall the manuscript of the poem, but in the published version, which omitted the description of Geraldine's body, it is not clear whether they represent the narrator's view of things or Christabel's.

The poem recalls the elusiveness of visionary experience described in the preface to 'Kubla Khan' – and then re-enacted by a speaker frustrated by his inability to revive what he has once seen. The dilemmas of 'Kubla Khan' thus help to direct focus towards both the elusive narrator in 'Christabel' and also the figure of the Bard in the second part. Since the narrator has difficulty telling his story, we are increasingly confused about his knowledge of Geraldine, or indeed, his role in the story, if any. He may be a representative of the poet, but he seems to have no control over the events being described, with his frequent questions and apparently helpless appeals. In Part II, Bard Bracy's dream suggests that poets are able to see more than other men, though their visions cannot be easily translated into ordinary language. His own inability to command the Baron's attention and the subsequent misinterpretation of his words shows that even when a poet tells the truth, it may not be heard – or if heard, not understood. It is a motif common in folklore and legend, but one which had special resonance for Romantic poets, frustrated by the political and commercial constraints imposed upon their art.

Though 'Christabel' works wonderfully as a compelling Gothic tale, it is also able to accomplish a great deal more. Despite the deceptively simple language, Coleridge's narrative embraces many of the major preoccupations of the period, from the literary concerns with imaginative experience, composition, transmission and interpretation, to psychological issues of the unconscious mind, sexuality and the will to power, to political questions of gender, class and inheritance. Like 'Kubla Khan', 'Christabel' is both incomplete and yet overflowing with interpretative hints and possibilities. Indeed, the poem is as resistant to explanation and ending as 'Kubla Khan', since the last section, added some years after the composition of Part II, is filled not with any concluding remarks, but with a series of tentative suggestions. If the little volume was presented to its original readers as a modest curiosity, however, its appearance from the House of John Murray, the foremost poetry publisher of the period, indicated that there might be more to the poems than the prefaces suggested.

Reading according to Composition or Publication?

When 'Christabel' is read beside 'Kubla Khan' and 'The Pains of Sleep', modern readers can make some attempt to imagine the experience of those who bought Coleridge's slim volume in 1816. Whether the original publication should influence the response of later readers, however, is a matter for further consideration, for by focusing exclusively on the first printed text, we are likely to ignore some aspects of the poem, not least the unpublished drafts that still survive. In the manuscript of 'Christabel', for example, we have seen that Coleridge was more explicit about what Geraldine revealed in the bedroom and therefore guided his readers more directly than in the published version. The version of 'The Pains of Sleep' which was sent to Southey in September 1803 also reveals a more physical, angry and self-punishing host of anxieties than the 'Fantastic passions' that appeared in print: 'Rage, sensual passion, mad'ning Brawl' (*Letters*, II, 983). Where the poem published with 'Kubla Khan' and 'Christabel' read 'For aye entempesting anew / The unfathomable hell within', the original letter was more confessional: 'Still to be stirring up anew / The self-created Hell within.' The simpler language, with its much more successful rhythm, means that the earlier, private version carries greater conviction, though the evasiveness of the elaborately awkward 1816 lines suggest an understandable reluctance to admit to – or less self-punishing reflection on – what had once seemed a specifically self-generated Hell.

When attention focuses on the period of composition rather than the publication, manuscripts often seem more important than the printed text. Detailed comparison of different surviving manuscript versions can become a rewarding study, raising numerous interpretative possibilities and often throwing light on hitherto unsuspected aspects of a familiar poem. Though traditionally the pursuit of scholars, tracing the evolution of a text has now become possible for any reader with a serious interest in Romantic poetry, because of the publication of excellent modern editions with textual variants. The magnificent *Cornell Edition of the Works of William Wordsworth*, which appeared in twenty two volumes from 1975 to 2008, set the highest standards for editing and offered printed versions of all the surviving manuscripts of Wordsworth's poems, as well as reading texts and extensive annotation. Photographs of the manuscripts were also reproduced to give readers a better sense of the original papers with which the team of editors had been working to establish the published texts. It is an invaluable resource, which has transformed modern understanding of Wordsworth and enabled kinds of criticism that were not possible in the past.

While the discovery of altered lines, cancelled stanzas, added glosses or deleted commas can be very illuminating, however, a mass of textual detail is sometimes rather daunting. Most editors of Romantic poetry accordingly aim to establish a 'reading text', whatever the variants, so that their readers can enjoy the poems in a state of completion even if they subsequently pursue their evolution or afterlives. For some poets of the period, the scale of variation is quite bewildering. Coleridge, for example, was an inveterate reviser of his own work, as Jack Stillinger demonstrated in his painstaking comparisons of the major poems, which uncovered as many as eighteen distinct versions of 'Christabel.' With a poem such as 'Dejection', the differences between the original verse letter to Sara Hutchinson and the Ode first published in the *Morning Post* in 1802 are extensive enough for some readers to treat them as separate poems. In the case of 'Dejection', the published 'Ode' has been chosen for inclusion in modern editions more frequently than the verse letter in manuscript, but for some major Romantic poems – most famously, the *Prelude* – opinion has favored the unpublished text. *The Prelude* belongs to 1805, 1850, or both – if it is a parallel edition. That is only the extended *Prelude*, however, because the briefer, 'Two-Part Prelude' was written in 1799, and then expanded into thirteen books six years later, though the Victorians who bought the first published edition in 1850 found a poem of fourteen books.

Modern readers have choices that were unavailable to Romantic audiences, because they are able to consider individual poems in different contexts – according to their history of composition or publication. With some poems, publication followed soon after composition, but with *The Prelude* or Coleridge's 1816 volume, a lapse of many years occurred. If poems are restored to their original moments of composition, 'Kubla Khan' and 'Christabel' may be read along with other poems written in 1797–8, when Coleridge was working closely with Wordsworth on *Lyrical Ballads*, as well as developing his 'Conversation Poems.' Many readers have regarded 'Kubla Khan' and 'Christabel' as among the most important works of this annus mirabilis, linking them to 'The Ancient Mariner' and finding numerous common images and concerns. When John Livingstone Lowes made his pioneering study of Coleridge's imagination in the 1920s, for example, he found that *The Road to Xanadu* went via 'The Rime of the Ancient Mariner'. More recently, Ted Hughes, attempting to assess Coleridge's chief contribution to English literary history, decided that his poetic reputation rested on 'the three great visionary poems – 'Kubla Khan', 'The Ancient Mariner', and 'Christabel' Part I' (*A Choice of Coleridge's Verse*, vii).

Hughes's selection was influenced by his own interests in myth and metre, but many modern editors group the same three poems, along with several others dating from 1797–8, on the grounds of their compositional proximity. The chronological principles guiding so many modern editions also place 'The Pains of Sleep' five years later, in 1803, when Coleridge, in the grip of opium, was doubly afflicted by the doomed passion and sense of failing poetic power that had found such anguished expression the previous year in 'Dejection: An Ode'. Although 'The Pains of Sleep' was composed in 1803, however, the version included in many editions is the one that was published in 1816 – so there can be some difficulties attendant on the chronological ordering of poems in modern editions. 'Christabel', too, provides a challenge, since the two parts were written in 1798 and 1800, with the conclusion some time later; a strict adherence to the compositional history would therefore split the poem into pieces, interspersed with other works.

Quite apart from the practical problems associated with the compositional history, there is much to be gained from seeing 'Christabel', 'Kubla Khan' and 'The Pains of Sleep' as a group, as we have seen. This was the way in which the reading public first encountered Coleridge's remarkable poems in 1816, and from which many contemporary reviewers recoiled in bewilderment. But these were also the exciting new poems that fired the imaginations of Byron, Keats, the Shelleys and a host of other creative talents, encouraging fresh interest in Gothic subjects and narrative poetry. Once we see Coleridge's poems coming hot off Regency presses, we are much more likely to trace Geraldine's snake-like eyes in the twists and turns of Keats's 'Lamia', or hear echoes of Christabel's urgent midnight prayers in 'The Eve of St Agnes'. It was Byron who prompted the publication of 'Kubla Khan' and his admiration for Coleridge can also be seen in many of his own poems, from 'Darkness' and 'The Dream' to the various 'Fragments' written in 1816. Byron and the Shelleys were reading 'Christabel' during the dark summer of 1816 in Switzerland, where they all turned their hands to ghost stories and Mary Shelley had her nightmare vision for *Frankenstein*. It may therefore prove as illuminating to see the *Christabel* volume in relation to Byron, Mary Shelley or Keats as it is to regard it as part of Coleridge's great collaboration with Wordsworth, for both the composition and publication of poems have implications beyond the texts themselves.

Whether Geraldine's eyes conjure up Lamia or the Ancient Mariner more readily will depend on the individual reader, but what should be emerging clearly is that any reading of a Romantic poem is likely to be influenced to some extent by the pages that surround it. The chronological ordering of many editions encourages a sense of the poet's development and often helps with understanding the biographical and historical dimensions of the work. Attention to the moment of publication and the text approved for readers, on the other hand, respects the integrity of the original volume as first published and received by contemporary readers. Both editorial principles have their historical justification, which is one reason why the issue has attracted so much debate in recent decades. Readers of Romantic poetry are fortunate to be able to consult both the *Cornell Edition of Wordsworth*, with its meticulous attention to the chronological order of composition, and to Jerome McGann's excellent edition of *The Complete Works of Lord Byron*, arranged according to the publication of Byron's numerous volumes. McGann was one of the leading critics in the move towards a careful contextualization of Romantic poetry, which has revolutionized modern understanding of the poetry and helped to establish the idea of a Romantic period. For McGann, Romantic poems needed to be understood in the context of their times and their authors in relation to the other people who had a bearing on the production of a literary work. His work on textual criticism argued that texts were achieved through complicated transformations, which turned 'an initially psychological phenomenon (the "creative process") into a social one' (*A Critique of Modern Textual Criticism*, 63). The argument was part of a general desire to demystify Romanticism and bring the major poets back from the sublime heights into which they sometimes seemed in danger of disappearing in the 1970s to a society of publishers, book-buyers and businessmen.

When Jerome McGann edited *The New Oxford Book of Romantic Period Verse*, in 1993, he accordingly opted to present the poems according to the dates when they were first published. This meant that 'Kubla Khan' appeared under '1816', but *The Prelude*, of course, did not appear at all. Just as startling as this omission was the way in which the works of different poets were dispersed through successive years – with poems by Burns, for example, appearing in the sections for 1786, 1790, 1791, 1792, 1796, 1799, and 1801, even though his death occurred in 1796. Since unpublished poems by Burns continued to appear well into the nineteenth century, McGann's principle runs the risk of becoming endless – but he wisely brought his sequence to a halt in 1832, finishing with Tennyson. In fact, 1832 also saw the appearance of the Dedication to *Don Juan*, 'The Mask of Anarchy' and a number of other important poems, but the collection ends with 'The Palace of Art' because, in the editor's view, 'that poem, and the volume in which it is taken, represent Tennyson's hail and farewell to Romanticism' (*New Oxford Book*, xx). Since the anthology appeared, a number of important books have in fact traced the influence of different Romantic poets on nineteenth and twentieth-century literature, not to mention their lasting effects on Tennyson. It is in the nature of anthologies and university courses, though, to define literary periods with significant dates, poems or events.

McGann's anthology represented an important challenge to ideas about Romanticism that had held sway in the middle of the twentieth century, generally centring on the 'Big Six' poets – Blake, Wordsworth, Coleridge, Byron, Shelley, Keats (though often a Big Five, with Byron somewhat marginalized). Here was a selection assembled on quite different principles from those that had determined Harold Bloom and Lionel Trilling's 1973 volume of *Romantic Poetry and Prose*, for it emphasised the work 'being read in the period' rather than singling out the greatest poems being written. In elevating Romantic audiences, however, McGann was also depriving his own readers of some of the most rewarding and challenging poems from the period. He was nevertheless reviving interest in many of the fine poems that had slipped from modern consciousness because of intense focus on the work of six major poets by formalist and philosophical critics. His choices also show the influence of the feminist criticism of the 1980s and early 90s, which did much to restore poets such as Anna Letita Barbauld, Charlotte Smith, Ann Yearsley, Felicia Hemans and Letitia Landon to readers of the Romantic period.

Twenty-first century editors, alert to the textual debates of the preceding decades, have generally maintained the tradition of grouping the poems by the same author, often chronologically – whether by composition or publication date – but they have also been keen to include a wider range of poets and different kinds of poetry. Whatever the arrangement of their own poetry anthology, twenty-first century readers benefit from recognizing the editorial policy, because of the often unobtrusive but decisive influence of such decisions on what may feel like a straightforward response to a poem on the page.

Editorial choices are generally influenced by contemporary critical attitudes, but they also do much to determine those of their readers. A glance at one of the popular Victorian anthologies, such as Francis Palgrave's *The Golden Treasury*, reveals at once that the general reader's sense of an earlier age is very much a part of his own cultural moment and so it is helpful to keep in mind the possible limitations of our own view. And yet, a survey of almost a century of poetry collections will still reveal that some poems seem to weather the storms of critical opinion more stoutly than others, attesting perhaps to their creators' hopes that they might live on to please the unknown generations of the future.

Further Reading

Much of the discussion above can be developed through consultation of the major, scholarly editions of Romantic poets, which are available in larger libraries – for details, see further reading section of Chapter 4. Different anthologies of Romantic poetry, published over the past two centuries are also illuminating in terms of their editorial selections, as well as providing texts for reading. See for example, M.H. Abrams (ed.) *The Norton Anthology of English Literature*, 2 vols (New York and London, 1962); Bloom, Harold and Lionel Trilling (eds.), *Romantic*

Poetry and Prose (London: Oxford University Press, 1973); Jerome McGann, *The New Oxford Book of Romantic Period Verse* (Oxford: Oxford University Press, 1993); H.S. Milford (ed.) *The Oxford Book of Regency Verse 1798–1837* (Oxford: Clarendon Press, 1928); Francis Palgrave, *The Golden Treasury*, ed. Christopher Ricks (Harmondsworth: Penguin, 1991). Successive editions of Duncan Wu (ed.) *Romanticism* (first published in 1994) also reveal significant changes in content.

For discussion of the Romantic volume, see Neil Fraistat, *The Poem and the Book: Interpreting Collections of Romantic Poetry* (Chapel Hill, NC.: University of North Carolina Press, 1985). For Keats's habit of writing poems in copies of his books, see Beth Lau, 'Keats and the Practice of Romantic Marginalia', *Romanticism* 2:1 (1996), 40–54.

On Blake's Illuminated books, see The Blake Archive (www.blakearchive.org) and the beautifully printed individual volumes of the major books, published by the Tate Gallery. The catalogue for the Blake Exhibition, R. Hamlyn and M. Phillips (eds.), *William Blake* (London: Tate Gallery, 2000) is also very informative. For critical readings, see Behrendt, Stephen, *Reading William Blake* (Basingstoke: Macmillan, 1992); David Bindman, *Mind-Forged Manacles: Blake and Slavery* (London: Hayward Gallery, 2007); Morris Eaves (ed.) *The Cambridge Companion to William Blake* (Cambridge: Cambridge University Press, 2003); Nelson Hilton and Thomas Vogler (eds), *Unnam'd Forms: Blake and Textuality* (Berkeley: University of California press, 1986); W.J.T. Mitchell, *Blake's Composite Art* (Princeton: Princeton University Press, 1978); Michael Phillips, *William Blake: The Creation of the Songs* (London and Princeton: British Library and Princeton University Press, 2000).

On Coleridge's 1816 collection of poems, see Patricia Adair, *The Waking Dream* (London, 1967); John Beer, *Coleridge the Visionary* (London: Chatto and Windus, 1959); Jennifer Ford, *Coleridge on Dreaming* (Cambridge: Cambridge University Press, 1997); Humphry House, *Coleridge* (London: Rupert Hart-Davies, 1953); Ted Hughes (ed) *A Choice of Coleridge's Verse* (London: Faber, 1996); Ann Janowitz, 'Coleridge's 1816 volume: Fragment as Rubric', *Studies in Romanticism* 24 (1985), 21–39; Alun Jones and William Tydeman (eds.) *The Ancient Mariner and Other Poems* (Basingstoke: Macmillan, 1973); John Livingstone Lowes, *The Road to Xanadu* (Boston: 1927); Marjorie

Levinson, *The Romantic Fragment Poem* (Chapel Hill: University of North Carolina Press, 1986); Paul Magnuson, *Coleridge's Nightmare Poetry* (Charlottesville: University of Virginia Press, 1974); Leonard Orr (ed.) *Christabel: Critical Essays on Coleridge's Poetry* (New York: G.K. Hall, 1994); Seamus Perry, 'Kubla Khan, Christabel and The Ancient Mariner', in D. Wu (ed.) *A Companion to Romanticism* (Oxford: Blackwell, 1995).

For critical discussion on textual variation of various kinds, the following will prove helpful: Robert Brinkley and Keith Hanley (eds), *Romantic Revisions* (Cambridge: Cambridge University Press, 1992); Tim Chilcott, *A Publisher and His Circle: The Life and Work of John Taylor, Keats's Publisher* (London: Routledge, 1972); Stephen Gill, 'Wordsworth's Poems: The Question of Text', *Review of English Studies*, 34 (1983), 172–90; *Wordsworth's Revisitings* (Oxford: Oxford University Press, 2011); Simon Kovesi, 'Beyond the Language Wars: Towards a Green Edition of John Clare', *John Clare Society Journal*, 27 (2007), 61–75; Zachary Leader, *Revision and Romantic Authorship* (Oxford: Oxford University Press, 1996); Jerome McGann, *A Critique of Modern Textual Criticism* (Chicago: University of Chicago Press, 1983); Jack Stillinger, *Coleridge and Textual Instability* (New York: Oxford University Press, 1994); Susan Wolfson (ed.), *Felicia Hemans* (Princeton: Princeton University Press, 2000).

On reading and reception, the *Critical Heritage* series is invaluable for tracing the reception of major poets. See also Jon Klancher, *The Making of English Reading* Audiences (Madison: University of Wisconsin Press, 1987); Lucy Newlyn, *Reading, Writing and Romanticism: The Anxiety of Reception* (Oxford: Oxford University Press, 2000); William St Clair, *The Reading Nation in the Romantic Period* (Cambridge: Cambridge University Press, 2004).

On the influence of Romantic poetry on later generations see for example, Robert Crawford (ed.) *Robert Burns and Cultural Authority* (Edinburgh: Edinburgh University Press, 1997); Andrew Elfenbein, *Byron and the Victorians* (Cambridge: Cambridge University Press, 1995); Stephen Gill, *Wordsworth and the Victorians* (Oxford: Clarendon Press, 1998); Karsten Engelberg, *The Making of the Shelley Myth* (London: Greenwood, 1988); Michael O'Neill, *The All-Sustaining Air* (Oxford: Oxford University Press, 2007); Nicholas Roe (ed.) *Keats and History* (Cambridge:

Cambridge University Press, 1995); Fiona Stafford, *Starting Lines in Scottish, Irish and English Poetry* (Oxford: Oxford University Press, 2000); *Local Attachments* (Oxford: Oxford University Press, 2010); Damian Walford Davies (ed) *The Monstrous Debt* (Detroit: Wayne State University Press, 2006). Several of the *Critical Heritage* volumes for the individual poets are also helpful resources for the later reception.

References

Abrams, M.H., *The Mirror and the Lamp* (London: Oxford University Press, 1953).
——*Natural Supernaturalism* (New York and London: Oxford University Press, 1971).
Anderson, Robert, *Ballads in the Cumberland Dialect* (Carlisle, 1805).
Anon., *The Yorkshire Dialect* (London, nd. c1810).
Austen, Jane, *Mansfield Park*, ed. Kathryn Sutherland (London: Penguin, 2003).
Austen, Jane, *Persuasion*, ed. Gillian Beer (London: Penguin, 2003).
Barbauld, Anna, *The Poems of Anna Letitia Barbauld*, ed. William MacCarthy and Elizabeth Kraft (Athens and London: University of Georgia Press, 1994).
Bate, W.J., *The Burden of the Past and the English Poet* (London: Chatto and Windus, 1971).
Blair, Hugh, *Lectures on Rhetoric and Belles Lettres*, 3 vols (Dublin, 1783).
Blake, *The Complete Writings of William Blake*, ed. Geoffrey Keynes (London: Oxford University Press, 1966).
——*The Letters of William Blake*, ed. Geoffrey Keynes (London: Oxford University Press, 1968).
Bloom, Harold, *The Anxiety of Influence* (New York: Oxford University Press, 1973).
——and Trilling, Lionel (eds), *Romantic Poetry and Prose* (London: Oxford University Press, 1973).
Burns, Robert, *The Poems and Songs of Robert Burns*, ed. James Kinsley, 3 vols (Oxford: Clarendon Press, 1968).
Byron, Lord, *The Complete Poems of Lord Byron*, ed. Jerome J. McGann, 7 vols (Oxford: Clarendon Press, 1980–1993).
——*The Complete Miscellaneous Prose* ed. Andrew Nicholson (Oxford: Clarendon Press, 1991).

Reading Romantic Poetry, First Edition. Fiona Stafford.
© 2014 Fiona Stafford. Published 2014 by John Wiley & Sons, Ltd.

Chandler, James, *England in 1819* (Chicago: University of Chicago Press, 1998).
Clare, John, *The Shepherd's Calendar*, ed. Tim Chilcott (Manchester: Carcanet, 2006).
—— *The Poems of John Clare*, 2 vols, ed. J.W. Tibble (London and New York: Dent, 1935).
Coleridge *Biographia Literaria*, ed. James Engell and W.J. Bate, 2 vols (Princeton and London: Routledge and Princeton University Press, 1983).
—— 'Lecture on the Slave Trade', *Lectures 1795 on Politics and Religion*, ed. Lewis Patton and Peter Mann (Princeton and London: Routledge and Princeton University Press, 1971), 231–51.
—— *The Collected Letters of Samuel Taylor Coleridge* ed. E.L. Griggs, 6 vols (Oxford: Clarendon Press, 1956–71).
—— *The Notebooks of Samuel Taylor Coleridge*, ed. Kathleen Coburn, vol III, (Princeton and London, Routledge and Princeton University Press, 1973).
—— *The Complete Poetical Works* ed. E.H. Coleridge, 2 vols (Oxford: Clarendon Press, 1912).
Cowper, William, *The Poems of William Cowper*, ed. John D. Baird and Charles Ryskamp, 3 vols (Oxford: Clarendon Press, 1980–1995).
Ford, Jennifer, *Coleridge on Dreaming* (Cambridge: Cambridge University Press, 1997).
Goethe, Johann Wolfgang von, *The Sorrows of Young Werther*, trans. Michael Hulse (Harmondsworth: Penguin, 1989).
Gray, Thomas, *The Poems of Gray, Collins and Goldsmith*, ed. Roger Lonsdale (London: Longman, 1969).
Hazlitt, William, 'Lectures on the English Poets' in Volume V of *The Complete Works of William Hazlitt*, ed. P.P. Howe, 21 vols (London: Dent, 1930–34).
Hazlitt, William, *The Complete Works of William Hazlitt*, ed. P.P. Howe, 21 vols (London: Dent, 1930–34).
Heaney, Seamus, *Finders Keepers* (London: Faber, 2000).
Hemans, Felicia, *Felicia Hemans*, ed. Susan J. Wolfson (Princeton: Princeton University Press, 2000).
Hogg, James, 'Memoir of the Author's Life', *Altrive Tales*, ed. Gillian Hughes (Edinburgh: Edinburgh University Press, 2003), 11–52.
—— *The Shepherd's Calendar*, ed. Douglas Mack (Edinburgh: Edinburgh University Press, 1995).
—— *Winter Evening Tales*, ed. Ian Duncan (Edinburgh: Edinburgh University Press, 2002).
Johnson, Samuel, *The Lives of the Poets*, ed. Roger Lonsdale, 4 vols, (Oxford: Oxford University Press, 2006).
Keats, John, *The Complete Poems*, ed. John Barnard, 3rd. edn (Harmondsworth: Penguin, 1988).
—— *The Letters of John Keats*, ed. Hyder Rollins, 2 vols (Cambridge, Mass.: Harvard University Press, 1958).

Macpherson, James, *The Poems of Ossian*, ed. Howard Gaskill (Edinburgh: Edniburgh University Press, 1996).

McGann, Jerome, *A Critique of Modern Textual Criticism* (Chicago: University of Chicago Press, 1983).

——— *The New Oxford Book of Romantic Period Verse* (Oxford: Oxford University Press, 1993).

Milton, John, *The Complete Poems*, ed. John Carey and Alastair Fowler, 2nd. edn (London: Longman, 1998).

Newlyn, Lucy, *Paradise Lost and the Romantic Reader* (Oxford: Clarendon Press, 1994).

O'Neill, Michael and Mahoney, Charles (eds.) *Romantic Poetry: An Annotated Anthology* (Oxford: Wiley-Blackwell, 2008).

Percy, Thomas, *Reliques of Ancient English Poetry*, 3 vols (London, 1765).

Pittock, Murray, *Scottish and Irish Romanticism* (Oxford: Oxford University Press, 2007).

Pope, Alexander, *The Poems of Alexander Pope*, ed. John Butt (London: Methuen, 1963).

Shelley, Mary, *The Novels and Selected Works of Mary Shelley*, ed. Nora Crook, 8 vols (London: Pickering and Chatto, 1996); vol I, *Frankenstein*.

Shelley, Percy Bysshe, 'A Defence of Poetry', in Percy Bysshe Shelley, *Poems and Prose*, ed. Timothy Webb (London: Dent, 1995).

Shelley, Percy Bysshe, *Poems and Prose*, ed. Timothy Webb (London: Dent, 1995).

——— *The Poetical Works*, ed. Thomas Hutchinson, rev. G.M. Matthews (Oxford: Clarendon Press, 1970).

St Clair, William, *The Reading Nation in the Romantic Period* (Cambridge: Cambridge University Press, 2004).

Thomson, James, *Poetical Works*, ed. J. Logie Robertson (London: Oxford University Press, 1908).

Wollstonecraft, Mary, *A Vindication of the Rights of Women*, ed. Janet Todd (Oxford: Oxford University Press, 1993).

Wordsworth, William, *William Wordsworth*, ed. Stephen Gill (Oxford: Oxford University Press, 2010).

——— *The Cornell Edition of the Works of William Wordsworth*, gen. ed. Stephen Parrish, 22 vols (Ithaca and London, 1975–2007).

——— *The Letters of William and Dorothy Wordsworth*, vol I, *The Early Years, 1797–1805*, ed. E. de Selincourt, rev. edn., Chester L. Shaver (Oxford: Clarendon Press, 1967).

——— *The Prose Works of William Wordsworth*, ed. W.J.B. Owen and Jane Worthington Smyser, 3 vols (Oxford: Clarendon Press, 1974).

Wu, Duncan (ed.) *Romanticism*, 3rd. edn (Oxford: Wiley-Blackwell, 2006).

Index

Abolition of the Slave Trade, 27, 30, 57–8, 66, 68–79, 92–3
Abrams, M.H., 7, 118
Addison, Joseph, 123, 137, 169
America, 27, 66
Amiens, Peace of, 124, 157
Anderson, Robert, poet, 157–8
Anderson, Robert, *Works of the British Poets*, 98
Anne, Queen, 27
Austen, Jane, 17, 73–4, 215
Ayrshire, 6, 156

Bailey, Benjamin, 40
Ballads, 123–5, 137, 144, 146, 157
Barbauld, Anna, viii, 7, 57, 72–3, 75, 78, 223
Bards, 12, 36, 127–8
Barnard, John, 199
Bastille, 13, 27
Bate, W.J., 99
Beattie, James, 127
Beddoes, Thomas Lovell, 66
Birds, 89, 164–85
Blackwood's Edinburgh Magazine, 149
Blair, Hugh, 145

Blake, William, viii, 22–3, 74–6, 113–16, 119, 122, 183, 201–8
'Chimney Sweeper, The', 23, 75
'Clod and the Pebble, The', 115–16
'Holy Thursday', 114
'Human Abstract, The', 205
'Little Black Boy, The', 75–6, 203–5
'Little Girl Lost, The', 204–6
'London', 114
Marriage of Heaven and Hell, The, 113–15, 203, 205, 207–8
Milton, 113, 206
'Poison Tree, A', 115, 205
'Prospectus', 202
Songs of Innocence and Experience, 23, 75–6, 114, 119, 202–8, 212
'Tyger, The', 206–8
'Vision of the Last Judgment, A', 203
Visions of the Daughters of Albion, 74

Reading Romantic Poetry, First Edition. Fiona Stafford.
© 2014 Fiona Stafford. Published 2014 by John Wiley & Sons, Ltd.

Bloom, Harold, 99, 222
Bloomfield, Robert, 6, 122, 149
Bowles, William, 52, 103, 105
Brawne, Fanny, 40–41
Brighton, 5
Bristol, 60, 71
Britain, 5, 22, 27, 73–4, 102, 124–6
Brown, Charles Armitage,
    40–41, 194
Bürger, Gottfried, 124
Burke, Edmund, 52, 66, 198
Burns, Robert, viii, 6, 11, 16, 18–19,
    28–9, 46–7, 53–6, 61, 122,
    126–7, 134, 138, 153–9,
    200, 222
  'Ae Fond Kiss', 18
  Amang the rigs o' barley', 11
  'Auld Lang Syne', 18
  'Author's Earnest Cry and
    Prayer', 28
  'Banks o' Doon', 18
  'Cotter's Saturday Night,
    The', 127
  'Despondency. An Ode', 16
  'Dream, The', 156
  'Dumfries Volunteers', 158
  'Epistle to Davie', 11,
    53, 126
  'Epistle to James Smith', 53
  'Epistle to Lapraik', 54–5,
    61, 126
  'Guidwife of Wauchope House,
    To the', 55
  'Hamilton, Gavin, Dedication
    to', 61
  'Holy Fair', 126
  'John Barleycorn', 138
  'Louse, To a', 23
  'Mouse, To a', 156–7
  Poems, Chiefly in Scottish Dialect
    (Kilmarnock edition), 53, 54,
    127, 200
  'Red, Red Rose, A', 11, 18
  'Tam O'Shanter', 29, 153–7
Byron, Lord, viii, 4, 5, 11–12, 16–17,
    19–20, 36–8, 43–5, 77–9,
    82, 85–92, 97, 110–111,
    122, 163, 186–9, 196–7,
    200, 212, 215, 221–2
  Beppo, 197
  Cain, 110
  Childe Harold's Pilgrimage, 5, 17,
    36–8, 43, 45, 49, 91, 110,
    127, 163
  Corsair, The, 110
  'Darkness', 16, 42, 45,
    85–92, 221
  Don Juan, 11–12, 25–7, 29,
    77–9, 85–92, 110–111,
    186–9, 196–7, 222
  Heaven and Earth, 79, 110
  Lara, 110
  Letters and Journals, 25, 30,
  'Manfred', 42–3, 215
  'Prisoner of Chillon, The', 42
  'Prometheus', 42, 77, 110
  'So we'll go no more a-roving',
    19–20
  'Stanzas to Augusta', 16, 42

Campbell, Thomas, 2
Carlisle, 157
Cary, Henry, 97
Celtic, 127–8
Chandler, James, 66
Chapman, George, 98, 122
Chatterton, Thomas, 34–7, 40,
    46–9, 53
Chaucer, Geoffrey, 98
Childhood, 7–10, 75, 84–6, 114, 117,
    125, 176
Christ, Christianity, 39–40, 72,
    79–82, 88–9, 111, 113,
    127, 183

'Christis Kirk on the Green', 126
Clairmont, Claire, 42–3
Clare, John, viii, 6, 30, 35, 122, 150–153, 169, 174–6, 199–200
Coleridge, George, 52
Coleridge, Samuel Taylor, viii, 1, 7–9, 16–17, 26, 28, 34–5, 41, 44, 47–52, 58–9, 69, 75, 89–92, 98–100, 107–8, 111, 122–4, 140, 143–8, 153, 162–8, 175, 178, 183, 186, 189, 199, 202, 210–223
    'Ancient Mariner', 48–9, 51, 89–91, 123–5, 143–7, 199, 220–221
    'Asra, To', 47
    Biographia Literaria, 1, 59, 98–9, 119, 148, 186, 189
    'Christabel', 13, 51, 91, 214–21
    Christabel volume, 1816, 202, 210–221
    'Dejection. An Ode', 17, 23, 47–8, 59, 65, 107–8, 123, 220–221
    'Eolian Harp, The', 107
    'Fears in Solitude', 28, 140
    Friend, The, 58–9
    'Frost at Midnight', 7–9, 140, 162
    'Kubla Khan', 5, 91, 133, 202, 210–214, 218, 220
    Lay Sermons, 91
    Lectures, 69, 75
    'Monody on the Death of Chatterton', 34, 48
    'Nightingale, The', 100, 140, 166–8
    'Pains of Sleep, The', 202, 214–15, 220
    'Revd. George Coleridge, To The', 98
    Sibylline Leaves, 91, 143
    'This Lime Tree Bower my Prison', 140
    'William Wordsworth, To', 51–2
Collins, William, 100, 104
Conversation Poems, 140–141
    see also Coleridge, Samuel Taylor, works
Cowper, William, viii, 6, 8, 13, 16, 39, 68–75, 140, 149, 166–7
    'Castaway, The', 16
    'Nightingale, To a', 166–7
    'Sweetmeat has Sour Sauce', 68–9
    The Task, 6, 8, 13, 39, 68–75, 140, 149
Crawford, Robert, 29

Daniel, Samuel, 98
Dante, 40, 96–7, 100–101, 108, 183
Derwent, 162
Dilke, Charles, 1, 41
Dolben, William, 68, 71
Donne, John, 98
Drayton, Michael, 98
Duff, William, 99
Dunlop, Frances, 55
Dyer, George, 166

Elegy, 38–41, 61–2, 100
Elgin marbles, 123
England, 9, 30, 58, 72
English language, 102–4 *see also* Standardisation
Epic poetry, 25, 100, 110–112, 116–22 *see also* Homer
Ettrick, 149

Fergusson, Robert, 53
Fenwick, Isabella, 117, 303, 314–15, 321
Ford, Jennifer, 213
Fox, Charles James, 22
France, 9, 27, 57–8, 124
French Revolution, 9, 13, 14, 27, 50, 57, 66, 116, 120
Friends, friendship, 28, 50–62

Gaelic, 134, 136
Garrick, David, 55
Geneva, 8, 42
Gerard, Alexander, 99
German literature, 123–4
George III, 28
Gill, Stephen, viii
Godwin, William, 42, 52, 111–12
Goethe, Johann Wolfgang von, *The Sorrows of Werther*, 36–7, 44–5, 53
Golden Treasury, The, 223
Goldsmith, Oliver, 149
Gothic, 6, 13, 69, 123, 214–15, 221
Grasmere, 149
Graveyard school, 13
Gray, Thomas, 103, 107, 109–10, 124, 127–8
Greece, 25, 45, 66, 109, 122–3, 127
Grose, Francis, 153

Hampstead Heath, 34
Hartley, David, 8
Hazlitt, William, 98–9
Heaney, Seamus, 158
Hemans, Felicia, viii, 61, 124–5, 127–8, 163, 197–8, 223
Highlands, 132–9
Hogg, James, 149–50, 155
Homer, 97–8, 101, 112, 122
Howard, John, 58

Hughes, Ted, 220
Hume, David, 12, 24
Hunt, James Leigh, 29, 40, 43, 65, 97–8, 182, 200
Hurd, Richard, 98
Hutchinson, Mary, 50
Hutchinson, Sara, 47, 50, 219

Invasion, fears of, 17, 124, 158–9
Ireland, 27, 29, 30, 66, 126
Italian, 101–4, 108–9
Italy, 4, 43, 106–9, 128, 183

Jamaica, 157
Jeffrey, Francis, 59
Johnson, Samuel, 98–9

Kean, Edmund, 95
Keats, Fanny, 40–41
Keats, George, 40–41
Keats, John, viii, 1–2, 10, 28–9, 34–5, 38–42, 65, 82–3, 95–103, 105, 109, 122–3, 133, 166, 169–74, 176–7, 179, 183, 193–6, 199–200, 221–2
  'Ailsa Craig', 195
  'Autumn, To', 190–191
  'Bright Star', 16
  'Dream, A,', 96–7, 195
  Endymion, 34, 40, 49, 195
  'Eve of St Agnes', 2, 10–11, 53, 127, 195, 200, 221
  'Hyperion', 30, 67, 100, 195
  'If by dull rhymes', 101–2, 190
  'Isabella', 30, 195
  'La Belle Dame Sans Merci', 2, 125, 195
  'Lamia', 82, 195, 221
  Lamia, 1820 volume, 194–5
  Letters, 1, 10, 41, 82, 95–6, 100

Index

Keats, John (cont'd)
    'Ode on a Grecian Urn', 62, 123, 133, 195, 199
    'Ode to a Nightingale', 41, 166, 169–74, 176–7, 179, 190, 195
    'On First reading Chapman's Homer', 97–8
    'On the Grasshopper and the Cricket, On the', 65
    'On Seeing a Lock of Milton's Hair', 97
    'On Sitting Down to read *King Lear* Once Again', 95–6, 109, 193–5
    Poems, 1817, 194
    'Sleep and Poetry', 99, 195
    'Written On the Day that Mr Leigh Hunt left Prison', 28
Kilmarnock edition *see* Burns, Robert

Lake District, 90
Lamb, Charles, 28, 52
Landon, Letitia, 61–2, 223
Lapraik, John, 53, 61
Lau, Beth, 194
Little, Janet, 55
Lloyd, Charles, 52
London, 6, 7, 25–6, 59, 98, 150, 155–6
Lowes, John Livingstone, 146, 220
Lucan, 40

Mackenzie, Henry, 56–7
Macpherson, James, 12, 36, 137–8
Mahoney, Charles, viii
Malta, 59
Manchester, 66, 109, 182
Mansfield, Lord Chief Justice, 74
Marlborough, John Churchill, Duke of, 26–7
Martin, John, 127

Marvell, Andrew, 100, 106
Mathew, George Felton, 40
McGann, J., 221–3
Mediterranean, 37, 128, 170
Medwin, Thomas, 43
Milton, John, 24, 39, 44, 72, 81, 88, 97–101, 105–8, 110–122, 140, 156, 163, 168–70, 174, 179, 183, 189–90 *see also* Epic poetry; 'Satan'
Moore, Thomas, 5, 19, 29, 40, 43, 126
More, Hannah, viii, 55–7, 60–61, 68–72, 75
Murray, John, 200, 218

Napoleon, 26, 27, 66
Native traditions, 122–8
Nelson, Horatio, 27, 125
Newlyn, Lucy, 110, 119
Newton, Isaac, 80–82
Northamptonshire, 6, 150

Odes, 100, 107–8, 126–7, 172–4, 190–191
O'Neill, Michael, viii, 108
Orality, 132–59
Ossian, 12, 36, 53, 138
Ottava rima, 187, 189
Otway, Thomas, 104
Ovid, 166–7
Owenson, Sydney, 126

Paine, Thomas, 29, 66
Paris, 13
Paulson, Ronald, 66
Peacock, Thomas Love, 163
Percy, Thomas, 123, 137
Peterloo, 28, 109, 182
Petrarch, 96, 103–5, 167, 173
Pittock, Murray, 154
Plato, 40, 163, 187

Pleasures of poetry, 1–31
Poetic form, 95–128 *see also* Ballads, Elegy, Epic poetry, Odes, Sonnets, Verse epistles
Pope, Alexander, 81, 185, 189
Portugal, 5
Print culture, 53–4, 65–6, 128, 136–8, 145–6, 149–9, 193–223
Proctor, Bryan Waller, 196
Prometheus, 43, 76, 112, 207
Protestantism, 112

Rainbow, 68, 80–92
Ramsay, Allan, 53
Reform, 66
Regent, Prince, 5, 27, 29
Regional identity, 126–8, 150–159
Regional poetry, 126–8, 152–9
Renaissance, 81, 83, 98–101, 127–8
Reynolds, John Hamilton, 40, 82
Robinson, Mary, 6, 102–3
Rogers, Samuel, 2, 196
Rome, 13, 34, 41
Rousseau, Jean Jacques, 8, 70
Ruins, 13–15

Satan, 110–113, 119 *see also* Milton, John
Science, 43, 67, 79–85
Schlegel, Friedrich and August Wilhelm, 98
Scotland, 18, 30, 126–7, 153–6
Scots language, 123, 126–7, 153–7
Scot, Elizabeth, 54–5
Scott, Walter, 13, 126, 196, 215
Scottish, 123, 126–7, 149, 153–6
Sensibility, 12, 18, 55–8, 60
Severn, Joseph, 40
Seville, 25
Seward, Anna, 45
Shakespeare, William, 82, 95–6, 98–9, 101–5, 183, 194

Shelley, Mary, 42–5, 66, 196, 207, 221
Shelley, Percy Bysshe, viii, 3–4, 13–14, 17, 22, 24–6, 34, 37–44, 76–7, 97, 106–10, 112, 122, 163–6, 175, 179–84, 196, 208, 221–2
Adonais, 38–42, 46, 55, 197
'Alastor', 10, 37, 49
'Cloud, The', 82
Defence of Poetry, A, 3, 13, 17, 23–4, 61, 107, 163–6, 175, 179, 181, 183–4, 188–9, 208
'England in 1819', 66, 109–10
'Julian and Maddalo', 4, 43
'Letter to Maria Gisborne', 43
'Mask of Anarchy, The', 28, 109, 125, 182, 222
'Mont Blanc', 42
'Ode to the West Wind', 106–10, 196
'Ozymandias', 13–14
Prometheus Unbound, 13, 42, 66–7, 76, 92, 112, 196
Necessity of Atheism, The, 39
'Rarely, rarely comest thou,' 3
'Skylark, To a', 179–84
'When the Lamp is Shattered', 84
'Wordsworth, To', 106, 196
Sheridan, Richard Brinsley, 52
Sidney, Algernon, 106
Sidney, Philip, 40, 98
Sillar, David, 53
Simson, William, 53
Smith, Adam, 23–4
Smith, Charlotte, 16, 36–7, 45–6, 103–5, 166–7, 223
Smith, Olivia, 66

Sociability, 35, 40–43 *see also* Friends, friendship
Solitude, 34–50
Song, 18–19, 100 *see also* Blake, William, *Songs of Innocence and Experience*
Sonnets, 36–7, 95–6, 100–110, 193–6
Sound, 132–9, 147, 162–91 *see also* Orality
Southey, Robert, 5, 25–6, 52, 90, 98, 143
Spain, 5, 37
Spectator, The, 58, 123, 137
Spenser, Edmund, 98, 112, 127
Spenserian stanza, 37, 127
de Stael, Germaine, 128
Standard Habbie, 126
Standardisation, 152–9
Sterne, Laurence, 127
Stillinger, Jack, 35, 219
Switzerland, 5, 38, 42–4
Sympathy, 23–5, 56–8

Taylor, John, 35, 40, 150, 152–3, 200
Tennyson, Alfred, 39, 222
Thames, 105
Thomson, James, 80–85, 87, 127, 148
Trafalgar, 27, 29, 157
Treason Trials, 29
Trees, 33, 102–3
Trelawney, Edward John, 43
Tristram Shandy, 127
Turkey, 5, 25, 77

United Irishmen, 6
Union, Act of, 126
Urbanisation, 22, 28, 137–8, 148–53

Vallon, Annette, 9
Vane, Henry, 106
Venice, 4, 19, 38

Verse epistles, 53–4
Victorian, 34–5, 40, 125, 151, 223
Virgil, 112, 117, 137

Wales, 30, 120, 126, 128
Wallis, Henry, 34, 40
War, French Revolutionary and Napoleonic, 14, 17, 22, 27, 29, 125–6, 157–9, 149, 157–9
Wardlaw, Lady, 146
Warton, Thomas, 95, 103, 105
Waterloo, 17, 27, 38, 66–7, 85, 124
Webb, Timothy, viii
Wellington, Duke of, 27
Wilberforce, William, 72–3, 78
Williams, Helen Maria, 57–8
Wollstonecraft, Mary, 42, 74
Women, Rights of, 42, 66, 70, 74–5, 122
Woodhouse, Richard, 200
Wordsworth, Dorothy, 50
Wordsworth, William, viii, 1–3, 7, 9–10, 14–16, 20–22, 24, 26, 28, 41, 44, 46–52, 84–5, 87, 98, 100, 105–8, 111, 116–23, 133–45, 147–9, 151, 162, 165–6, 176–80, 183–6, 189–90, 196–7, 199, 219–20
  'Addressed to the Sons of Burns', 135
  'Cuckoo, To the', 176–80
  'Composed in a Valley Near Dover', 124
  'Daffodils, The', 36
  'Elegiac Stanzas', 16
  Essays upon Epitaphs, 59
  Excursion, The, 13
  'Expostulation and Reply', 140
  'Glen Almain', 135

'Goody Blake and Harry Gill', 139
'Great Men have been among Us', 106
'Green Linnet, The', 179
'Highland Girl, To a', 135
'Home at Grasmere', 165
'Idiot Boy, The', 51
'Immortality Ode', 15, 47–8, 59, 85, 108, 135
Letters, 22, 105
'Lines left upon a Seat in a Yew Tree', 49–50
'Lines written a few Miles above Tintern Abbey', 2–3, 9, 50, 100
'London, 1802', 105
Lyrical Ballads, 1, 20–22, 24–5, 48–52, 59, 90, 139–49, 185–6, 189, 199
'Michael', 21–2, 149
'Nuns Fret Not', 105
'Ode, There was a Time', 65, 84
Poems, 1815, 85, 184–5, 190–191
Poems, in Two Volumes, 65, 85, 106, 135, 176, 178
'Poems on the Naming of Places', 52
'Poet's Epitaph, A', 162, 186
Prelude, The, 7, 9–10, 28–9, 50–52, 59, 116–22, 162, 196–7, 219–20, 222
'Prospectus to The Recluse', 121
'Rainbow, The', 5, 85, 151, 176
'Resolution and Independence', 46–7, 49, 59, 65, 135, 181–2, 185
'Rob Roy's Grave', 135
'Ruined Cottage, The', 13–15
'Simon Lee', 125
'Skylark, To a', 178–9
'Small Celandine, To a', 25
'Solitary Reaper, The', 36, 132–9, 141, 144, 147
'Stepping Westward', 135
'Tables Turned, The', 140
'Tintern Abbey', 3, 9, 50
'Thorn, The', 51, 141–3
Wu, Duncan, viii, 193

Yearsley, Ann, viii, 30, 60–61, 68, 71, 75, 223
Young, Edward, 99
Yorkshire, 127, 158

once supporting and refuting his dead friend's argument, in language that could not have been further from the imagery of fading coals and flowers. His poem was nevertheless a defence of poetry, not just in its witty engagement with the literary concerns of the period, but also in its persistent emphasis on rhyme, form and genre.

Don Juan is Byron's major contribution to the contemporary debate over poetry and prose and, as such, part of his general retort to Wordsworth and Coleridge. His very choice of form indicates that as far as Byron was concerned, the difference between prose and verse was too obvious to waste any time over. Wordsworth had devoted considerable attention to the question in his preface to *Lyrical Ballads* in 1800, making points which Coleridge had brought back to the fore in *Biographia Literaria*, only a year before Byron began writing *Don Juan*. The lengthy cogitations of his contemporaries were, however, dismissed with a characteristically brusque comment, 'Prose poets like blank verse; I'm fond of rhyme' (*Don Juan*, I, 201), a preference borne out by the stanza chosen for his new heroic poem.

Among Coleridge's remarks on meter was the squashing judgement of 'Double and tri-syllable rhymes', which he regarded as 'a lower species of wit', occasioning nothing more than 'momentary amusement' (*Biographia Literaria*, II, 67). For Byron to select ottava rima with its multiple rhyming possibilities for his epic gave a clear enough indication of what he thought of Coleridge's pronouncements. Byron was just as interested in poetic technique as Wordsworth or Coleridge, as his admiration for Pope and Dryden's 'innumerable metres' and 'the exquisite beauty of their versification' shows (Byron, *Prose*, 111). Rather than attempt to analyze the complicated pleasures deriving from rhyme and meter, however, he allowed the brilliant and self-evidently enjoyable rhyming stanzas of *Don Juan* to make their own case. *Don Juan*'s rhymes are impossible to miss and so every reader is constantly made aware of the poem's sounds, whatever might be made of the sense.

The question of whether rhyme presented a kind of 'bondage' was, however, one that continued to preoccupy poets of the period. Milton had famously rejected 'the modern bondage of rhyming' in his choice of blank verse for *Paradise Lost* and so any later poet with epic ambition had to grapple with the memory of the great master's unequivocal decision. Byron's relish for such literary bondage is abundantly evident in his self-styled epic poem, but other poets of the period were rather more tentative in confessing their attraction to rhyme. Wordsworth clearly had

Milton in mind when he wrote of the 'bondage of definite form' in his preface to the 1815 *Poems*, a comment that may well have influenced Keats's remarkable image of Andromeda in 'If by dull rhymes our English must be chain'd' (discussed in Chapter 4). If the figure of Andromeda led readers to expect a Perseus poet liberating the sonnet from the chains of dull rhymes into something freer, what Keats actually offers is an image of poetry 'bound with garlands of her own' (14; O'Neill and Mahoney, 442). It was not that he rejected formal rhyme or meter, but rather that he was advocating a much more careful and therefore innovative approach to poetic acoustics: binding was not the same as bondage. 'Sound and syllable' were as precious to the poet as gold was to King Midas, and although there is a certain self-mockery in the parallel, it does bring home the point. The suggestion that Midas has come to mind because of his aural resemblance as well as legendary connection with 'Misers' is all part of the witty self-consciousness that Keats's sonnet shares with *Don Juan*.

Since Keats composed 'If by dull rhymes' in May 1819, the same month that he wrote 'Ode to a Nightingale', it is easy to see how quickly his new awareness of the need to 'weigh the stress / Of every chord' (7–8) and rely on the 'ear industrious' (9) informed his own creative practice (O'Neill and Mahoney, 442). The Odes allowed Keats to develop his own garlands for the English Muse, and to achieve a new kind of interwoven completeness. By the time he composed 'To Autumn', in late September, the self-sustaining nature of poetry seemed assured, the sounds of the season essential to its fullness. The last stanza of 'To Autumn' is a quiet affirmation of the beauty of season, expressed chiefly through its distinctive music:

> Then in a wailful choir the small gnats mourn
>   Among the river sallows, borne aloft
>   Or sinking as the light wind lives or dies;
> And full-grown lambs loud bleat from hilly bourn;
>   Hedge-crickets sing; and now with treble soft
> The red-breast whistles from the garden-croft;
>   And gathering swallows twitter in the skies.
>   ('To Autumn', 27–33;
>   O'Neill and Mahoney, 457–8)

'To Autumn' is just as concerned with sound as 'Ode to a Nightingale', but in this late-summer poem, there is none of the urgent exploration of the spring. Instead, the mood of calm acceptance finds its own harmonies, in the slow adagio of the small gnats and full-grown lambs, the high

7

Poems on Pages

Modern readers are most likely to encounter 'On Sitting Down to Read *King Lear* Once Again' in the pages of an anthology of Romantic literature, or an edition of Keats's poetry. The poem will be neatly laid out on the page, alongside other poems, all sharing the same typography, style of title and line numbering. So familiar are the conventions for printing poetry that few will pause to think about the original appearance of the individual poems, whether in the poet's own handwriting or in a nineteenth-century publication. And, arguably, that is at it should be. A successful poem, once composed, has a completeness that allows it to stand alone through the years, apparently inviting successive generations to interpret it as they please. The words are so well placed, the rhythms so perfectly balanced, the images so striking, that readers can experience a powerful personal response whether or not they know anything of the poet or the circumstances in which it was first composed. The self-sufficiency of a poem is a major part of its enduring appeal. Most readers nevertheless find reassurance in knowing that the poem is one of Keats's, while their understanding of the individual work may be deepened immeasurably through noticing connections with other poems, letters, contemporary contexts or critical theories. Modern editors will, accordingly, include information about a poem's composition and publication, to help readers set it in illuminating contexts. Duncan Wu, for example, presents 'On Sitting Down to read *King Lear* Once Again' with the following details: 'composed 22 January 1818; published 1838; edited from manuscript' (Wu, 1351).

The facts about a poem's original publication may initially seem little more than incidental historical detail, interesting to editors, of course, but

Reading Romantic Poetry, First Edition. Fiona Stafford.
© 2014 Fiona Stafford. Published 2014 by John Wiley & Sons, Ltd.

hardly to those who just want to read the poem. What does it matter if Keats's sonnet was first published in 1838? And yet, facts of this kind may lead to a train of puzzling questions, which can, in turn, transform a reading that had been based entirely on the words of the poem on the page. By 1838, Keats had been dead for seventeen years, so why did his sonnet appear then? And how did it come to be published for the first time in a provincial newspaper, the 8 November issue of the *Plymouth and Devonport Weekly*? Where had it been for the last twenty years? With the help of literary scholarship, it is easy enough to answer such questions and to begin to understand that friends of Keats, such as Charles Armitage Brown, played a crucial role in the survival of his manuscripts. And while this may seem largely a biographical or bibliographical, rather than critical, matter, the discovery of the sonnet's strange, posthumous appearance in Plymouth serves as a reminder that it was never published in Keats's lifetime. Why not?

The publication or non-publication of Romantic poems has always been a puzzling question. Keats's failure to publish the '*King Lear*' sonnet, for example, does not necessarily reflect a negative self-assessment: his despatch of one copy of the poem to his brothers and insertion of another into an edition of Shakespeare, is hardly indicative of disappointment. Some critics, including Beth Lau, have suggested that by copying the sonnet into a volume of Shakespeare, Keats was claiming equality with England's greatest poet, and if that were the case, his decision not to publish it seems even more surprising. The exclusion of 'On Sitting Down to Read *King Lear* Once Again' from Keats's 1820 collection of poems may be explained, however, by considering the arrangement of the volume. The title, *Lamia, Isabella, The Eve of St Agnes, and Other Poems*, announces itself as a collection of narrative verse, while the table of contents reveals at once that the 'other poems' are principally Odes. There are no sonnets in this volume, unlike Keats's first collection of *Poems*, published in 1817, which had included seventeen. Soon after its appearance in 1820, Keats was in no position to publish anything; his literary remains, including several unpublished sonnets, were destined to become posthumous works, their publication dependent on the survival of manuscripts in the hands of friends.

The realization that Keats's first collection of poems had included numerous sonnets, his last collection, none, offers a new dimension to the *King Lear* sonnet. When read in isolation, it may seem to be capturing a particular moment with great intensity, as the speaker lays aside the enjoyable 'Golden-Tongued Romance' in order to 'burn through' the searing pages of Shakespearean tragedy. Once seen in the light of Keats's writing career, however, the moment is magnified. *Poems*, 1817, had included many sonnets, but it concluded with 'Sleep and Poetry', which, though fretted with uncertainty, was still a public announcement of Keats's literary ambitions. In this poem, which ran to over four hundred lines, Keats set out his intention to devote the next ten years to poetry, moving from the delights of pastoral to the nobler heights of the epic. His next major publication was the long narrative poem, *Endymion*, in 1818, and then the 'Lamia' volume in 1820, with its epic fragment, 'Hyperion', the great odes and the narrative poems, 'Lamia, 'Isabella', 'The Eve of St Agnes'.

'Ode on a Nightingale', 'Ode to a Grecian Urn' and 'La Belle Dame Sans Merci' appeared in journals before their inclusion in the 1820 collection, but the only sonnets Keats published after 1817 were 'To Ailsa Craig' and 'A Dream'. The moment described in the *King Lear* sonnet, when the young poet girds himself to tackle literary challenges of Shakespearean magnitude may therefore reflect the public persona that Keats was projecting, even though the sonnet remained unknown. For the small circle of privileged readers who did see the sonnet at the time it was written, it probably revealed the same soaring poetic ambition that had been visible to the world in 'Sleep and Poetry' and which influenced Keats's momentous decision to abandon his medical studies. The tone of the *King Lear* sonnet thus intensifies, once it becomes apparent that Keats was not merely deciding what to read on a winter afternoon, but rather what he might do with the rest of his life.

Later generations of readers were to discover that Keats not only continued to write sonnets but also to extend its formal possibilities; during his lifetime, however, only those who knew him well were aware of his private literary experiments. A poet's public presentation was often at odds with the private practice, though such apparent discrepancies sometimes resulted from the influence of editors, friends or family. Decades of scholarship mean that we are now privileged to see works that remained inaccessible to the Romantic reading public, although the very richness of the material and the editorial expertise can at times obscure some legitimate considerations. What may appear to be an outspoken contribution to a political debate, for example, can seem a little less bold once we realize that it was not published until many years after the public crisis. If the poem appears in a smooth sequence ordered by a modern editor according to the chronology of composition, however, it may not be obvious to modern readers that the poet's contemporaries were unaware of its existence. This chapter focuses on the appearance of poems on printed pages and the implications for readers of considering both the original publications and subsequent editions.

Reading Romantic Poetry: Then and Now

In the twenty-first century, readers equipped with well-informed editions of Romantic poetry may easily fail to grasp the difference between their own perceptions of canonical poets and those of the original reading public. We see at once that the literary language, form and references of the early nineteenth century are often quite unlike those of modern poems, but we may not find it so easy to gauge the gulf between our readerly expectations and those of the Romantic period. It is difficult to imagine a time when Keats and Shelley were virtually unknown, but Bryan Waller Proctor and Samuel Rogers were the height of fashion. Keats's *Endymion* was remaindered after four years, leaving his publishers with unsold copies and considerable losses, while Shelley's *Prometheus Unbound* volume, which included poems such as 'Ode to the West Wind', has become famous for selling fewer than twenty copies. When these figures are put next to Scott's sales, for example, and we learn that *The Lay of the Last Minstrel* rapidly ran to six editions enjoying sales of 27,000 copies within a decade, the contemporary obscurity of those now generally described as 'major Romantic poets' is only too apparent. Whether this should affect our reading of the poems is a matter for debate, but it certainly sheds new light on Shelley's firm focus on a more enlightened future.

It is also salutary to remember that many of the poems that have come to be regarded as defining texts of the Romantic period were not known to those living at the time. We may not be surprised to learn that Byron was unaware of 'On Sitting Down to read *King Lear* Once Again', but what of the realisation that he never read *The Prelude*? The poem now generally considered to be Wordsworth's masterpiece and often singled out as *the* major Romantic text, was not published until 1850 and so remained hidden from the public throughout Wordsworth's long writing life. Anyone who reads Shelley's 'To Wordsworth' or the 'Dedication' to *Don Juan* today might pause to remember, then, that neither Shelley nor Byron's view of Wordsworth was influenced by *The Prelude*. Since it is rather difficult for a modern reader to think seriously about Wordsworth without *The Prelude*, the gulf between twenty-first century and Romantic readers becomes startlingly apparent. The issue is further complicated by the realization that the Dedication to *Don Juan* was not published until 1832, so the poem's first readers of 1819, unaware of Byron's opening attack on Wordsworth and Coleridge, were doubly unaware of what may now seem a startling unawareness of *The Prelude*.

Alertness to the original date of publication can often prevent critical errors that seem perfectly reasonable when a reading has been based on a later text. For those who read Felicia Hemans's 'The Lost Pleiad' for the first time in the pages of her 1829 collection, *The Forest Sanctuary*, for example, the poem, with its epigraph from *Beppo*, may have seemed a direct response to the shocking death of Byron. The poem was first published in *The New Monthly Magazine* in January 1823, however, several months before Byron died, so it can hardly have been a response to the news. Since some of the sentiments and imagery are reminiscent of *Adonais*, it is more likely to have been inspired by Shelley – whether by the poem on Keats, or his own death, or both. And yet, as O'Neill has observed, the poem can perhaps be read as a 'proleptic elegy' for Byron, because after 1824 the lament for the lost star took on fresh significance (O'Neill and Mahoney, 413).

The premature deaths of poets in the Romantic period often meant that the poems they influenced, as well as their own works, could acquire new dimensions with dismaying rapidity. As Mary Shelley commented when she edited *Adonais* for her husband's *Poetical Works*, in 1839, 'There is much in Adonais which now seems more applicable to Shelley himself, than to the young and gifted poet whom he mourned.'

Nor were the meanings of poems transformed by the death of poets alone. Hemans's 'The Graves of a Household' can similarly be seen to accrue meaning with successive publications, for when it originally appeared in the *New Monthly Magazine* in 1825, the poet's mother was still alive. By the time it was collected for publication in *Records of Woman* in 1828, the death of Hemans's mother in the previous year amplified the poignant recollection of the childhood home into a deeply felt lament:

> The same fond mother bent at night
> O'er each fair sleeping brow;
> She had each folded flower in sight, –
> Where are those dreamers now?
> (5–8; O'Neill and Mahoney, 409)

This later version of the poem concludes with a direct address to the earth:

> Alas, for love! If thou wert all,
>   And nought beyond, oh, earth!
>   (31–2)

In 1825, however, the poem printed in the magazine had concluded, 'And nought beyond, on earth', which suggests that the lines were addressed to 'love', not the earth. This might seem a minor amendment – a single letter changed, an additional comma – but it entirely alters the meaning of the poem. For what had been a fairly standard reflection on the loneliness and mortality of human love became, in the collected volume, an anguished comment on the possibility of a universe entirely material and therefore deaf to human misery. Whether the revision was made by the poet, the publisher, or even the compositor in the printing house, the poem itself was changed for readers of *Records of Woman* – and for modern audiences, whose texts are based on the later version in the 1828 collection.

Any idea of 'Romantic Poetry' must be influenced by the individual reader's knowledge of certain texts, but responses to the poems are often colored by their surroundings. If a poem is read in a modern edition, alongside works of other writers, it may offer readers a different aspect from what is most visible in another context. As part of a sequence, poems gather meaning from those that precede and succeed them, while understanding of their original publication may cast a different light on their meaning. When 'The Graves of a Household' appeared in *Records of Woman*, for example, it was part of a collection that highlighted female experience, including many examples of women's perspectives on masculine action around the world. In the *New Monthly Magazine*, the poem had been sandwiched between some 'Original Letters of Burke' and a description of visiting Beirut, which meant that the first readers had also been confronted with Hemans's poem in contrast to international and male views. They were, however, much less likely to notice the distinctly feminine slant of a piece that offered no direct clue to the speaker's identity and whose author was designated only by the initials 'F.H.'. The question for modern readers, therefore, is whether reading 'The Graves of a Household' in a modern edition of *Records of Woman* helps to illuminate its meaning, or whether there are advantages to reading it in isolation, an experience that might be closer to that of its earliest readers?

Often poems published more than once alter subtly with each fresh appearance, so a reader's experience may depend on decisions taken by editors or publishers. It always makes a difference to discussion of 'The Ancient Mariner' if the participants have read a text based on the poem first published in *Lyrical Ballads*, or the later version of 1817, with its extensive marginal glosses. In the case of 'Ode on a Grecian Urn', the varying punctuation of the enigmatic closing lines has led to enormous debate over their meaning.

When the Ode was originally published in *Annals of the Fine Arts* in January 1820, its final lines were presented as follows:

> Beauty is Truth, Truth Beauty. – That is all
> Ye know on Earth, and all ye need to know.

In the 1820 collection of Keats's *Poems*, however, the lines acquired the inverted commas that now appear in some modern editions, turning 'Beauty is Truth, Truth Beauty' into a quotation within the poem. Since there is no surviving manuscript in Keats's hand, the position of the inverted commas continues to divide his editors and, in some texts, the quotation marks open before 'beauty', but close only after 'know', to indicate continuing speech. John Barnard, who edited Keats's poems for Penguin neatly sums up the interpretative possibilities arising from the textual crux:

1 both lines are spoken by the urn, and addressed to man.
2 the lines are spoken by the poet to the urn.
3 the lines are spoken by the poet to the figures on the urn
4 'Beauty is truth, truth beauty' is spoken by the urn, and the remainder is the poet speaking to his readers.
5 the motto, as in preceding reading, is spoken by the urn, but the poet then addresses the urn, not mankind.

(Keats, *Complete Poems*, 676).

With so many different meanings hanging on a pair of speech marks, the decision of an individual editor can quietly determine the possibilities open to the reader.

Some Romantic poets, notably Wordsworth, were extremely concerned with the appearance of their poems, furiously revising the texts for each new edition or insisting on errata slips after spotting an imperfection on the printed page. Others were more content to leave such matters to their editors, although, in the case of John Clare, such willingness to be 'improved' has been seen by later readers as a confession of inadequacy – the anxiety of a writer packaged as the 'peasant poet'. In general, the relationships between poets and their publishers were cooperative and collaborative, but at times their different perspectives led to serious disagreements. John Taylor was Keats's publisher as well as Clare's, and although he gave both poets crucial support, he was also alert to the tastes of the reading public and keen to avoid either hostile reviews or disastrous sales.

Some stanzas of Keats's 'The Eve of St Agnes' struck Taylor as unpublishable, because in his view, the explicit depiction of premarital sex would alienate many readers and render the entire volume unfit for ladies' eyes. Taylor's legal adviser, Richard Woodhouse, reported that although Keats had made some changes to the poem, he remained adamant that

> he does not want ladies to read his poetry; that he writes for men, and that if in the former poem there was any opening of doubt what took place, it was his fault for not writing clearly and comprehensibly, that he should despise a man who would be such a eunuch in sentiment as to leave a maid, with that character about her in such a situation.
>
> (Wu, 1042)

Taylor felt so strongly about the matter, however, that he threatened to refuse publication of the 1820 volume altogether and, in the end, Keats conceded to some further modifications. It is possible now to read the lines from the 1820 publication in the editorial notes to modern editions of the poem and to see the poem not just as a finished work of art, but also in the process of becoming one. Modern readers can decide for themselves whether Taylor's worries helped to enhance or diminish Keats's poem.

Those in more powerful social and financial positions were able to assert their authorial rights more strongly than poets such as Keats or Clare, but even Byron agreed to suppress the Dedication to *Don Juan*. His relationship with John Murray, however, became more and more strained after the first two cantos were published in 1819, and eventually, they parted company over the risqué epic, leaving any risks surrounding the later cantos of *Don Juan* to be borne by Leigh Hunt. Such details from publishing history can shed important light on the poetry of the period, by revealing the hidden pressures that sometimes influenced the development of a poem. Romantic poets might be given to making memorable declarations about moments of inspiration, but their poems were also subject to the forces of public taste, prevailing morals, commercial considerations and the critical reception.

Many poems of the period changed very little from the original version, scribbled down by the poet, but some were transformed through the process of publication and continued to be modified through successive editions. Modern readers can easily ignore the history of a poem, trusting to editorial decisions and concentrating solely on the text presented in their chosen edition. However, those who pursue the evolution of Romantic poems often discover new dimensions and find their reading greatly enriched. In the successive transformations from manuscript to print, or from edition to edition, Romantic poems might gain or lose titles, epigraphs, punctuation, names, illustrations, prose prefaces and notes, not to mention entire stanzas or passages of blank verse. In the case of Blake, the distinction between the poet's hand and the press was unusually close, and so special consideration is necessary. Even works that issued from the presses with uniform print and standard layout, however, can still reveal significant changes between editions. While some poems were printed in magazines, others appeared in modest pamphlets, or grand volumes designed for gentlemen's libraries. Collections of poetry might be financed by subscription, like Burns's first volume, or left, like most of Byron's collections, to trust to the pockets of the book-buying public. The most popular volumes of the period attracted a readership of thousands, not to mention illegal imitations pirated from the original edition. Still many fine works remained unpublished, or known only to the author's immediate circle, a fate that might reflect personal reticence, political considerations, publisher's preferences or commercial constraints.

Details such as these might have a decisive bearing on how a modern reader interprets a Romantic poem, once aware of the original publication. Today, poems of the period are generally read in selections and anthologies, but would the individual text be interpreted in other ways if seen in the volume in which it first appeared? Electronic resources are making versions of the original printed texts accessible to a wider audience than ever before and so it is increasingly possible for students to consider Romantic poems as they appeared to their first readers. This makes possible comparisons between modern editions and first publications, enabling a greater sense of individual poems as part of a volume and highlighting those that were not included for publication. Such information has long been available through the work of scholars in the field, but is now easier to visualize. Given the scale of the topic and the variety of textual issues that arise in relation to almost every major poet, this chapter can do no more than open some avenues for reading. Since some of the questions relating to poems on pages can be introduced through more careful consideration of certain volumes, the discussion focuses on the visual dimension of Blake's *Songs of Innocence and Experience* and the arrangement of Coleridge's *Christabel, Kubla Khan and The Pains of Sleep*. This choice also enables some revisiting of poems mentioned in earlier chapters, to show how new contexts can reveal different aspects of an already familiar text.

Illuminated Books

When he composed his *Songs of Innocence and Experience*, Blake was evoking popular song culture and the old tradition of the poet as a singer. The appeal of his little book, however, was as much visual as aural, because he printed the poems himself, presenting the lyrics of each 'Song' in an intricate design that filled the entire page. Although many of the poems have been reprinted in modern anthologies with standard type and without illuminations, the original audience for Blake's *Songs* were viewers as much as readers. Blake was an artist and engraver, earning a living from illustrating books, so it came naturally to him to present his own poetry in a form that offered visual as well as literary beauty. Since Blake not only composed the poems, but also designed, printed and colored the plates, each edition of the *Songs* was unique, even though the words of the poems remained unchanged.

The effort invested by Blake in creating works which combined 'the Painter and the Poet' ('Prospectus', 1793), suggests a desire to encourage readers to perceive words visually, as well as interpreting them more conventionally. The skill with which he created the plates, using a specially developed kind of mirror writing to allow for a new printing technique, shows that for Blake, making poems called on many different faculties. Composition was a physical as much as a mental activity, a craft both manual and imaginative. For a modern reader, conditioned by print, to ignore the appearance of Blake's poetry is to strip away a whole dimension of his creative endeavor. This is needlessly self-denying, too, since the advent of electronic technology means that we are fortunate enough to be able to see Blake's works in their original format, with vibrant clear colors or strong contrasts, depending on which copy is consulted. Although modern readers often read only Blake's words, their experience of his work can be utterly transformed by consulting beautifully printed library editions of the *Illuminated Books* or the online Blake Archive, which offers a chance to compare the different versions of his dazzling texts. For poems that are made of words alone, comparison of variant editions usually throws up typographical changes, but with Blake's work, different versions can seem like different poems.

Reading 'The Little Black Boy', for example, is changed utterly by seeing the different surviving versions of the second image, which depicts the two boys at the knee of the Jesus-like seated figure (O'Neill and Mahoney, 26). For although Blake developed a method of color printing, each book was also hand-colored, allowing for great individuality in each copy. In the case of 'The Little Black Boy', some versions represent the two children as white, some as dark, and some suggest a contrast between a pink figure and a darker one. In the copy held at the Yale Center for British Art, which dates from 1795, the figure in profile is very light, while the child slightly behind, who faces outwards towards the reader is so dark that his features can hardly be distinguished. The existence of so many different images thus complicates what is already a difficult lyric in terms of its play on the literal and metaphorical meanings of 'black' and 'white'. The variety of the colors and contrasts shows that outward appearances are subject to complete transformation and that what is perceived by the eye is not necessarily the whole truth.

This is, of course, quite consistent with a passage in Blake's *Vision of the Last Judgment*, about the essential subjectivity of the eye. For Blake, the entire world could be altered by imaginative energy, as is clear from his comparison between the contrasting perceptions of the miser and the visionary:

> "What", it will be Question'd, "When the Sun rises, do you not see a round disk of fire somewhat like a Guinea?" O, no, no, I see an Innumerable company of the Heavenly host crying 'Holy, Holy, Holy is the Lord God Almighty'. I question not my Corporeal or Vegetative Eye any more than I would Question a Window concerning a Sight. I look thro'it & not with it"'
> (*A Vision of the Last Judgment, Complete Writings*, 617)

Blake had made the same point more succinctly in *The Marriage of Heaven and Hell*, including among the Proverbs of Hell the observation that 'A fool sees not the same tree that a wise man sees' (Wu, 209). For Blake, perception of the external world was colored from within, and by producing books that showed how the same image could appear radically altered by a fresh colour wash, he challenged readers to rethink their assumptions.

If we see with our minds and not with our eyes, the appearance of a child depends on the perceiver. The speaker in Blake's Song may be looking forward to a time when he will be free of the conditioning that has made him grow up with a sense of innate inferiority. Instead of superficial differences, he, too, will see the essential similarities between people of different races and nations. If the reader perceives the words of the Black Boy with a spiritual, rather than corporeal eye, then both boys will look glowing and beautiful. However, the image that shows the starkest contrast between the two figures may also be read as an ironic comment on the speaker's vision, by emphasizing the gulf between the children and the relative obscurity of the black boy. In this reading, the speaker's reference to stroking 'silver hair' may suggest not a gleaming visionary but an old man, because any realisation of his ideal equality is still many years away. The look of the poem on the page, then, opens up numerous interpretative possibilities – all of which are based on verbal details, but which the visual dimension magnifies and multiplies.

The less optimistic reading of 'The Little Black Boy' is most apparent in a 1795 copy of *Songs of Innocence and Experience* and differs from the first versions of the poem, printed in the *Songs of Innocence*, in 1789. It is not that an ironic reading was impossible in the original poem, but it certainly seems more obvious in the later text, which post-dated the failure of the Abolition Bill in 1791. The distinctions between 'innocence' and 'experience' become further confused by more extensive exploration of the different versions of Blake's volume, when it becomes clear that several of the poems of *Experience* were originally published in *Songs of Innocence*. 'The Voice of the Ancient Bard', 'The Little Girl Lost' and 'The Little Girl Found', for example, were originally poems of *Innocence*, transferring to *Experience* only when the second book was printed in 1794. Such a discovery encourages us to look again at these poems, for if we read them solely in the second part of a modern edition of *Songs of Innocence and Experience*, we may well fail to consider the possibility of an 'innocent reading'.

If 'The Little Girl Lost' is encountered under the label 'Experience', for example, readers are more likely to find images of sexual menace in the leopards, tigers and the 'lion old' that surround the sleeping girl. Once restored to 'Innocence', however, the poem might yield Biblical resonances from Isaiah's vision of an ideal future, where 'The wolf also shall dwell with the lamb, and the leopard shall lie down with the kid; and the calf and the young lion and the fatling together; and a little child shall lead them' (Isaiah. 11, 6). The opening stanzas of the poem take a prophetic voice, to conjure up a future in which the sleeping earth will wake, and the 'desert wild / Become a garden mild' (7–8). If this possibility is embraced, then the image of the sleeping girl being undressed and carried away by the animals becomes less disturbing, for it may suggest either a recovery of the innocence of Eden, where human beings were as naked as the birds and beasts, or the state of the new born child, as yet unconfined by adult constraints and social conventions. At the same time, the knowledge that when Blake rearranged his poetic sequence, the poem was placed in *Songs of Experience*, makes readers conscious of its more disturbing possibilities. Images of the child, lost in a place filled with predators, and her distraught parents searching through the night, trigger fairly straightforward anxieties, while the details of the 'kingly lion' viewing 'the virgin' suggest metaphorical dangers, just as troubling.

The movement of poems between *Innocence* and *Experience* and the variations in their visual appearance alert Blake's readers to the difficulty of assigning definite meanings to his work. His use of commonplace imagery – children, nurses, old men, trees, gardens, animals, flowers – in poems that are far from commonplace often encourages symbolic interpretation. While Blake is clearly exploring the metaphorical and allegorical possibilities of language, however, it is debatable whether he is creating a private symbolic system whereby his images have consistent meanings. As he observed in a letter to Dr Trusler, 'The tree which moves some to tears of joy is in the eyes of others only a green thing that stands in the way' (Blake, *Letters*, 23 Aug, 1799). To suggest, after reading 'A Poison Tree', that all the trees in *Songs of Innocence and Experience* are somehow sinister may therefore be unwise. That the Little Black Boy's mother teaches him underneath a tree might suggest its shadows are internal as well as external, but it could also be an image of protective love. Just because *Songs of Experience* includes 'A Poison Tree' and 'The Human Abstract' does not mean that all the trees in the collection are growing dangerously in the human brain – though they might be. The image accompanying 'The Human Abstract', after all, looks more like a spider in the undergrowth than a tree. The more readers see in Blake's illuminated books, the less certain do their readings tend to become and once the illuminations are understood to be intrinsic to the poems, new connections begin to emerge, complicating initial responses to the words on the page. Since fixed opinions are condemned in the *Marriage of Heaven and Hell* as the breeding ground for reptiles of the mind, the fluidity that seems consequent on seeing the poems in their original format should nevertheless be welcomed as refreshing rather than vexing to anyone sympathetic to Blake's art.

Perhaps the most baffling of Blake's songs is 'The Tyger', which seems to leap into the midst of *Songs of Experience*, scattering the surrounding poems with their more familiar images of gardens, sunflowers, roses, and flies, with its unexpected force:

> Tyger, tyger, burning bright
> In the forests of the night
> What immortal hand or eye
> Could frame thy fearful symmetry?
> (1–4; O'Neill and Mahoney, 35)

Even more disconcerting than the lyrics themselves, however, is the discovery that in the illuminated plate, they are set beside a tall, leafless tree, where a decidedly unthreatening tiger is standing quietly. In some copies, the dramatic colors and contrasting stripes suggest something burning brightly in a dark rainforest, but in others, the tiger has a large smile, and is more reminiscent of a marmalade cat sunning itself in the back garden. So, what are we to make of this startling disjunction between words and image?

Perhaps the image offers an answer to the question, 'Did he who made the Lamb make thee?' by showing that a tiger can be just as peaceful as a lamb and that it is only man's conventional attitude that renders it terrifying. The reminiscence of Isaiah in 'The Little Girl Lost' may also echo in the background of this poem, suggesting a vision of an ideal world in which all living creatures exist in harmony and freedom. From the perspective of experience, such a vision can only be realized in the future, so perhaps the stirring lyrics are a call to rouse dormant imaginative faculties into action. The lines 'On what wings dare he aspire? What the hand dare seize the fire?' may be an early version of the pledge made in *Milton*:

> Bring me my bow of burning gold!
> Bring my arrows of desire!
> Bring me my spear – oh clouds unfold!
> Bring me my chariot of fire!
>
> I will not cease from mental fight,
> Nor shall my sword sleep in my hand,
> Till we have built Jerusalem
> In England's green and pleasant Land.
> (Wu, 245)

A. Phillips and G. Summerfield (eds.) *John Clare in Context* (Cambridge: Cambridge University Press, 1994); James McKusick, 'The Return of the Nightingale', *The Wordsworth Circle* 38 (2007), 34–40; Jeremy Mynott, *Birdscapes* (Princeton: Princeton University Press, 2010); Sam Ward, ' "To List the Song and Not to Start the Thrush": John Clare's Acoustic Ecologies', *John Clare Society Journal*, 29 (2010), 15–33.

For Keats's Odes, see S. Robert Barth and John L. Mahoney (eds.) *Coleridge, Keats and the Imagination* (Columbia, Mo.: Columbia University Press, 1990); Cleanth Brooks, *The Well-Wrought Urn* (New York: Harcourt Brace, 1947); John Minahan, *Word like a Bell: John Keats, Music and the Romantic* Poet (Kent, Oh., University of Ohio Press, 1992); James O'Rourke, *Keats Odes and Contemporary Criticism* (Gainesville: University of Florida Press, 1998); Christopher Ricks, *Keats and Embarrassment* (Oxford: Clarendon Press, 1974); Helen Vendler, *The Odes of John Keats* (Cambridge Mass.: Harvard University Press, 1983).

For *Don Juan*, see Anne Barton, *Byron: Don Juan* (Cambridge: Cambridge University Press, 1992); Bernard Beatty, *Byron's Don Juan* (London: Croom Helm, 1985); Michael Joseph, *Byron the* Poet (London: Gollancz,1964); Jerome McGann, *Fiery Dust: Byron's Poetic Development* (Chicago: University of Chicago Press,1968); Michael O'Neill, *Romanticism and the Self-Conscious Poem* (Oxford: Clarendon Press, 1997); Jane Stabler, *Byron, Poetics and History* (Cambridge: Cambridge University Press, 2009).

staccato of the robin and the twittering swallows. The pentameter lines move at their own unhurried pace, varying their steps to accompany the well-orchestrated gathering of autumnal noises. Keats's last Ode employs alliteration, assonance, puns and rhymes just as skilfully as his spring poem to the nightingale, but its slower movement, languid syllables and longer stanzas create a very different kind of beauty.

Further Reading

On Shelley's poetic theory and style, see Timothy Clark, *Embodying Revolution: The Figure of the Poet in Shelley* (Oxford: Clarendon press, 1989); Paul De Man, 'Shelley Disfigured', in Harold Bloom (ed.) *Deconstruction and Criticism* (London: Routledge, 1979); Judith Chernaik, *The Lyrics of Shelley* (Cleveland: Ohio University Press, 1972); Jerrold Hogle, *Shelley's Process* (Oxford: Oxford University Press, 1988); 'Language and Form', in *The Cambridge Companion to Shelley*, ed. Timothy Morton (Cambridge: Cambridge University Press, 2006); William Keach, *Shelley's Style* (New York and London: Methuen, 1984); Angela Leighton, *Shelley and the Sublime* (Cambridge: Cambridge University Press, 1984); Michael O'Neill, *The Human Mind's Imaginings* (Oxford: Clarendon Press, 1989); Earl Wasserman, *Shelley: A Critical Reading* (Baltimore: Johns Hopkins University Press, 1971); Timothy Webb, Shelley: A Voice Not Understood (Manchester: Manchester University Press, 1977).

For Wordsworth's meter and metrical theory, see Jared Curtis, *Wordsworth's Experiments with Tradition: The Lyric Poems of 1802* (Ithaca: Cornell University Press, 1971); Paul Fry, *Wordsworth and the Poetry of What We Are* (New Haven and London: Yale University Press, 2008); Brendan O'Donnell, *The Passion of Meter: A Study of Wordsworth's Metrical Art* (Kent, Oh.: Kent State University Press, 1995); W. J. B. Owen, *Wordsworth as Critic* (London: Oxford University Press, 1969); Stephen Parrish, *The Art of Lyrical Ballads* (Cambridge Mass.: Harvard University Press, 1973); Christopher Ricks, *The Force of Poetry* (New York: Oxford University Press, 1987); Susan Wolfson, 'Romanticism and the Measures of Meter', *Eighteenth Century Life* (1992), 162–80.

For Romantic birds, see Alison Brackenbury, 'Birdsnesting with John Clare', *Poetry Review* 100, no 1 (Spring 2010), 70–5; H. Houghton,

www.ingramcontent.com/pod-product-compliance
Lightning Source LLC
LaVergne TN
LVHW021658060526
838200LV00050B/2414